THE BEST OF
BEHAVIOUR RESEARCH AND THERAPY

Titles of Related Interest

Behaviour Research and Therapy

Journal of Behavior Therapy and Experimental Psychiatry

Personality and Individual Differences

Journal of Anxiety Disorders

Clinical Psychology Review

THE BEST OF BEHAVIOUR RESEARCH AND THERAPY

Editor

S. Rachman

Founding Editor

H. J. Eysenck

PERGAMON

UK	Elsevier Science Ltd, The Boulevard, Langford Lane, Kidlington, Oxford, OX5 1GB, UK
USA	Elsevier Science Inc., 660 White Plains Road, Tarrytown, NY 10591-5153, USA
JAPAN	Elsevier Science Japan, Tsunashima Building Annex, 3-20-12 Yushima, Bunkyo-ku, Tokyo 113, Japan

First edition 1997

Library of Congress Cataloging in Publication Data
A catalog record for this book is available from the Library of Congress

British Library Cataloging in Publication Data
A catalogue record for this book is available from the British Library

ISBN 008 043 0783

Printed in Great Britain by BPC Wheatons Ltd, Exeter

CONTENTS

THE BEST OF BEHAVIOUR THERAPY AND RESEARCH

Contents

PREFACE

Thirty-five Years of BRAT

The journal was established in 1962 and the first issue appeared in May 1963. It contained 11 articles, dealing with: the concept of behaviour therapy, the conditioning treatment of enuresis, the "new science of psychotherapy", an evaluation of outcome data on child psychotherapy, operant conditioning therapy for psychotic behaviour, three articles on desensitization treatment, and Kurt Freund's original description of his plethysmographic method for assessing sexual responsiveness. The authors included Ayllon, Blakemore, Freund, Lazarus, Lovibond and Wolpe. That first issue was a portent of the range and style of the journal in its first ten years. Later on the emphasis shifted from the description of new methods of treatment and their applications to experimental analyses of abnormal behaviour and studies of therapeutic mechanisms. In the early eighties the scope of the journal expanded to include behavioural medicine and medical psychology.

The original editors and publishers had two main aims. The first was to provide a forum for the new conception of psychological therapy, for the rationale and methods of behaviour therapy. At that time it was extremely difficult to persuade editors and reviewers of existing journals to publish articles on something called "behaviour therapy", or even to take them seriously. The submissions were rejected, sometimes by return of post, as highly speculative or outlandish, or both. "We do not publish this type of article", was the huffy reply received from a prominent journal of the day.

The second and grander aim was to help promote and guide this new approach to therapy, to encourage research and promulgate the results.

How well were these aims met? The journal certainly succeeded in providing a forum. We have published 35 volumes of research, thousands of papers, and given a platform to many thousands of scientists and clinicians—including the most prominent contributors in the field. We have been privileged to publish the works of Agras, Arntz, Allyon, Azrin, Bandura, Beck, Borkovec, Chambless, Clark, D. A., Clark, D. M., Costello, Craske, DeSilva, Ehlers, Emmelkamp, Eysenck, Foa, Fordyce, Freund, Frost, Gelder, Hodgson, Hallam, Hemsley, Kazdin, Lang, Leitenberg, Marks Margraf, Mathews, McLeod, McNally, Martin, Marshall, Meyer, Michelson, Mineka, Ost, Philips, Salkovskis, Seligman, Teasdale, Turk, van den Hout, Velten, Wilson, Wolpe, Yule and many others, too numerous to mention. Indeed, a fully representative collection of authors and papers published since 1963 would require not this single volume but another four equally large books. So we apologise in advance to readers who feel that their favoured papers or authors have not been included in this collection.

The selections cover three areas: Theory, Methods and Treatment. I have tried to pick the most interesting historically and to ensure that they are representative. Articles that were topical ten or twenty years ago but have been superseded by new collections of facts were not chosen. Hence, the many articles on the treatment of phobias were omitted, as were treatment outcome trials that are without historical interest, and ideas/methods that failed (e.g. aversion therapy).

Instead, we have included six papers on theory: Professor Eysenck's statement of his theory of neurosis, Clark's heavily quoted landmark paper on the cognitive theory of panic, the correspondingly important paper on OCD by Salkovskis, Teasdale on depression, Philips on a cognitive view of pain, and a model of emotional processing. From a wide range of papers on method, two stand out because of their widespread adoption (in modified forms)—Freund's plethysmographic method and Velten's mood-induction technique.

On the treatment side, preference has been given to innovative techniques such as Vic Meyer's treatment of OCD, Fordyce on pain control, Azrin on habit reversal, Turk on cancer pain and new approaches to the treatment of bulimia and of bereavement. Selecting the articles for this section was particularly difficult because there was such a wide choice available.

It is our hope that readers will find much value in these papers—and some surprises. All too often we lose sight of the origins of our current ideas and tools, and this collection of historical pieces should come as a welcome and occasionally amusing reminder. We also hope to convey in the selections the thrust of journal policy over the years, including the search for originality, a commitment to rigorous scientific investigations, an insistence on validated (or validating) therapeutic procedures and fast publication. I believe that much of the time we were successful in these pursuits and that as a result the journal made a tangible and large contribution to the promotion of this vigorous new form of thinking and treatment. Behavioural therapy, and its latest form, cognitive behaviour therapy, have flourished. Science has been advanced, students informed and large numbers of patients have benefitted.

Along the way we have made our share of mistakes, occasionally accepting work that later turned out to be unimportant or even misleading. Our hopeful expectations for some forms of innovative treatment, such as operant reinforcement of the speech of autistic children, were not fulfilled. Some theoretical pieces that appeared to be enlightening sank like lead balloons, methods that seemed promising turned out to be hopelessly impractical, and so on. But we did get it right much of the time, and *Behaviour Research and Therapy* has an enviably high citation index—greater than the Journal of Abnormal Psychology on some comparisons.

Did the journal make a difference? We prefer to think so, and for the pioneers in this field, *Behaviour Research and Therapy* was for many years the only vehicle for their work. No doubt the pioneers would have persisted until they obtained a platform, but this Journal provided for them a welcoming and positively encouraging forum. The editors understood their language.

S. Rachman

THE LEARNING THEORY MODEL OF
NEUROSIS—A NEW APPROACH

H. J. EYSENCK*

Department of Psychology, Institute of Psychiatry, De Crespigny Park Road,
Denmark Hill, London S.E.5, U.K.

(*Received* 18 *June* 1975)

Summary—This paper is concerned with the development of a learning theory model of neurosis which would not be susceptible to the many criticisms which can be made of former models. Two widely favoured models—those of Freud and Skinner—are rejected because they are either non-falsifiable or tautological. The Watson and Mowrer models are rejected because they have been experimentally invalidated. The model here suggested differs from previous ones in several important respects. In the first place, it replaces the classical law of extinction by a more modern version which allows for incubation (enhancement) effects of exposure to *CS*-only stimuli, as well as for extinction effects. In the second place, the model emphasizes the importance of individual differences, and suggests precise relations between personality and the conditioning of neurotic behaviours. In the third place, the model lays stress on innate fear patterns and 'preparedness' as important factors in the genesis of conditioned fear responses. In the fourth place, the concept of 'pain' in the classical animal literature, and its use in creating models of neurosis, is supplemented by other concepts ('frustrative non-reward', 'approach-avoidance' conflict) which are more relevant to human neurosis. In the fifth place, and most important, the notion of 'traumatic', single-trial conditioning is abandoned, and a new theory based on incubation is proposed. It is suggested that the new theory is more adequate than previous ones to account for the known facts of human neurosis, and that it suggests novel types of experiment in both the animal and human fields which can be used to test its adequacy.

There is no agreed model of neurosis in psychiatry, although there are several theories which claim to explain the phenomena commonly subsumed under the term, 'neurosis'. Among the authors of such theories are such well known figures as Freud, Watson, and Skinner. It will be argued here that the theories of Freud and Skinner are incapable of presenting us with an acceptable scientific model of neurosis, and it will be further argued that Watson's model, although containing the seeds of a viable theory, is not sufficiently in line with what is known about the development of neurotic illness to be useful. Taking up the detailed criticisms of Watson's model, we shall then try to put forward a theory which avoids these critisisms, and seems more adequate than those mentioned above to explain what Mowrer (1950) has called 'the neurotic paradox.'

At the beginning of his paper, Mowrer invites us 'to consider what, in many respects, is the absolutely central problem in neurosis and therapy. Most simply formulated, it is a paradox—the paradox of behavior which is at one and the same time self-perpetuating and self-defeating!' (p. 486.) As he goes on to say, 'common sense holds that a normal, sensible man, or even a beast to the limits of his intelligence, will weigh and balance the consequences of his acts: if the net effect is favorable, the action producing it will be perpetuated; and if the net effect is unfavorable, the action producing it will be inhibited, abandoned. In neurosis, however, one sees actions which have predominantly unfavorable consequences; yet they persist over a period of months, years, or a lifetime.' (*ibid.*) Mowrer examines, in the course of his book, the theories of Freud and of Watson; he did not consider Skinner's theory because this had not yet been extended to deal with psychiatric disorders.

(1) *The Freud and Skinner models*

We shall not here take space to formulate in detail criticisms of the Freudian theory. As Slater (1975) has argued, following the almost unanimous view of philosophers of

* I am indebted to Dr. J. Gray, Dr. M. Seligman, Dr. S. Rachman, and Dr. I. Marks for valuable criticisms and suggestions. I am indebted to the Science Research Council for the support of some of the work upon which most of my theorising is based.

science like Popper, Kuhn, Lakatos and others, Freudian theories are untestable because they cannot be falsified by any conceivable experimental or clinical event; such theories therefore are outside the realm of science. Some psychologists have argued that this view is mistaken, and that parts at least of Freud's theories can be formulated in such a way that experimental tests are possible; Eysenck and Wilson (1973) have examined what are generally believed to be the most convincing examples of such experimental confirmation, and have concluded that they fail to provide any support for psychoanalytic theory. Some psychiatrists have argued that the curative effects of psychoanalytic methods can be used as evidence for the value of the underlying theories; Rachman (1971) has examined all the published evidence on the effects of psychotherapy, and has failed to find any support for these hypothetical curative effects. In view of these very negative findings, we shall abjure closer examination of these theories.

Skinner, his colleagues and pupils have in recent years advanced a theory which is offered as a general theory of human conduct; this is based essentially on operant behaviour and the effects of positive and negative reinforcements (Blackman, 1974). Summaries of recent attempts to apply these principles to neurotic and psychotic behaviour (Krasner, 1971; Ullman and Krasner, 1969) are interesting in that they fail to deal with the central paradox of neurosis, as defined by Mowrer; as he indicates, it is precisely because neurotic behaviour does not follow Thorndike's law of effect, or Skinner's laws of reinforcement, that a special theory is required to account for these departures from lawful behaviour! Simply to reiterate the laws which by definition do not account for the observed behaviour is to leave us in fact without any theory of neurotic behaviour at all. Actions followed by negative reinforcement should be eliminated from conduct; in neurotic patients this does not happen. Restatement of the general theory does not solve the riddle.

In recent years, Skinner and his followers have followed Freud into the realm of non-disconfirmable theories, by defining positive and negative reinforcements in terms of their consequences. In other words, we do not know whether a stimulus is positively or negatively reinforcing until we have discovered its consequences; however, as these consequences are to be explained in terms of the positive or negative reinforcing properties of the stimuli used, we have here a completely circular explanation which is incapable of being disproved. Circularity of explanations, and refusal to take seriously alternative explanations, are characteristics of many Skinnerian theories.

As in the case of Freud, Skinner too can rescue his theories from being considered unfalsifiable, and hence non-scientific, by accepting independent criteria of the positively or negatively reinforcing nature of stimuli. Consider Premack's (1965) reformulation of the principle of reinforcement, which now reads that a high probability (or preferred event) can be used contingently to strengthen a low probability (or non-preferred) event. How can we establish, independently of consequences, the probability of the events in question? Premack (1963) has recommended a 'free-operant' procedure in which the subject is allowed to engage in a variety of activities with unlimited access; per cent time spent on the activities or response frequencies can then be used as an index for rank ordering a given subject's preferences. This does furnish us with an external criterion of the degree to which a given reinforcer is positively or negatively active; it also furnishes us with the possibility of testing the Premack principle. Studies by Polidora and Thompson (1964) on animals, and by Schutz and Naumoff (1964) on kindergarten children have indicated marked inconsistencies among different methods, and Alter (1968) and Whitehurst (1971) found little predictive accuracy in 'cafeteria' choices for behaviour modification. Free operant 'menu' choices and verbal choices failed to show any agreement (Whitehurst and Domash, 1974), and Eysenck (1973a), in a detailed examination of the law of effect, has shown that experimental studies failed to indicate agreement between independent measures of the reinforcing effects of stimuli, and their value in producing behaviour modification. As with Freud, we may say in the case of Skinner's major principle that it is either experimentally falsified, or else that it remains inviolate because it is tautological, and untestable. From the point of view of a proper model for neurotic behaviour, we must conclude that Skinner's theory in its present form is not of any great help.

It might be possible to breathe life into it by introducing the concept of anxiety, perhaps along the lines of Mowrer's (1947) two-process theory of avoidance conditioning, but Skinnerians explicitly reject this theory, presumably because it introduces (as every scientific theory must) certain unobservables; Schoenfeld (1950) has presented a clear argument rejecting this approach, thereby cutting off Skinner's theory from any support that might have rescued it from the fate adumbrated above.

(2) *The Watson and Mowrer model*

When we now turn to Watson's theory, we find that it has not in fact been elaborated in any detail; we have to reconstitute it from a few words in his study of little Albert, the 11-months-old infant in whom he conditioned a fear of rats (Watson and Rayner, 1920), and from the early behaviour therapy experiments of his student, Mary Cover Jones (1924a, 1924b.) From these sources it would appear that Watson thought of neurotic disorders essentially as of conditioned emotional responses, the process of conditioning being entirely Pavlovian in nature. Watson never worked out his theory (if that be the right term for what is in effect merely a pointer in the direction which the prolegomena to a proper theory might take), and none of his successors have taken the task seriously, even though many have light-heartedly spoken of a 'conditioning theory' of neurosis. Such a theory has never been accepted absolutely by psychologists or psychiatrists, for the simple reason that any attempt to construct a proper model along these lines immediately runs into insuperable difficulties.

(1) One of the obvious objections to Watson's 'theory', based as this is on one single case (little Albert), is that later investigators have been unable to replicate his results (English, 1929; also Bregman, 1934). This suggests that the phenomenon in question may be affected powerfully by individual differences, and Watson's model makes no room for these. He does indeed say that 'one may possibly have to believe that such persistence of early conditioned responses will be found only in persons who are constitutionally inferior' (Watson and Rayner, 1920, p. 14.) However, this single sentence goes counter to his insistence in his major books on the absolute supremacy of environment, and the lack of genetic causes in differentiating human behaviour. Furthermore, the notion of 'constitutional inferiority' has no experimental backing, has no theoretical meaning, is untestable in its present form, and simply reinstates Victorian notions which psychiatry has already sloughed off. Watson is paying lip service to genetics, just as Freud and Skinner have done; none of these writers has taken seriously the task of specifying the precise nature of the genetic component, or of performing the necessary experiments to demonstrate the correctness of the hypothesis.

(2) Watson postulates 3 major original patterns of emotional reaction (fear, rage and love); fear is produced by simple stimuli falling into one of three categories: loud noises, loss of support, and physical constraint. Later writers have concentrated on pain (excessive sensory stimulation) as the major (or only) unconditioned source of fear responses. It is true that one or more of these supposedly 'natural' fear producers sometimes occur at the beginning of a neurosis (this is particularly true of simple phobic reactions), but it is by no means universally true of all neuroses, and is in fact probably rather unusual (except in war neuroses.) Traumatic single-trial conditioning is relatively rare in human neurosis, yet something like this is required by Watson's theory. Even multiple sub-traumatic conditioning is not often observed in the genesis of human neurosis, particularly if we restrict ourselves to these 'natural' unconditioned stimuli specified by Watson and his successors.

(3) There is direct evidence of other sources of strong fears than those postulated by Watson. Ethologists have provided good support for the notion of innate fears, which may be quite specific (see Seligman, 1972, Hinde *et al.*, 1973 and Breland and Breland, 1966) and Bandura (1969) and his colleagues have shown that 'modeling' or imitation can also produce fear responses which, while learned, are not acquired through

classical conditioning. Marks (1969) discusses these alternative methods of 'anxiety acqui-sition' in some detail. This objection is perhaps not fatal to Watson's theory, as far as it concerns neurosis; it seems unlikely that either of these two ways of producing fear and anxiety is directly and solely responsible for the production of neuroses, although they may be partly involved in directing its course.

As we shall see, it is possible to overcome the difficulties presented by these three objections; they invalidate certain aspects of Watson's theory, but leave its essential nature intact. Eysenck and Rachman (1965) have suggested a theory which effectively integrates personality with neurotic behaviour, and Gray (1971) has shown that frus-tration ('frustrative non-reward') can be shown to have physiological and behavioural consequences which are identical with those of pain. We can thus substitute frustration for pain (or loud noise, loss of support, and physical constraint) in the Watson formula, and thus extend its reach to causes much more likely to play a part in the genesis or neurosis (Eysenck, 1975a). These modifications would certainly change the Watson model in major respects, but they would also have the effect of bringing it closer to psychiatric reality. Even this revamped model, however, is still subject to damaging criticism; indeed, the two remaining criticisms would seem fatal to its survival.

(4) Unreinforced conditioned reactions extinguish quickly (Kimble, 1961), and neurotic reactions should be no exception to this rule. Eysenck and Rachman (1965) have sug-gested that the well-documented prevalence of spontaneous remission in neurosis (Rach-man, 1971) may be due to extinction of this type; however, in many cases extinction does not take place, and it is the task of a good theory to account for these 'non-fitting' cases as well as for those which behave according to expectation. Mowrer (1947) pro-posed his two-process theory of conditioning in part to account for this difficulty; according to this theory the original conditioning is 'protected' by a second stage of instrumental or operant conditioning, in which the relief from anxiety which is produced by avoidance of the CS leads to a conditioned avoidance reaction. This is analogous to the avoidance of 'reality testing' which psychiatrists have postulated, and there is no doubt that for certain cases of neurosis Mowrer's theory fits the facts very well. However, Mowrer's theory does not seem to explain the majority of clinical cases, and in any case has been criticized on experimental grounds by Herrnstein (1969) and by Seligman and Johnston (1973). It is very doubtful if the Watson–Mowrer theory can really offer convincing arguments to explain the astonishing failure of extinction to occur after many years of exposure to the unreinforced CS. Unless this fact can be explained in a satisfactory manner, the theory becomes untenable. Indeed, as the essence of the 'neurotic paradox' is precisely the failure of extinction to occur (anxiety fails to extinguish although no reinforcement is offered; behaviour which is punished continues to occur), we may say that the Watson theory fails to come to grips with the problem which it was designed to solve.

Watson himself gave it as his opinion, based on his experiments with little Albert, that 'conditioned emotional responses as well as those conditioned by transfer ... persist and modify personality throughout life.' (Watson and Rayner, 1920.) And he explicitly maintains that 'emotional disturbances in adults ... must be retraced along at least three collateral lines—to conditioned and transferred responses set up in infancy and early youth in all three of the fundamental human emotions.' (p. 14) (By 'transferred responses' Watson means what would now be called 'stimulus and response generaliza-tion', a term not then widely used.) Watson must have known of the experimental phenomenon of extinction; it is difficult to see why he did not mention the difficulties this would present to any such theory as that advocated by him. Of course Pavlov's work had not been translated at this time, and he had to base himself on casual reports; this may account for his failure. Later writers do not have this excuse.

(5) Several writers have of course noted the difficulty which the failure of extinction to occur in avoidance responding causes for a two-process fear mediation theory, begin-ning with Ritchie (1951), Solomon and Wynne (1954), and Solomon and Brush (1956). Several systems would seem to generate predictions of almost total resistance to extinc-

tion (e.g. Miller, 1951a, 1951b, 1963). Soltysik (1960, 1964) has suggested that the occurrence of an avoidance response may protect the warning stimulus from extinction. Solomon and Wynne (1954) have proposed the principle of the conservation of anxiety as a way out of this difficulty. Kimble and Perlmutter (1970) have suggested the principle of 'automatization', i.e. a process by which well-practiced responses come to be initiated without direct motivational antecedents. Schoenfeld (1950), Sidman (1953), and Dinsmoor (1954) have proposed a two-process aversion theory which aims to overcome some of the difficulties encountered by two-process fear mediation theory. Herrnstein (1969) has formulated a discriminative stimulus theory that dispenses both with fear and aversion. Last and perhaps most acceptable, Seligman and Johnston (1973) have proposed what they call a 'cognitive theory', following the tradition of Ritchie (1951), Tolman (1949), and Irwin (1971). In this theory, learned avoidance responses come to be controlled by expectations and preferences, and responses therefore can be postulated to occur even in the absence of fear.

But even if we could agree that any of these attempts to explain, rather than postulate, the lack of extinction were successful, they would still leave unexplained a further difficulty in which the Watson–Mowrer theory is involved. In many neuroses, we not only fail to observe the expected extinction of the unreinforced CS, but we find an incremental (enhancement) effect, such that the unreinforced CS actually produces more and more anxiety (CR) with each presentation of the CS. This fact is obvious when we consider the notion of 'sub-traumatic UCSs' which is sometimes introduced to salvage the Watson theory from the failure to discover traumatic UCSs in the history of development of a neurotic disorder. In the theory of Pavlovian conditioning, there is no provision for CRs to achieve greater strength than UCRs; the dog never salivates more to the bell than to the food. As Mackintosh (1974) points out, 'CRs even if they resemble the UCR very closely, are usually weaker and of lesser amplitude.' (p. 97.) Yet the very notion of 'sub-traumatic UCSs' implies something of this sort—the final CR (the neurotic breakdown) is stronger (involves more anxiety) than the UCR! This goes counter to all we know of the fate of UCRs; these are known to habituate, rather than to increase in strength.

We shall rely here more on experimental work than on clinical experience, although both in fact concur on the 'enhancement' effect postulated. Figure 1 shows the development of a UCR with repetition; the diagrammatic presentation is derived from data reported by Napalkov (1963). The experimental animals were dogs, and the UCS was a pistol shot, fired behind the dog's ear. It will be seen that after 25 repetitions habituation has reduced the UCR (increment in blood pressure) to nothing. Compare this with the fate of the conditioned stimulus, studied in another group of dogs. The CS (variable in different experiments) was paired with the UCS just once; after this one pairing the CS (unreinforced) was repeated several hundred times. It will be seen that the CR does not extinguish; it increments to many times the value of the UCR! This enhancement effect is similar to the development of neurotic disorders, and cannot be explained in terms of Watson's and Mowrer's theory. This 'enhancement' of the unreinforced CR, even more than the failure of extinction, would seem to be the central paradox of the neurotic reaction. It requires a serious modification of learning theory before it can be incorporated within such a theory.

There is much material in the literature on 'experimental neurosis' which indicates that quite frequently sub-traumatic (and in fact even mild) fear-producing stimuli, when accompanied by CSs, fail to habituate, but instead show enhancement effects leading ultimately to some form of 'neurotic' breakdown. Wolpe (1958) has given an account of many such experiments; they produce a considerable problem for the Watson-type theory. The writers concerned with these experiments tend to give *ad hoc* explanations for their results, but they fail to provide us with any general theory which might subsume all the examples given. Wolpe (1958) himself gives an explanation which is probably along the right lines, but is not deduced from general theory, or supported by specific experiments. It will be the task of the next section to provide such a theory.

Before turning to the elaboration of this theory, two points may be worth mentioning. The first point is that behaviour therapists often seem to work along the lines of an oversimplified conditioning theory which does not make use of quite well supported experimental work. Thus the efficacy of backward conditioning is often denied, although there is ample evidence that such conditioning can be produced under special *CS-UCS* conditions (Eysenck, 1975; Keith-Lucas and Guttman, 1975). Backward conditioning may play an important part in both the acquisition and the extinction of neurosis. Similarly, the relationship between number of conditioned trials and size and persistence of the *CR* is much more complicated than is usually thought. Thus for instance Kimmel (1966) pointed out that in *GSR* conditioning the *CR* increases in magnitude and reaches a peak early in conditioning; it then becomes attenuated and may even disappear completely although the *UCS* is still being paired with the *CS*. The peak *CR* is usually reached in a very few acquisition trials (2 or 3). Additional training appears to produce extinction, rather than further strengthening of the *CR*. Silver and Kimmel (1969) similarly studied resistance to extinction as a function of the number of post-peak acquisition trials; they found that greatest resistance was shown by groups given two trials past the peak. Further acquisition trials lowered resistance. A group given two trials post-peak required 40 extinction trials, while a group given 16 post-peak acquisition trials required only 15 extinction trials. Thus extinction can be facilitated by lengthy conditioning procedures, and retarded by short post-peak conditioning procedures. It is unknown whether human neurotic conditioning follows this rule, or the more usual one linking peak performance with increasing number of *CS-UCS* pairings in a monotonic manner.

In suggesting a theory of human neurosis formation, it has been necessary to go considerably beyond ascertained fact, and to extrapolate to a considerable extent from animal work. The purpose of the exercise is of course that of alerting therapists and experimentalists to certain factors which are not usually paid much attention to, but which may be of crucial importance in this field. In science, the postulation of a theory often precedes the collection of data to support or disprove it; in Popper's words, we deal with conjectures and refutations. The conjectures here put forward lack certainty because the necessary experimental work has for the most part not been done; it is one of the purposes of putting forward the theory to encourage the collection of relevant data, both by therapists and by experimentalists. Until this has been done successfully, much uncertainty must of course attend the application of the theory.

(3) *The Incubation model of anxiety*

Classical extinction theory has always been beset by experimental anomalies. In a review of forty years of American and Russian experimentation, Razran (1956) stated that 'extinction continues to be clearly a less than 100 per cent phenomenon. Instances of difficult and even impossible extinction are constantly reported by classical *CR* experimenters.' (p. 39.) Eysenck (1968) has proposed to rewrite the law of extinction completely; in his formulation there are two consequences which may follow upon the *CS*-only

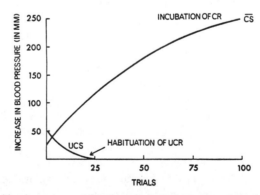

Fig. 1. Increase in blood pressure as a function of repeated exposure of the dog to *UCS* (habituation) or to *CS*-only presentation (incubation.) From Eysenck, 1975a.

presentation. We may either obtain *extinction* or *enhancement* of the *CR*. The condition for the latter effect Eysenck calls 'incubation of the anxiety/fear response'. So far, this restatement is simply a factual account of the results of numerous experiments; theoretical interest centres on the postulation of two classes of *CR* which give rise, respectively, to these two alternative types of response. According to Eysenck's argument, we must distinguish carefully between two types of *CR*, viz. those which have drive properties, and those which have not. Pavlov's bell produced a response (salivation), but this response had no drive properties. The experiment only worked when the hunger drive was already present in the dog; it did not produce the hunger drive. (It may be possible to produce a conditioned hunger drive through periodical feeding schedules; the evidence is not too clear on this point. As Mackintosh (1974) points out, 'the presentation of a stimulus established as a classical *CS* for appetitive reinforcement does not appear to increase the vigour or rate of appetitive instrumental responding' (p. 231). Also, 'stimuli paired with a reinforcing event become signals for that event rather than generators of a motivational state.' (p. 227)). Giving rats shock after a *CS* (e.g. in a shuttle box) does produce a *CS*-induced drive (Miller, 1951a); rats will learn new activities, and practice established ones, in order to avoid the *CS*. Sexual *CSs* may also be drive-producing; tumescence can be conditioned to a *CS* (Rachman, 1966; Rachman and Hodgson, 1968), and being pleasurable, may constitute a drive. However, *CSs* other than anxiety ones are poorly researched with regard to this effect, and we shall here concentrate entirely on anxiety-producing conditioned stimuli.

Our argument is that *CSs* which do not produce drives are subject to the classical law of extinction, while *CSs* which do produce drives follow the law of enhancement (incubation).* The reason for this difference is quite simple. When it is anxiety (or any other class of responses where the *CS* possesses drive properties) that is being conditioned, it is not strictly speaking true to say that the *CS* is not reinforced when the *UCS* is missing. Originally the *UCS* produces fear/anxiety, the *CS* does not. However, pairing the two leads to *CR* effects which are identical with *UCR* effects; the *CS* produces fear/anxiety responses, just as does the *UCS*! Apparently, the *CS* (after conditioning) produces fear/anxiety, i.e. the *UCR*, even though the *UCS* may now be absent. This process should set up a positive feedback cycle, with each presentation of the *CS*-only reinforcing itself, and thus continuing to increment the *CR*. It is possible to put this argument into an arithmetic form, although very crudely, and omitting such effects as habituation, etc. These are important in actual experimental work, but they do not affect the argument.

Table 1 shows the effect of the postulated incubation effect, assuming that the *CR* increments at a rate of 20% of the combined *CR–UCR* effect. It is also assumed that the *UCR* remains at uniform strength, and that no extinction of the *CR* occurs. It will be seen that under these conditions the combined *CR–UCR* effect becomes much stronger than the original *UCR* alone. We can complicate the picture somewhat by assuming that the *UCR* shows habituation at a 5% rate per trial, and that the *CR* shows extinction at a rate of 10% per trial. When these effects are added, we obtain the results shown in Table 2. Quite possibly these habituation and extinction effects should themselves be progressive, rather than equal, but there would be little point in complicating the picture by making rather arbitrary assumptions about these matters.

* The term 'incubation' has in the past sometimes been used to refer to the so-called Kamin effect (Kamin, 1957), i.e. to an increment in conditioned anxiety responses over time when *no CR* is being administered. McAllister and McAllister (1967) have reviewed the literature on this phenomenon. Eysenck (1968) and Grossman (1967) have argued that this effect is simply an example of the well known reminiscence phenomenon, i.e. the transfer of short-term memory traces to long-term storage. As such it does not deserve a separate name; if such a name is desired, the well established eponymous 'Kamin effect' should suffice, leaving the term 'incubation' for the increase in responses due to *CS*-only exposure. There certainly exists a tendency for physiological indices to show a steady increase over time (Diven, 1937; Bindra and Cameron, 1953), without *CS* presentation, but many of the behavioural studies have used active avoidance responses (Kamin, 1957; Denny and Ditchman, 1962) which make it difficult to assess whether a fear component is still present at later stages. The Kamin effect can certainly be observed clinically upon occasion, with neurotic patients, but it is doubtful if it plays an important part in the genesis of neurosis.

Table 1

	1st	2nd	3rd	4th	5th	6th
UCR:	100	100	100	100	100	100
CR:	0	20	44	73	108	150
Σ:	100	120	144	173	208	250
Added to CR:	20	24	29	35	42	50

Table 2

	1st	2nd	3rd	4th	5th	6th
UCR:	100	95	90	85	81	77
CR:	0	20	41	64	91	122
Σ:	100	115	131	149	172	199
Added to CR:	20	21	23	27	31	36

Clearly, only empirical study can furnish us with the appropriate figures for particular instances.

What would happen in a situation such as that depicted in Fig. 1, i.e. with just one conditioning trial, sub-traumatic, followed by a large number of *CS*-only trials? The answer is given in Table 3, which again makes the assumption that there are no extinction effects; it will be seen that the first *CS*-only trial shows a marked drop from the *UCS–UCR* trial, but that thereafter the *CR* increments at a slow rate. This rate, however, is gradually increasing; after 11 *CS*-only trials the strength of the *CR* surpasses the strength of the *UCR*. Inclusion of extinction effects would of course slow down this rapidly increasing enhancement effect, and would make the general shape of the curve closer to that shown in Figure 1. (It should of course be remembered that successive increments of *CR* cannot be presumed to be equal in size. As Hull, 1943, has shown, successive units of $_sH_R$ become progressively smaller as they approach the ceiling; he shows how to compute habit strength on p. 119 of his book. We have omitted this feature of the *CR* growth curve as it is irrelevant to our argument.) Despite the rough and ready nature of the calculations, and the arbitrariness of the assumptions, these calculations do show that the mechanisms postulated can succeed in producing the effect empirically observed, namely the existence of a positive feedback cycle which works in the absence of the *UCS*.

(4) *Empirical support for the incubation hypothesis*

Clearly the postulated enhancement effect should be experimentally verifiable, and equally clearly such verification is most likely to come from animal studies specially designed for the purpose. Before briefly commenting on the few studies which comply with these conditions, we may mention a series of studies which clearly show the postulated effect, although they were not carried out in an attempt to test the writer's hypothesis. Lichtenstein (1950) and Dykman, Mack and Ackerman (1965) have reported instances of 'fixation' of fear responses during attempted extinction trials with dogs. As the latter authors state, 'apparently to dogs the threat is more traumatic than the presence of the shock' (p. 222). Maatsch (1959) has reported a similar continued increase in an avoidance *CR*, in rats subjected to a single shock trial, over a fixation criterion of 100 massed extinction trials. Napalkov's (1963) study has already been mentioned; his work was followed by that of Reynierse (1966) who found that both time and

Table 3

	1st	2nd	3rd	4th	5th	6th
UCR:	100	—	—	—	—	—
CR:	0	20	24	29	35	42
Σ:	100	20	24	29	35	42
Added to CR:	20	4	5	6	7	8

duration of CS-only exposure were influential in deciding on the course of extinction/enhancement (see also Baum, 1972, and Sartory and Eysenck, 1975b). In human subjects, Campbell, Sanderson and Laverty (1964) found enhancement effects after a single, traumatic experience of respiratory paralysis; despite repeated extinction trials, 30 administered 5 min after conditioning, 30 one week later, and 40 two weeks after that, GSR continued to gain strength over time. These and other slightly less relevant studies have been reviewed in Eysenck (1968).

More recently, Rohrbaugh and Riccio (1970), Silvestri, Rohrbaugh and Riccio (1970) and Rohrbaugh, Riccio and Arthur (1972) have attempted to test the writer's incubation theory directly. They exposed rats to CS-only, in the form of apparatus cues, between conditioning and testing, and succeeded in demonstrating enhancement effect. They also tested the hypothesis that duration of CS-only exposure was an important variable, and succeeded in demonstrating that short CS-only exposures produced enhancement, long CS-only exposures extinction. More recently still, Sartory and Eysenck (1975a) studied five different strains of rats which were repeatedly subjected to extinction trials following Pavlovian fear conditioning, the duration of the extinction trials being varied for different groups of animals. Results showed that fearfulness of the animals (strain differences) and duration of extinction trials were jointly and severally causal in determining the degree of extinction of the conditioned fear response.

Relevant to this discussion, and in particular the duration effects of CS-only presentation, is work on response-prevention or 'flooding' techniques, both in the animal field and in the field of behaviour therapy with human patients. Rapid extinction of responses has been found with this technique in animals (e.g. Baum, 1966; Page and Hall, 1953; Polin, 1959), and also with neurotics (e.g. Rachman et al., 1971; Hodgson et al., 1972; Rachman et al., 1973; see also review by Baum, 1970.) These studies all used lengthy CS-only presentations; with short presentations failures of extinction to occur have been observed, and in many cases incubation (enhancement) effects (review by Wood, 1974). Thus in a study reported by Rachman (1966), one of three spider-phobic subjects, exposed for ten sessions to CS-only presentation of spiders for 2-min periods, reported that her fear of spiders *increased* during treatment. Periods of 1–1½ hr seems best for producing extinction effects. Wolpe (1958) has also reported that desensitization procedures, which require gradually increasing exposure to ever more anxiety-provoking stimuli, can have their effects destroyed by accidental exposure during treatment to stimuli which produce too high a level of anxiety; such short-term exposures to CS-only apparently produce strong enhancement effects, as would be expected from the experimental animal work. Thus studies on neurotic patients bear out the main conclusions of the animal studies.

A number of recent studies with human subjects have investigated experimentally the effects of short vs. long exposure to CS-only. Miller and Levis (1971) succeeded in verifying the importance of length of CS-only exposure on the fate of the CR. Proctor (1968) and Watts (1971) studied the influence of intra-item exposure time to aversive stimuli on systematic desensitization. Ross and Proctor (1973) found long single exposure to hierarchy items more effective in reducing avoidance behaviour than short exposure. Sue (1975) has reviewed a number of successful and unsuccessful extinction-like studies in humans (exposure only), and found that success depended crucially on length of exposure; his own study gave similar results. There are also studies showing that exposure to symbolic representations of feared stimuli can elicit unexpected *increases* in autonomic responses, whether these stimuli were visual (Borkovec and Glasgow, 1973), verbal descriptions (Boulougouris, Marks and Marset, 1971), or self-induced thoughts (Rankin et al., 1964; Bresnitz, 1967.) Stone and Borkovec (1975) also found evidence of a paradoxical effect of brief CS-only exposure on analogue phobic subjects, in a study replicating that of Miller and Levis (1971), but with certain additions which served to test (and disprove) hypotheses regarding the phenomenon of fear incubation advanced by Staub (1968) and others.

These studies are important, not only in supporting the general theory here offered, but also because they specify in detail one of the parameters determining the effect of the *CS*-only presentation. Time and duration of *CS*-only presentation are apparently crucial in determining whether extinction or enhancement are observed. Future research will no doubt look for other determinants; such parameter studies are essential if any real understanding and control of this phenomenon is to be achieved. Perhaps the most important of the variables to be investigated would appear to be personality; both *E* (extraversion–introversion) and *N* (neuroticism–stability) would seem to be involved in determining the effects of *CS*-only presentation. We would expect stable extraverts to extinguish more readily than other groups, and we would expect neurotic introverts to show most evidence of incubation.* These predictions follow directly from the writer's general biological theory of personality (Eysenck, 1967). *N* is implicated in the strength of the *UCR*, *E* in the development of the *CR* (introverts condition more readily than extraverts, particularly under conditions unfavourable to the development of conditioned responses.) Under identical experimental conditions, we can see that this prediction is reasonable by substituting in Tables 2 and 3 differential values for extraverts and introverts, stable and high-*N* subjects. Instead of using the figure of 100 as the average *UCR*, we might write 120 for high-*N* subjects, and 80 for low-N subjects. Similarly, instead of using an average figure of 20% for the *CR*, we might use 10% for extraverts and 30% for introverts. These figures are not too far removed from the sort of results obtained in experimental work, and they provide material for working out expected differences in extinction or incubation of *CS*-only produced responses. Unfortunately there is no published work on differential response rates in conditioning experiments which simulate the type of design used by Rohrbaugh and Riccio (1970).† Possibly relevant are such studies as those of Franks (1963) showing that subjects who condition well also extinguish poorly, even though matched with poor conditioners on level of *CR* strength reached. The study of Campbell, Sanderson and Laverty (1964) already mentioned would be relevant, but they used too few subjects to make correlation with personality feasible.

Another parameter variable which must be presumed to be important in relation to the appearance of extinction or enhancement effects after *CS*-only presentation is the strength of the *UCS* (Annau and Kamin, 1961). The theory would assume that each *CS*-only presentation has consequences leading to extinction, and also consequences leading to enhancement; it is the *relative* strength of these tendencies which determine whether extinction or enhancement will occur, and how quickly and strongly it will occur. As Table 2 makes clear, much will depend on the strength of the *UCR*; the stronger this is, the greater will be the probability that enhancement will occur. Equally, the weaker the *UCR*, the more likely is extinction to occur (Appel, 1961). Strength of the *UCS* and the *UCR* are therefore important variables, although little systematic work has been done in this connection. The fact that the Campbell, Sanderson and Laverty study is the only experimental study to note enhancement effects in humans, and that it is also the one study to use a very strong *UCS*, reinforces the suggestion made, although in the absence of planned parameter studies it cannot serve as sufficient proof for the hypothesis. The strength of the *UCS* must of course always be related to the personality of the subject; identical stimuli may produce quite different *UCRs* in different people, depending on their standing on the *E* and *N* dimensions, on their

---

* Both *E* and *N* have a strong genetic component (Eysenck, 1957b.) It seems likely, therefore, that Watson's 'constitutional inferiority' suggestion may in fact refer to the dysthymic personality which, while certainly more susceptible to neurotic disorders than most, is certainly not 'inferior' in any more general sense. In one study, for instance, a group of extremely gifted creative visual artists was found to be made up entirely of dysthymics (Eysenck, 1973b, p. 268.) Looked at from this point of view, 'high *N*/low *E*' people would appear constitutionally superior rather than inferior! Personality qualities usually lead to both positive and negative pay-offs, and cannot be regarded as 'good' or 'bad' in any absolute sense.

† Studies have been published which make use of differentially-bred strains of rats in this connection; the relevance of these depends on the degree to which it is judged reasonable to accept the comparability of 'emotional reactivity' in rats and high *N* scores in humans. For a discussion of such studies, see Sartory and Eysenck (1975a).

past history of reinforcement and conditioning, and perhaps also on specific heritable fear responses.

It may be asked why it is that *UCRs* habituate, while on the account given in this section *CRs* may show no such habituation. There are two possibilities. The first is that *CRs* under conditions of *CS*-only exposure do habituate, but that the rate of habituation–extinction is less than that of enhancement. Our theory would suggest that this would only happen in certain types of personality, e.g. high *N*/low *E* individuals. The other possibility is that habituation is linked with *UCRs*, and not with *CRs*, because although the nocive end-effect is similar in the two, there are also important differences. Extraction of a tooth (*UCS*) is followed by a short, sharp pain (*UCR*). Anticipation of the visit to the dentist (*CS*) is followed by a lengthy period of increasing anxiety (*CR*). Both types of response are nocive, and hence have drive properties, but it seems quite possible that the *UCR* may habituate, having no *anticipatory* properties, while the *CR* might not do so, being entirely anticipatory. This difference also suggests another important point. The actual strength of the *UCR* may be much greater than that of the *CR*, but its duration is much shorter; the nocive nature of the response may be a product of strength and duration. This again brings into the picture individual differences; high *N*/high *E* individuals (psychopaths) are known to have much steeper anticipatory fear gradients than others, thus producing a much weaker *CR* (Hare, 1970, p. 82). This may be responsible for their failure to produce anticipatory fear conditioning, and thus account for their psychopathic behaviour and their lack of anticipation of punishment. Habituation is to an event already past (the *UCR*); failure to experience habituation is connected with events yet to come (the *CR*). The physiological mechanisms involved may thus be quite different. Unfortunately little is in fact known about this differential response; the problem is raised in the hope that future research may be directed to its solution.

(5) *The Place of preparedness*

The concept of incubation (enhancement of the unreinforced *CS*) may not be enough to give a satisfactory explanation of neurotic behaviour, even if we also take into account the factor of individual differences. Seligman (1970, 1971) has advanced the hypothesis of 'preparedness' to account for certain features of neurotic, and particularly phobic behaviour which would seem to create difficulties for our theory as much as for previous ones. As he points out, 'phobias comprise a nonarbitrary and limited set of objects, whereas fear conditioning is thought to occur to an unlimited range of conditioned stimuli. Furthermore, phobias, unlike laboratory fear conditioning, are often acquired in one trial and seem quite resistant to change by "cognitive" means' (p. 307).

Seligman argues that the failure of extinction to occur in typical animal experiments (e.g. Solomon, Kamin and Wynne, 1953; Seligman and Campbell, 1965) is quite different in many ways from the failure of extinction to occur in neurotic human subjects. In animal work, 'it does not follow from failure of avoidance to extinguish that classical conditioning of fear does not extinguish' (p. 309). Typically, contingencies are arranged so that if the animal avoids on every trial (i.e. responds to the *CS* and terminates it before the shock would have appeared) it is no longer exposed to the fact that the tone no longer predicts shock; when the avoidance response is prevented, thus forcing the animal to 'reality test', avoidance readily extinguishes (e.g. Baum, 1970.) 'Avoidance extinguishes after blocking because fear is extinguished, since the subject is exposed to the *CS* no longer predicting the *UCS*. Avoidance fails to extinguish before blocking because the response is continually reinforced by shock prevention and by *CS* termination' (p. 310). Seligman goes on to suggest that in humans 'the problem we are tackling is that phobics actually exposed to the *CS* do not extinguish.... For example, a spider phobic individual will think about spiders, see pictures of spiders, and even actually see spiders. All of these situations constitute exposure to the *CS* (more or less) no longer paired with the original *UCS*. Yet it is commonplace that such inadvertent exposures rarely weaken, and may even strengthen, the phobia' (p. 311).

The answer to this objection is two-fold. In the first place, phobias and even obsessive-compulsive symptoms readily extinguish when escape-prevention exposure to the CS is introduced (e.g. Hodgson et al., 1972; Rachman et al., 1973). And in the second place, these casual exposures Seligman mentions are usually of very short duration, and we have seen that the experimental literature on incubation supports the hypothesis that short exposures to the unreinforced CS strengthen, rather than weaken, the CR; it is long-continued exposure that extinguishes the CR. So far, there is no reason to add new concepts to our general theory.

Seligman's second point is more cogent. He points out that in Pavlovian conditioning, one CS is as good as another; 'Any natural phenomenon chosen at will may be converted into a conditioned stimulus ... any visual stimulus, any desired sound, and odor and the stimulation of any part of the skin' (Pavlov, 1928, p. 86). This does not seem true of phobias, however; 'they comprise a relatively nonarbitrary and limited set of objects: agoraphobia, fear of specific animals, insect phobias, fear of heights, and fear of the dark, etc. All these are relatively common phobias. And only rarely, if ever, do we have pyjama phobias, grass phobias, electric-outlet phobias, hammer phobias, even though these things are likely to be associated with trauma in our world.' (Seligman, 1971, p. 312). The set of potentially phobic stimuli thus seems to be nonarbitrary, and to be related to the survival of the human species through the long course of evolution, rather than to recent discoveries and inventions which potentially are far more rational sources of phobic fears, such as motor cars, aeroplanes, and guns (Geer, 1965; Landy and Gaupp, 1971; Lawlis, 1971; Rubin et al., 1968; Wolpe and Lang, 1964). Another important peculiarity about phobias is that they are frequently acquired by single-trial conditioning; such conditioning is rare in the experimental laboratory, where usually some half-dozen trials are required (e.g. Kamin, 1969; Seligman, 1968). We have argued in a previous section that single-trial conditioning is in fact relatively rare in the acquisition of neurotic disorders, even of phobias; nevertheless it does occur, and perhaps more frequently than one might have expected on the basis of laboratory experiments. This fact, together with the previously mentioned nonarbitrary nature of the CS, had led Seligman to argue for a theory of *preparedness*, according to which fears may not be innate, as we have postulated, but rather that 'phobias are highly prepared to be learned by humans, and, like other highly prepared relationships, they are selective and resistant to extinction, learned even with degraded input, and probably are non-cognitive' (Seligman, 1971, p. 312). Seligman gives examples of the fact that some contingencies are learned much more readily than others, i.e. with highly degraded input, such as single-trial learning, long delay of reinforcement, etc.; the work of Garcia et al., (1971) has become a classical example of this.

This conception of preparedness helps to explain, among other things, why Bregman (1934) and English (1929) failed to get fear conditioning in their replication of Watson's experiment with little Albert; they used common household goods, such as curtains and blocks, or a wooden duck, none of which would have the 'preparedness' value of furry animals. Another problem which may be explained by this concept is the choice of CS—why, in a traumatic situation (or, in our theory, in a series of sub-traumatic situations) does the person concerned pick on one rather than another equally prominent stimulus to become *the CS?* On Seligman's showing, the choice would be determined very much by innate preparedness, in addition to the usual chance factors.

The notion of preparedness integrates well with the hypothesis of innate fears; presumably it is mainly a question of *degree* of fear experienced which separates the two concepts. When the fear is strong upon first encountering the stimulus object, it is considered innate; when it is weak, but easily conditioned, we think of preparedness. The underlying physiological connections, and the hypothetical evolutionary development, are identical. The concept is a valuable one, and appears necessary for a full understanding of phobic neuroses in particular. Presumably it, too, must be seen in the context of individual differences; it seems likely that extraversion and neuroticism are as relevant to preparedness as they are to the development of neurotic illnesses, or to incubation.

There exists the possibility, of course, that preparedness may interact with incubation, in the sense that incubation will be more readily established in connection with stimuli which are high on the 'preparedness' rank order. This may explain the relative paucity of reports of incubation with laboratory stimuli; incubation may only occur in certain people (high N, low E) or rat strains (emotional reactive), with certain stimuli (high preparedness), under specified conditions (short exposure to unreinforced CS, strong UCS.) Clearly there is here the beginning of an extensive research programme which will have to be completed before we can assert that the theory here advanced can in fact be used to explain all the details of neurotic behaviour. However, it seems likely that neither the Watson–Mowrer model, nor the Seligman 'preparedness' model, can by themselves explain important features of neurotic behaviour. We have already discussed the weaknesses of the Watson–Mowrer model; the 'preparedness' model suffers from the fact that it postulates, in terms of innate propensities, what requires to be explained. In this sense, therefore, it does not seem possible to disprove it by any particular experimental paradigm. Its main usefulness lies in accounting for the specificity (nonarbitrariness) of CSs, and the relative ease with which these can be learned with highly degraded input. Even these points, of course, have not received sufficient experimental clarification, but the indirect evidence quoted by Seligman (1970, 1971) is certainly telling, and may justify the inclusion of this hypothesis here.

SUMMARY AND CONCLUSIONS

It has been suggested in this paper that the theories associated with Freud and Skinner cannot serve to explain the main 'neurotic paradox', and it has also been suggested that the theories associated with Watson and Mowrer fail to do so satisfactorily. It is, however, possible to make these theories more adequate for the purpose by making certain important changes in the way that Pavlovian conditioning is supposed to work; these changes are congruent with more recent experimental work in conditioning and in behaviour therapy. It may be useful to present the main features of our new theory of neurosis in the form of short statements of its major characteristics.

(1) Maladaptive and unreasoning fears can be innate, or they can be acquired through 'modeling' (imitation). Innate processes, however, are more likely to *sensitize* a person to certain types of stimuli, and *facilitate* the conditioning of fear responses to these stimuli ('preparedness').* 'Modeling', by itself, also does not seem likely to produce the strong and long-continued fear/anxiety reactions which characterise neurotics.

(2) The main process leading to neurotic fear/anxiety responses is probably Pavlovian (classical) conditioning. This may be either of traumatic, single-trial kind, or may be sub-traumatic, repeated presentation of the CS–UCS combination.

(3) The main UCS in human conditioning outside the laboratory is probably not pain, or the three types of stimuli suggested by Watson (loud noises, loss of support, and physical constraint,) but frustration ('frustrative non-reward', as it is technically known.) Physical pain may play a part in the genesis of certain neurotic disorders, particularly in war-time, but frustration, and conflict giving rise to frustration, is probably a more pervasive UCS in peace time.†

(4) Conditioned responses, under conditions of non-reinforcement (CS-only presentation), may extinguish; this is probably the fate of neurosis-producing stimuli during

---

* It is possible that the importance of preparedness is not in relation to the conditioning of fear responses but rather to their failure to extinguish. There is some experimental evidence in favour of this hypothesis (Öhman, Erixon and Löfberg, 1975), and it would go well with the incubation hypothesis and the general stress in this article on failure to extinguish as a characteristic of neurotic responses.

† Much of this paper is worded in terms of pain as the UCR; this is inevitable in view of the fact that most of the experimental literature, particularly the animal literature, has traditionally employed this concept and experimental model. The use of 'frustrative non-reward', 'approach-avoidance' conflict, and other sources of 'psychic pain' in this connection is relatively recent; it is hoped that future research will make more frequent use of these sources of abient behaviour than has been the case in the past. Until such research is done the extension of the experimental results obtained with the use of pain as the UCR to these alternative responses is somewhat speculative.

'spontaneous remission'. However, extinction is not the only possible consequence of the presentation of CS-only stimuli.

(5) Under certain specified conditions, presentation of CS-only stimuli produces incubation (enhancement) of the CR; the more frequently the CS-only is presented, the greater will be the CR. It is this process which is believed to be responsible for the growth and the continuation of neurotic responses.

(6) Incubation is postulated to occur in one class of CSs only, namely those which acquire *drive properties* as a result of the conditioning process. It is these drive properties which make the CR functionally equivalent to the UCR, thus providing reinforcement for the CS-only presentation. In this way, a positive feedback cycle is set up which produces CR incrementation (enhancement) instead of extinction.

(7) Fear/anxiety responses are the prime example of CRs which possess drive properties which can become linked with the CS.* It is possible that sex is another type of response which may fall into this category. This may account for the frequency with which sexual disorders are found in neurosis, and for the easy conditioning of sexual behaviours, even of the most deviant form.

(8) Conditions which favour the emergence of incubation of fear/anxiety responses after CS-only presentation are suggested to be the following: (a) short as opposed to long presentation; (b) strong as opposed to weak UCS; (c) personality characteristics of subjects—high N vs. low N, and introversion vs. extraversion. There is strong evidence for (a), but only weak evidence for (b) and (c) to date.

(9) Incubation allows CRs to exceed in strength the UCR, and it also permits the slow growth of neurotic responses over time, with occasional exposure to CS-only. There is good experimental evidence, both in animals and in humans, for the existence of this process.

(10) The 'learning theory' model of neurosis here presented is not subject to the objections made to earlier models employing Pavlovian conditioning as their main mechanism. It is not subject to experimental objections, as were the Watson and the Mowrer models, and it is not subject to clinical objections of failure to account for observed processes in the development of human neuroses. Many anomalies are likely to remain; these may make necessary further changes in the details of the model.† However, the revision of the law of extinction has removed what was the essential stumbling block in the acceptance of a conditioning model; what is now most urgently needed is further research guided by the postulates of the model, both to test its adequacy, and to explore the parameters suggested in (3) above. When this has been done, it may prove possible to give the model a more adequate quantitative formulation.

REFERENCES

ALTER M. (1968) *Identification of high probability responses and their use as reinforcers.* Unpublished doctoral dissertation, University of Utah.
ANNAU Z. and KAMIN L. J. (1961) The conditioned emotional response as a function of intensity of the US. *J. comp. physiol. Psychol.* **54**, 428–432.

* There may be need of further explication of this point, in relation to point 3 above, as the postulation of 'frustrative non-reward' (which finds its experimental support mainly in animal work) as the cause of nocive stimulation seems to conflict with the postulation of fear/anxiety responses as drive-producing CSs. Frustration does not normally lead to fear/anxiety in humans, and although the physiological and behavioural responses of animals to the two classes of stimuli (pain and frustration) are similar, we can say nothing about resulting 'mental states' from animal experimentation. Emotions are named in response to the situation, as well as the physiological response; this may make the term 'fear/anxiety' unsuitable for responses to frustration. Possibly Seligman's concept of 'learned helplessness' (Seligman, 1975) might be helpful here. Another alternative is Mowrer's (1960) analysis of major effects into fear, relief, hope, and disappointment; Mowrer directly links frustration with fear. His system of course is based on animal experimentation, but he himself also extends it to human neurosis.

† One extension of the whole conception of 'fear' which has not been treated in detail in this account is that referred to as 'desynchrony' by Rachman and Hodgson (1974) and Hodgson and Rachman (1974). They refer to the observation that the three major components of fear (subjective experience, avoidance behaviour, and physiological disturbance) do not necessarily covary, but may on occasion vary independently, or even inversely (Lang, 1970). Desynchrony of fear responses certainly complicates the picture here presented, but it does not seem at present to invalidate our theory.

APPEL J. A. (1961) Punishment: the Squirrell Monkey Saimiri Sciurea. *Science* **36**, 133.

BANDURA A. (1969) *Principles of behavior identification*. Rinehart and Winston. New York.

BAUM M. (1966) Rapid extinction of an avoidance response following a period of response prevention in the avoidance apparatus. *Psychol. Rep.* **18**, 59–64.

BAUM M. (1970) Extinction of avoidance responding through response prevention (flooding). *Psychol. Bull.* **74**, 276–284.

BAUM M. (1972) Flooding (response prevention) in rats: the effects of immediate *vs* delayed flooding and of changed illumination conditions during flooding. *Can. J. Psychol.* **26**, 190–200.

BINDRA D. and CAMERON L. (1953) Changes in experimentally produced anxiety with the passage of time: incubation effect. *J. exp. Psychol.* **45**, 197–203.

BLACKMAN D. (1974) *Operant conditioning*. Methuen, London.

BORKOVEC F. D. and GLASGOW R. E. (1973) Boundary conditions of false heart-rate feedback effects on avoidance behavior: a resolution of discrepant results. *Behav. Res. and Therapy* **11**, 171–177.

BOULOUGOURIS J. C., MARKS I. and MARSET P. (1971) Superiority of flooding (implosion) to desensitization for reducing pathological fear. *Behav. Res. and Therapy* **9**, 7–16.

BREGMAN E. (1934) An attempt to rectify the emotional attitudes of infants by the conditioned response technique. *J. genet. Psychol.* **45**, 169–198.

BRELAND K. and BRELAND M. (1966) *Animal behavior*. Macmillan, New York.

BRESNITZ S. (1967) Incubation of threat and duration of anticipation and false alarm as determinants of the fear reaction to an unavoidable frightening event. *J. exp. Res. Personality* **2**, 173–179.

CAMPBELL D., SANDERSON R. E. and LAVERTY S. A. (1964) Characteristics of a conditioned response in human subjects during extinction trials following a simple traumatic conditioning trial. *J. abnorm. soc. Psychol.* **68**, 627–693.

DENNY M. R. and DITCHMAN R. E. (1962) The locus of the 'maximal' Kamin effect in rats. *J. comp. Physiol. Psychol.* **55**, 1069–1070.

DINSMOOR J. A. (1954) Punishment. I. The avoidance hypothesis *Psychol. Rev.* **61**, 34–46.

DIVEN E. (1937) Certain determinants in the conditioning of anxiety reactions. *J. Psychol.* **3**, 291–308.

DYKMAN R. J., MACK R. L. and ACKERMAN P. T. (1965) The evaluation of autonomic and motor components of the nonavoidance conditioned response in the dog. *Psychophysiol.* **1**, 209–230.

ENGLISH H. B. (1929) Three cases of the 'conditional fear response'. *J. abnorm. soc. Psychol.* **34**, 221–225.

EYSENCK H. J. (1967) *The biological basis of personality*. C. C. Thomas, Springhill.

EYSENCK H. J. (1968) A theory of the incubation of anxiety/fear responses. *Behav. Res. and Therapy* **6**, 319–321.

EYSENCK H. J. (1973a) Personality and the law of effect. In: *Please, reward, preference* (Eds. D. E. Berlyne and M. B. Madsen). Academic Press, New York.

EYSENCK H. J. (1973b) *The Inequality of Man*. Temple Smith, London.

EYSENCK H. J. (1975a) Anxiety and the natural history of neurosis. In: *Stress and Anxiety* (Eds. C. Spielberger and I. Sarason). Hemisphere Publishing Corp., New York.

EYSENCK H. J. (1975b) Genetic factors in personality development. In: *Human Behavior Genetics* (Ed. A. R. Kaplan). C. C. Thomas, Springfield.

EYSENCK H. J. (1975) A note on backward conditioning. *Behav. Res. and Therapy* **13**, 201–202.

EYSENCK H. J. and RACHMAN S. (1965) *Causes and cures of neurosis*. Routledge and Kegan Paul, London.

EYSENCK H. J. and WILSON G. D. (1973) *The experimental study of Freudian theories*. Methuen, London.

FRANKS C. M. (1963) Ease of conditioning and spontaneous recovery from experimental extinction. *Br. J. Psychol.* **54**, 351–357.

GARCIA J., McGOVAN B. and GREEN K. (1971) Sensory quality and integration: constraints on conditioning? In: *Classical conditioning* (Eds. A. H. Black and W. F. Prokasy). Appleton-Century-Crofts, New York.

GEER J. H. (1965) The development of a scale to measure fear. *Behav. Res. and Therapy* **3**, 45–53.

GRAY J. (1971) *The psychology of fear and stress*. World University Library, London.

GROSSMAN S. P. A. (1967) *A textbook of physiological psychology*. Wiley, New York.

HARE R. D. (1970) *Psychopathy*. John Wiley & Son, London.

HERRNSTEIN R. J. (1969) Method and theory in the study of avoidance. *Psychol. Rev.* **76**, 49–69.

HINDE R. A. and STEVENSON-HINDE J. (1973) *Constraints on learning*. Academic Press, London.

HODGSON R. J., RACHMAN S. and MARKS I. M. (1972) The treatment of chronic obsessive-compulsive neurosis: follow up and further findings. *Behav. Res. and Therapy* **10**, 181–189.

HODGSON R. L. and RACHMAN S. (1974) II Desynchrony in measures of fear. *Behav. Res. and Therapy* **12**, 319–326.

HULL C. L. (1943) *Principles of behaviour*. Appleton-Century-Crofts, London.

IRWIN F. W. (1971) *Intentional behaviour and motivation: A cognitive theory*. Lippincott, New York.

JONES M. C. (1924a) A laboratory study of fear: the case of Peter. *Pedagogical Seminar* **31**, 308–315.

JONES M. C. (1924b) The Elimination of childrens' fear. *J. exp. Psychol.* **7**, 383–390.

KAMIN L. (1957) The retention of an incompletely learned avoidance response. *J. comp. physiol. Psychol.* **50**, 457–460.

KAMIN L. (1969) Predictability, surprise, attention and conditioning. In: *Punishment and aversive behavior* (Eds. B. A. Campbell & R. M. Church). Appleton-Century-Crofts, New York.

KEITH-LUCAS T. and GUTTMAN N. (1975) Robust single-trial delayed backward conditioning. *J. comp. physiol. Psychol.* **88**, 468–476.

KIMBLE G. (1961) *Hilgard and Marquis, 'Conditioning and Learning'*. Appleton-Century-Crofts, New York.

KIMBLE G. and PERLMUTTER L. C. (1970) The problem of volition. *Psychol. Rev.* **77**, 361–384.

KIMMEL V. D. (1966) Inhibition of the unconditioned response in classical conditioning. *Psychol. Rev.* **73**, 232–240.

KRASNER L. (1971) The operant approach in behaviour therapy. In: *Handbook of Psychotherapy and Behavior Change* (Eds. A. E., Bergin and G. L. Garfield). J. Wiley & Son, New York. 612–652.

LANDY F. J. and GAUPP L. A. (1971) A factor analysis of the fear survey schedule III. *Behav. Res. and Therapy* **9**, 89–93.

LANG P. (1970) Stimulus control, response control and desensitization of fear. In: *Learning Approaches to Behavior Change* (Ed. D. Lewis). Aldine, Chicago.

LAWLIS G. F. (1971) Response syles of a patient population on the fear survey schedule. *Behav. Res. and Therapy* **9**, 95–102.

LICHTENSTEIN P. E. (1950) Studies of anxiety: I. The production of a feeding inhibition in dogs. *J. comp. physiol. Psychol.* **43**, 16–29.

MAATSCH J. L. (1959) Learning and fixation after a single shock trial. *J. comp. physiol. Psychol.* **52**, 408–410.

MACKINTOSH N. J. (1974) *The Psychology of Animal Learning*. Academic Press, London.

MARKS I. M. (1969) *Fears and phobias.* Heinemann, London.

McALLISTER W. R. and McALLISTER D. E. (1967) Incubation of fear: an examination of the concept. *J. exp. Res. Personality* **2**, 180–190.

MILLER B. V. and LEVIS D. J. (1971) The effects of varying short visual exposure times to a phobic stimulus on subsequent avoidance behaviour. *Behav. Res. and Therapy* **9**, 17–21.

MILLER N. E. (1951) Learnable drives and rewards. In: *Handbook of Experimental Psychology* (Ed. S. S. Stevens). John Wiley & Son, New York.

MILLER N. E. (1951b) Comments on multiple process conceptions of learning. *Psychol. Rev.* **58**, 375–381.

MILLER N. E. (1963) Some reflections on the law of effect produce a new alternative to drive reduction. In: *Nebraska Symposium on Motivation* (Ed. M. R. Jones). University of Nebraska Press, Lincoln, Nebraska, 65–112.

MOWRER O. H. (1939) A stimulus-reponse analysis of anxiety and its role as a reinforcing agent. *Psychol. Rev.* **46**, 553–565.

MOWRER O. H. (1947) On the dual nature of learning as a reinterpretation of 'conditioning' and 'problem-solving'. *Harvard Educational Review*, 102–148.

MOWRER O. H. (1950) *Learning theory and personality dynamics.* Arnold Press, New York, 483–530.

MOWRER O. H. (1960) *Learning theory and the symbolic processes.* John Wiley & Son, New York.

NAPALKOV S. V. (1963) Information process and the brain. In: *Progress in brain research* (Eds. N. Wiener and J. Schadel), Vol. 2, 59–69. Elsevier, Amsterdam.

ÖHMAN A., ERIXON G. and LÖFBERG I. (1975) Phobias and preparedness: phobic versus neutral pictures as conditioned stimuli for human autonomic responses. *J. abnorm. Psychol.* **84**, 51–45.

PAGE H. A. and HALL J. F. (1953) Experimental extinction as a function of the prevention of a response. *J. comp. physiol. Psychol.* **46**, 33–34.

PAVLOV I. P. (1928) *Lectures on conditioned reflexes.* International Publishers, New York.

POLIDORA V. J. and THOMPSON W. J. (1964) Stimulus correlates of visual pattern discrimination by monkeys: area and contour. *J. comp. physiol. Psychol.* **58**, 264–269.

POLIN J. T. (1959) The effect of flooding and physical suppression as extinction techniques on the anxiety-motivated locomotor response. *J. Psychol.* **47**, 253–255.

PREMACK D. (1963) Rate differential reinforcement in monkey manipulation. *J. exp. Anal. Behav.* **6**, 81–89.

PREMACK D. (1965) Reinforcement theory. In: *Nebraska Symposium on Motivation* (Ed. D. Levine). University of Nebraska Press, Lincoln, 123–180.

RACHMAN S. (1966) Studies in desensitization: II. Flooding. *Behav. Res. and Therapy* **4**, 1–6.

RACHMAN S. (1966b) Sexual fetishism: an experimental analogue. *Psychol. Res.* **16**, 293–296.

RACHMAN S. (1971) *The effects of psychotherapy.* Pergamon, London.

RACHMAN S. and HODGSON R. J. (1968) Experimentally induced 'sexual fetishism.' *Psychol. Rec.* **18**, 25–27.

RACHMAN S., HODGSON R. J. and MARKS I. M. (1971) Treatment of chronic obsessive compulsive neurosis. *Behav. Res. and Therapy* **9**, 237–247.

RACHMAN S., MARKS I. M. and HODGSON R. J. (1973) The treatment of obsession-compulsive neurotics by modelling and flooding *in vivo. Behav. Res. and Therapy* **11**, 463–471.

RACHMAN S. and HODGSON R. J. (1974) I. Synchrony and desynchrony in fear and avoidance. *Behav. Res. and Therapy* **12**, 311–318.

RANKIN N. O., NOMIKOS M. S., OPTON E. M. and LAZARUS R. S. *The roles of surprise and suspense in a stress reaction.* Paper delivered at Western Psychological Association Meeting, June 1964. Quoted by Stove and Borkovec, 1975.

RAZRAN G. (1956) Extinction re-examined and re-analysed: a new theory. *Psychol. Rev.* **63**, 39–52.

REYNIERSE J. H. (1960) Effects of CS-only trials on resistance to extinction of an avoidance response. *J. comp. physiol. Psychol.* **61**, 156–158.

RITCHIE B. F. (1951) Can reinforcement theory account for avoidance? *Psychol. Rev.* **58**, 382–386.

ROHRBAUGH M. and RICCIO D. V. (1970) Paradoxical enhancement of learned fear. *J. abnorm. Psychology*, **75**, 210–216.

ROHRBAUGH M., RICCIO D. V. and ARTHUR S. (1972) Paradoxical enhancement of conditioned suppression. *Behav. Res. and Therapy* **10**, 125–130.

ROSS S. M. and PROCTOR S. (1973) Frequency and duration of hierarchy item response in a systematic desensitization analogue. *Behav. Res. and Therapy* **11**, 303–312.

RUBIN B. M., KATKIN E. S., WEISS B. W. and EFRAN J. S. (1968) Factor analysis of a fear survey schedule. *Behav. Res. and Therapy* **6**, 65–75.

SARTORY G. and EYSENCK H. J. (1975a) Strain differences in the acquisition and extinction of fear responses in rats. *Psychol. Rep.*, in press.

SARTORY G. and EYSENCK H. J. (1975b) The effects of immediate and delayed extinction trials on a classically conditioned fear response. *Psychol. Rep.*, in press.

SCHOENFELD W. N. (1950) An experimental approach to anxiety, escape, and avoidance behaviour. In: *Anxiety* (Eds. P. H. Hoch and J. Zubin). Grune and Stratton, New York, 70–90.

SCHUTZ R. E. and NAUMOFF H. (1964) The relationship between paired comparison scale values of stimuli and their function as reinforcers of a free operant response with young children. *Psychol. Rec.* **14**, 89–93.

SELIGMAN M. E. P. (1968) Chronic fear produced by unpredictable electric shock. *J. comp. physiol. Psychol.* **66**, 402–411.

SELIGMAN M. E. P. (1970) On the generality of the laws of learning. *Psychol. Rev.* **37**, 406–418.

SELIGMAN M. E. P. (1971) Phobias and preparedness. *Behav. Ther.* **2**, 307–320.

SELIGMAN M. E. P. (1972) *Biological boundaries of learning.* Appleton-Century-Crofts, New York.

SELIGMAN M. E. P. and CAMPBELL B. L. (1965) Effects of intensity and duration of punishment on extinction of an avoidance response. *J. comp. physiol. Psychol.* **59**, 295–297.

SELIGMAN M. E. P. and JOHNSTON J. C. (1973) A cognitive theory of avoidance learning. In: *Contemporary Approaches to Conditioning and Learning* (Eds. F. J. Guigan and D. B. Lumsden). V. N. Winston & Sons, Washington, 69–110.

SIDMAN M. (1953) Avoidance conditioning with brief shock and no exteroceptive warning signal. *Science* **46**, 253–261.

SILVER S. I. and KIMMEL H. D. (1969) Resistance to extinction in clinical GSR conditioning as a function of acquisition trials beyond peak *CR* size. *Psychonomic Science* **14**, 53–55.

SILVESTRI R., ROHRBAUGH M. and RICCIO D. C. (1970) Conditions influencing the retention of learned fear in young rats. *Devl. Psychol.* **2**, 389–395.

SLATER E. (1975) The psychiatrist in search of science: III—The depths psychologies. *Br. J. Psychiat.* **126**, 205–224.

SOLOMON R. L. and BRUSH E. G. (1956) Experimentally derived conceptions of anxiety and aversion. In: *Nebraska Symposium on Motivation* (Ed. M. R. Jones) Vol. 4. University of Nebraska Press, Lincoln, 212–305.

SOLOMON R. L., KAMIN L. J. and WYNNE L. C. (1953) Traumatic avoidance learning: the outcomes of several extinction procedures with dogs. *J. abnorm. soc. Psychol.* **48**, 291–302.

SOLOMON R. L. and WYNNE L. C. (1954) Traumatic avoidance learning: The principles of anxiety conservation and partial irreversibility. *Psychol. Rev.* **61**, 353–385.

SOLTYSIK S. (1975) Studies on the avoidance conditioning: III. Alimentary conditioned reflex model of the avoidance reflex. *Acta biol. exp.* **20**, 183–192.

SOLTYSIK S. (1964) Inhibitory feedback in avoidance conditioning. In: *Feedback Systems controlling nervous activity* (Ed. A. Escobar), pp. 316–331. Sociedad Mexicana de Ciencias Fisiologicas, Mexico.

STAUB E. (1968) Duration of stimulus as determinant of the efficacy of flooding procedures in the elimination of fear. *Behav. Res. and Therapy* **6**, 131–192.

STONE N. M. and BORKOVEC T. D. (1975) The paradoxical effect of brief CS exposure on analogue phobic patients. *Behav. Res. and Therapy* **13**, 51–54.

SUE D. (1975) The effect of duration of exposure on systematic desensitization and extinction. *Behav. Res. and Therapy* **13**, 55–60.

TOLMAN E. C. (1949) There is more than one kind of learning. *Psychol. Rev.* **56**, 144–155.

ULLMAN Z. P. and KRASNER L. (1969) *A psychological approach to abnormal behaviour.* Prentice-Hall, New Jersey.

WATSON J. B. and RAYNIER R. (1920) Conditioned emotional reactions. *J. exp. Psychol.* **3**, 1–14.

WHITEHURST C. (1971) *The application of the Premack principle to reading and maths behaviour in elementary school children.* Unpublished doctoral dissertation, University of Illinois.

WHITEHURST C. and DOMASH M. (1974) Preference assessment for application of the Premack principle. *Psychol. Rep.* **35**, 919–924.

WOLPE J. (1958) *Psychotherapy by reciprocal inhibition.* Stamford: University Press, Stamford.

WOLPE J. and LANG P. J. (1964) A fear survey schedule for use in behaviour therapy. *Behav. Res. and Therapy* **2**, 27–30.

WOODS D. J. (1974) Paradoxical enhancement of learned anxiety response. *Psychol. Rep.* **35**, 295–304.

A COGNITIVE APPROACH TO PANIC

DAVID M. CLARK

Department of Psychiatry, University of Oxford, Warneford Hospital, Oxford OX3 7JX, England

(*Received 3 December 1985*)

Summary—A cognitive model of panic is described. Within this model panic attacks are said to result from the catastrophic misinterpretation of certain bodily sensations. The sensations which are misinterpreted are mainly those involved in normal anxiety responses (e.g. palpitations, breathlessness, dizziness etc.) but also include some other sensations. The catastrophic misinterpretation involves perceiving these sensations as much more dangerous than they really are (e.g. perceiving palpitations as evidence of an impending heart attack). A review of the literature indicates that the proposed model is consistent with the major features of panic. In particular, it is consistent with the nature of the cognitive disturbance in panic patients, the perceived sequence of events in an attack, the occurrence of 'spontaneous' attacks, the role of hyperventilation in attacks, the effects of sodium lactate and the literature on psychological and pharmacological treatments. Finally, a series of direct tests of the model are proposed.

INTRODUCTION

Ever since Freud's (1894) classic essay on anxiety neurosis, it has been accepted that panic attacks are a frequent accompaniment of certain types of anxiety disorder. However, it is only relatively recently that panic attacks have become a focus of research interest in their own right. This shift in emphasis is largely a result of the work of Donald Klein. In a series of studies which started in the 1960s, Klein and his colleagues (Klein, 1964; Zitrin, Klein and Woerner, 1980; Zitrin, Woerner and Klein, 1981; Zitrin, Klein, Woerner and Ross, 1983) appeared to demonstrate that anxiety disorders which are characterized by panic attacks respond to imipramine while anxiety disorders which are not characterized by panic attacks fail to respond to imipramine. This 'pharmacological dissociation' led Klein (1981) to propose that panic anxiety is *qualitatively* different from non-panic anxiety. A view which was subsequently endorsed by the writers of DSM-III (APA, 1980) when they created the two diagnostic categories of 'panic disorder' and 'agoraphobia with panic' and used the presence or absence of panic attacks as a major criteria for distinguishing between different types of anxiety disorder. Following the publication of DSM-III, there has been an enormous increase in research on panic attacks. Perhaps because drug studies were the major stimulus for the creation of the diagnostic category of panic disorder, most recent research has concentrated on biological approaches to the understanding of panic. However, there are a number of reasons for supposing that panic attacks might be best understood from a cognitive perspective. After a brief description of the phenomenology of panic attacks, the present article presents a cognitive approach to the understanding of panic. A literature review indicates that the proposed cognitive model is consistent with existing information on the nature of panic and the article concludes with a set of specific predictions which could be used to test the model.

THE PHENOMENOLOGY OF PANIC ATTACKS

A panic attack consists of an intense feeling of apprehension or impending doom which is of sudden onset and which is associated with a wide range of distressing physical sensations. These sensations include breathlessness, palpitations, chest pain, choking, dizziness, tingling in the hands and feet, hot and cold flushes, sweating, faintness, trembling and feelings of unreality. Panic attacks occur in both phobic and non-phobic anxiety disorders. Within phobics, attacks occur in feared situations (such as a supermarket for an agoraphobic) but some attacks occur in 'safe' situations such as at home. Some attacks follow a clearly identifiable precipitating event or short period of anxious rumination but other attacks are perceived by patients as occurring 'out of the blue'. The latter are commonly termed 'spontaneous' panic attacks. The majority of people who suffer frequent panic attacks fall into the DSM-III categories of panic disorder or agoraphobia with panic. In order to be diagnosed as suffering from panic disorder an individual must have had at least three panic attacks in the last 3 weeks and these attacks must not be restricted to circumscribed phobic situations. In order to be diagnosed as suffering from agoraphobia with panic, an individual must show marked fear and avoidance of the agoraphobic cluster of situations and also have a history of panic attacks.

A COGNITIVE MODEL OF PANIC ATTACKS

Paradoxically, the cognitive model of panic attacks is perhaps most easily introduced by discussing work which has focused on neurochemical and pharmacological approaches to the understanding of panic. This work has established that in patients, panic attacks can be provoked by a wide range of pharmacological and physiological agents including: infusions of lactate (Appleby, Klein, Sachar and Levitt, 1981; Leibowitz, Fyer, Gorman, Dillon, Appleby, Levy, Anderson, Levitt, Palij, Davies and Klein, 1984), yohimbine (Charney, Beninger and Breier, 1984) and isoproterenol (Rainey, Pohl, Williams, Knitter, Freedman and Ettedgui, 1984); oral adminis-tration of caffeine (Charney, Beninger and Jatlow, 1985); voluntary hyperventilation (Clark, Salkovskis and Chalkley, 1985) and inhalation of carbon dioxide (van den Hout and Griez, 1984). These agents rarely provoke panic attacks in individuals without a history of panic. However, they produce some of the bodily sensations which are associated with panic attacks in most individuals. The success of the agents at producing panic attacks in panic patients and their less marked effects on normals have been taken to indicate that certain biochemical changes have a direct panic-inducing effect, and that individuals who are vulnerable to the agents have a biochemical disorder. These conclusions have provided a rationale for the further exploration of drug treatments for panic (Chouinard, Annabie, Fontaine and Solyom, 1982; Zitrin, 1983) and also for studies which attempt to identify neurochemical abnormalities in panic patients (Charney et al., 1984; Nesse, Cameron, Curtis, McCann and Huber-Smith, 1984).

However, two recent studies (Clark and Hemsley, 1982; van den Hout and Griez, 1982) suggest an alternative, psychological, explanation for the panic-inducing effects of these diverse agents. These studies investigated the effects of two panic-inducing agents—hyperventilation (Clark and Hemsley, 1982) and CO_2 inhalation (van den Hout and Griez, 1982)—in normal Ss. It was found that individuals varied considerably in their affective response to the procedures and there was tentative evidence that the extent to which individuals experienced the procedures as pleasurable or aversive was determined by cognitive factors such as expectation and the recall of previous experiences with the induced sensations. This suggests that the various pharmacological and physiological agents which have been shown to promote panic in patients may not have direct panic-inducing effects but instead may provoke panic only if the bodily sensations which they induce are interpreted in a particular fashion. This is the central notion behind the cognitive theory of panic which is described below.

It is proposed that panic attacks result from the catastrophic misinterpretation of certain bodily sensations. The sensations which are misinterpreted are mainly those which are involved in normal anxiety responses (e.g. palpitations, breathlessness, dizziness etc.) but also include some other bodily sensations. The catastrophic misinterpretation involves perceiving these sensations as much more dangerous than they really are. Examples of catastrophic misinterpretations would be a healthy individual perceiving palpitations as evidence of impending heart attack; perceiving a slight feeling of breathlessness as evidence of impending cessation of breathing and consequent death; or perceiving a shaky feeling as evidence of impending loss of control and insanity.

Figure 1 illustrates the sequence of events that it is suggested occurs in a panic attack.* A wide range of stimuli appear to provoke attacks. These stimuli can be external (such as a supermarket for an agoraphobic who has previously had an attack in a supermarket) but more often are internal (body sensation, thought or image). If these stimuli are perceived as a threat, a state of mild

---

*Although derived independently, the present model has similarities with the models of panic which have recently been proposed by Beck, Emery and Greenberg (1985) and by Griez and van den Hout (1984).

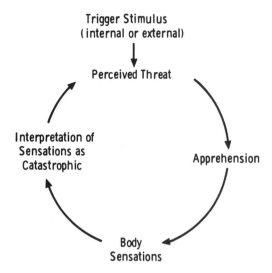

Fig. 1. A cognitive model of panic attacks.

apprehension results. This state is accompanied by a wide range of body sensations. If these anxiety-produced sensations are interpreted in a catastrophic fashion, a further increase in apprehension occurs. This produces a further increase in body sensations and so on round in a vicious circle which culminates in a panic attack.

The model shown in Fig. 1 can deal both with panic attacks which are preceded by a period of heightened anxiety and also with panic attacks which are not preceded by a period of heightened anxiety but instead appear to come 'out of the blue'. In the case of attacks which are preceded by heightened anxiety two distinct types of attack can be distinguished. In the first the heightened anxiety which precedes the attack is concerned with the anticipation of an attack. This is often the case when agoraphobics experience an attack in a situation (such as a supermarket) where they have previously panicked. On entering such a situation they tend to become anxious in anticipation of a further attack, then selectively focus on their body, notice an unpleasant body sensation, interpret this as evidence of an impending attack and consequently activate the vicious circle which produces an attack. In other cases the heightened anxiety which precedes an attack may be quite unconnected with anticipation of an attack. For example, an individual may become nervous as a result of the particular topics which are being discussed in a dispute with a spouse, notice their bodily reaction to the argument, catastrophically interpret these sensations and then panic.

In the case of panic attacks which are not preceded by a period of heightened anxiety, the trigger for an attack often seems to be the perception of a bodily sensation which itself is caused by a different emotional state (excitement, anger) or by some quite innocuous event such as suddenly getting up from the sitting position (dizziness), exercise (breathlessness, palpitations) or drinking coffee (palpitations). Once perceived the body sensation is interpreted in a catastrophic fashion and then a panic attack results. In such attacks patients often fail to distinguish between the triggering body sensation and the subsequent panic attack and so perceive the attacks as having no cause and coming 'out of the blue'. This is understandable given the patients' general beliefs about the meaning of an attack. For example, if an individual believes that there is something wrong with his heart, he is unlikely to view the palpitation which triggers an attack as different from the attack itself. Instead he is likely to view both as aspects of the same thing—a heart attack or near miss.

In Fig. 1 it is hypothesized that the misinterpretation of bodily symptoms of anxiety is always involved in the vicious circle which culminates in a panic attack. However, other sensations can also play a role in panic, particularly as triggering stimuli. We have already mentioned sensations such as breathlessness and palpitations which sometimes are produced by anxiety but other times can initially be produced by innocuous events or positive emotions. In addition, occasionally panic attacks are triggered by sensations which are never part of an anxiety response. For example, floaters in the visual field are not symptoms of anxiety. However, if an individual was concerned about the possibility of a deterioration in sight then perception of a floater could trigger a panic.

The individual might interpret the floater as a sign of impending visual deterioration, become anxious, as a product of this anxiety experience blurred vision, this would further reinforce the belief that there was something seriously wrong with his or her vision and so activate a vicious circle of misinterpretation and increasing blurred vision which culminates in a panic attack.

So far our discussion of the sensations whose misinterpretation results in a panic attack has mainly concentrated on sensations which arise from the perception of internal physical processes (e.g. palpitations). These are the most common sensations involved in the production of panic attacks. However, sensations which arise from the perception of mental processes can also contribute to the vicious circle which culminates in a panic attack. For example, for some patients the belief that they are about to go mad is partly based on moments when their mind suddenly goes blank. These moments are interpreted as evidence of impending loss of control over thinking and consequent insanity.

A final aspect of the cognitive model which requires comment concerns the temporal stability of patients' catastrophic interpretations of bodily sensations. For some patients the panic-triggering sensations and their interpretations of those sensations remain fairly constant across time. However, in other patients both the sensations and interpretations change over time. For example, some patients appear to have a rather vague belief that they are going to suffer from some serious illness, this leads them to misinterpret a very wide range of bodily sensations and the particular misinterpretations will vary depending on which bodily sensations are noticed, what illnesses they have information about and what illnesses they have already been able to discount.

A BRIEF REVIEW OF RESEARCH ON PANIC ATTACKS

Having presented a cognitive model of panic, I will now briefly review the literature on panic to determine the extent to which it is consistent with the proposed model.

(1) Ideational components of panic anxiety

If the above model is correct, one would expect that the thinking of patients who suffer from panic attacks would be dominated by thoughts which relate to the catastrophic interpretation of bodily sensations. A recent interview study has provided data which is broadly consistent with this hypothesis. Hibbert (1984a) compared the ideation of non-phobic patients who experienced panic attacks ($n = 17$) and non-phobic patients who did not experience panic attacks ($n = 8$). Panic patients were significantly more likely than non-panic patients to have thoughts concerned with the anticipation of illness, death or loss of control (includes 'going mad'), but did not differ from non-panic patients in the frequency of thoughts concerned with general feelings of being unable to cope or with the anticipation of social embarrassment. In discussing these results Hibbert (1984a, p. 622) concluded that "the ideational content of those experiencing panic attacks can be understood as a reaction to the somatic symptoms, a connection insisted upon by all but 2 of the patients".

(2) Perceived sequence of events in a panic attack

As the cognitive model specifies that panic attacks result from the catastrophic interpretation of bodily sensations, one would expect that a bodily sensation would be one of the first things which individuals notice during an attack. Two studies have asked patients about the perceived sequence of events in an attack and both have provided results consistent with this expectation. Hibbert (1984a) and Ley (1985) both found that panic patients frequently report that the first thing they notice during an episode of anxiety is a physical feeling. In addition, Hibbert (1984a) found that this sequence of events was reported significantly more often by patients with panic attacks than by patients without panic attacks (53 and 0%, respectively).

(3) The role of hyperventilation in panic attacks

The bodily sensations which are produced by voluntary hyperventilation are very similar to those experienced in naturally occurring panic attacks. This observation has led a number of writers (Clark, 1979; Clark and Hemsley, 1982; Gibson, 1978; Hibbert, 1984b; Kerr, Dalton and Gliebe, 1937; Lewis, 1957; Lum, 1976; Wolpe, 1973) to suggest that hyperventilation may play an important role in the production of panic attacks. Consistent with this suggestion it has been shown that in some panic patients (i) voluntary hyperventilation produces a panic-like state (Clark *et al.*, 1985) and (ii) hyperventilation accompanies naturally occurring panic attacks (Hibbert, 1986; Salkovskis, Warwick, Clark and Wessels, 1986c), panic attacks produced by contrived psychological stress (Salkovskis, Clark and Jones, 1986a) and panic attacks induced by sodium lactate (Liebowitz, Gorman, Abby, Levitt, Dillon, Gail, Appleby, Anderson, Palij, Davies and Klein, 1985b). These observations suggest that hyperventilation plays a role in some panic attacks. However, it is clear that hyperventilation *per se* does not produce panic. As already mentioned, studies of the effects of hyperventilation in normals (Clark and Hemsley, 1982; Svebak and Grossman, 1986) have shown that individuals vary considerably in their affective response to hyperventilation with some individuals actually finding the experience enjoyable. It is therefore suggested that hyperventilation only induces panic if the bodily sensations which it induces are (a) perceived as unpleasant and (b) interpreted in a catastrophic fashion.

(4) Lactate-induced panic

Infusions of sodium lactate are the most frequently used technique for inducing panic attacks in the laboratory. Between 60–90% of panic patients and 0–20% of normals and non-panic anxious patients experience an attack when given an i.v. infusion of 0.5–1.0 M racemic sodium lactate (Appleby *et al.*, 1981; Liebowitz *et al.*, 1984, 1985a; Rainey *et al.*, 1984). Even when Ss do not panic, lactate infusions are accompanied by a wide range of physiological and biochemical changes. Liebowitz *et al.* (1985b) reported that lactate produces significant increases in heart rate, systolic blood pressure, pyruvate, prolactin and bicarbonate, and significant decreases in cortisol, pCO_2, phosphate and ionized calcium. As some of these changes in bodily function are likely to be perceived, the cognitive model could account for the panic-inducing effects of lactate by proposing that individuals who panic do so because they catastrophically interpret the induced sensations. This is consistent with Liebowitz *et al.*'s (1985b, p. 718) observation that individuals who panic during lactate infusion perceive bodily changes such as tremor and parasthesias well before the onset of panic. The fact that more patients than controls panic on lactate would mainly be explained by supposing that patients have, as a relatively enduring characteristic, a particularly marked tendency to interpret certain bodily sensations in a catastrophic fashion. However, in some studies part of the difference in response between patients and controls may be due to differences in the instructions given to the two groups. For example, in their pre-infusion instructions, Appleby *et al.* (1981) told patients that they "might experience a panic attack" (p. 413) but told controls that they "might experience an attack with symptoms analogous to those of 'public speaking'" (p. 413). As the controls presumably had never experienced a panic attack but probably had been slightly nervous during public speaking these instructions are likely to lead controls to expect a less-frightening experience than patients. Such differences in expectation can have marked effects on the affect produced by biochemical interventions (cf. van den Hout and Griez, 1982).

(5) Effects of psychological treatment

The proposal that panic attacks result from the catastrophic interpretation of certain bodily sensations suggests both a cognitive–behavioural and a behavioural approach to the treatment of panic attacks. The cognitive–behavioural approach would involve identifying patients' negative interpretations of the bodily sensations which they experience in panic attacks, suggesting alternative non-catastrophic interpretations of the sensations and then helping the patient to test the validity of these alternative interpretations through discussion and behavioural experiments. The behavioural approach would capitalize on the observation that fear of specific stimuli can often be treated by repeated, controlled exposure to those stimuli and would consist of graded exposure to the body sensations which accompany panic. Recently both of these approaches have been tried and the initial results are highly encouraging.

Clark *et al.* (1985) adopted the cognitive–behavioural approach and concentrated on one particular alternative interpretation—the view that the bodily sensations which patients experience in a panic attack are the result of stress-induced hyperventilation rather than the more catastrophic things which patients usually fear (impending heart attack, insanity, loss of control). The treatment had five stages:

(1) Brief voluntary hyperventilation. This was intended to induce a state which patients recognized as similar to their panic attacks.

(2) Explanation and discussion of the way hyperventilation induces panic. On the basis of the results of the brief period of voluntary hyperventilation, it was suggested to patients that during a panic attack they may be overbreathing. This then produces a wide range of bodily sensations which they interpret in a catastrophic fashion leading to greater anxiety, more overbreathing and so on round in a vicious circle which culminates in a panic attack. Patients attempted to fit their own recent experience of panic attacks into this model and where doubts were expressed these were carefully considered. Attacks which initially appeared inconsistent with the model were carefully discussed. After reviewing details of these attacks with the therapist, the patient was often able to see ways in which the model could account for the attacks.

(3) Training in a pattern of slow, controlled breathing to use in a coping technique during attacks.

(4) Training in more appropriate cognitive responses to bodily symptoms. These responses were based on the discussion described above.

(5) Identification and modification of panic triggers. By reviewing panic diaries, it was often possible to identify hitherto unrecognized triggers for panic. This helped some patients to see their panic attacks as more understandable, made them less frightening and suggested control techniques. Examples of triggers identified in this way were high caffeine intake, misinterpretation of the bodily symptoms of a hangover, postural hypotension, phase in the menstrual cycle and fleeting, bizarre images.

To date, two evaluations of this treatment approach have been reported. In the first evaluation (Clark *et al.*, 1985) patients were selected who perceived a similarity between the effects of overbreathing and naturally occurring panic attacks. Substantial reductions in panic attack frequency were observed during the first few weeks of treatment. These initial gains, which occurred in the absence of exposure to feared external situations, were improved upon with further treatment and maintained at 2-yr follow-up. In the second evaluation (Salkovskis, Jones and Clark, 1986b), an unselected group of panic patients were studied. Again a substantial reduction in attack frequency was observed. In addition, there was some evidence that outcome was positively correlated with the extent to which patients perceived a marked similarity between the effects of voluntary overbreathing and naturally occurring attacks. Neither study employed a waiting-list control group. However, it is unlikely that the observed improvements are due to spontaneous remission as, in both studies, a stable baseline was established before treatment, and significant improvements from baseline took place in a treatment period shorter than the baseline. It therefore appears that the cognitive–behavioural package is an effective treatment for panic, especially in patients who perceive a marked similarity between hyperventilation and naturally occurring panic. Patients who fail to perceive a marked similarity between the effects of hyperventilation and naturally occurring panic would probably benefit from the inclusion of additional procedures which concentrate on other, non-catastrophic explanations of bodily sensations (cf. Clark, 1986).

Griez and van den Hout (1983, 1986) adopted the behavioural approach to treatment and used inhalations of 35% CO_2/65% O_2 as a way of repeatedly exposing patients to the bodily sensations which accompany panic attacks. Inhalation of 35% CO_2/65% O_2 is a highly effective technique for inducing the bodily sensations of panic (van den Hout and Griez, 1984). Its effects appear to result from the sudden drop in pCO_2 (hyperventilation) which follows exhalation of the gas rather than from the increase in pCO_2 (hypercapnia) which accompanies inhalation (van den Hout and Griez, 1984). When used as a treatment, inhalations are introduced in a graded fashion. Initially, *S*s take small inhalations, as their anxiety drops they are encouraged to take a full-depth inhalation and eventually take several full-depth inhalations each session. Griez and van den Hout (1986) evaluated the short-term effectiveness of this treatment using a cross-over design in which 2 weeks of CO_2 inhalation therapy was compared with 2 weeks of propranolol. CO_2 inhalation therapy was associated with significant reductions in panic attack frequency and fear of autonomic sensations. Propranolol failed to have significant effects on either of these measures. However, the difference in change scores between treatments only reached significance on the measure of fear of autonomic sensations. In view of the unusually brief duration of therapy, it is possible that Griez and van den Hout's (1986) results are an underestimate of the effectiveness of CO_2 inhalation therapy. Although the therapy was associated with substantial drops in panic attack frequency, most patients were not panic-free at the end of 2 weeks and it is possible that further improvements would have been observed if the therapy had been extended over a longer and more normal period of time.

At this stage, neither Clark et al.'s (1985) cognitive–behavioural treatment nor Griez and van den Hout's (1984) behavioural treatment have been compared against an alternative psychological treatment in order to control for non-specific therapy ingredients. Until this is done it is not possible to say whether the apparent effectiveness of the treatments is due to their specific emphasis on fear of internal sensations. However, it is encouraging to note that both treatments appear to be effective with panic disorder patients as these patients form a group for whom there is no generally accepted psychological treatment. In Clark et al.'s (1985) study, these patients (termed 'non-situationals') did extremely well. Indeed most were panic-free by the end of treatment.

In contrast to panic disorder, there is a generally accepted psychological treatment for agoraphobia with panic. Numerous studies (cf. Mathews, Gelder and Johnston, 1981) have shown that graded, in vivo exposure to feared external situations is an effective treatment for agoraphobic avoidance and situational fear. Early studies did not include direct measures of panic but it was assumed that panic attacks would decline as situational fear declined and recent studies have confirmed this assumption (Marks, Grey, Cohen, Hill, Mawson, Ramm and Stern, 1983; Michelson, Marchione and Mavissakalian, 1985; Mavissakalian and Michelson, 1986). The question therefore arises of whether the cognitive–behavioural and behavioural treatments described above have anything to add to graded, in vivo exposure. Several authors (Freud, 1895; Goldstein and Chambless, 1978; Hallam, 1978; Klein, 1981; Westphal, 1872) have argued that in many cases agoraphobia is best viewed as a fear of panic rather than a fear of specific situations. This suggests that treatments which directly tackle panic may produce more generalized change. In particular, they may be more effective than graded exposure alone in reducing the frequency of 'spontaneous' panic attacks and panic attacks which occur in patient's homes. Certainly there is room for further improvement in these areas. In a recent study, Michelson et al. (1985) found that 45% of patients given the DSM-III diagnosis of agoraphobia with panic were still experiencing panic attacks at home without obvious environmental provocation after 3 months of in vivo, therapist-assisted exposure to feared situations.

(6) The role of biological factors in panic

By specifying that the catastrophic interpretation of certain bodily sensations is a necessary condition for the production of a panic attack, the cognitive model provides a different perspective to that offered by biological models of panic and also provides a rationale for psychological approaches to treatment. However, it would be wrong to assume that biological factors have no role to play in panic attacks. In principle, there are, at least three ways in which biological factors might increase an individuals' vulnerability to the vicious circle shown in Fig. 1.

First, biological factors may contribute to the triggering of an attack. As already mentioned, panic attacks are often triggered by a perceived body sensation such as breathlessness or palipitations, and such sensations appear to be reported more frequently by panic patients than by other patients or normals. Body sensations are particularly likely to be noticed when there is a change in bodily processes (Pennebaker, 1982). It is therefore possible that the increase in perceived body sensations observed in panic patients occurs because such patients experience more, or more intense, benign fluctuations in body state than others.

Second, biological factors are likely to influence the extent to which a perceived threat produces an increase in bodily sensations, as shown in Fig. 1. The reduced efficiency of central adrenergic α_2-autoreceptors, which it has been suggested is characteristic of panic patients (Charney et al., 1984), would be an example of such an effect. Noradrenergic neurons in the locus coerulus and other brain-stem areas play an important role in the control of the autonomic nervous system. The α_2-adrenergic autoreceptor has an inhibitory influence on presynaptic noradrenergic neurons. A deficiency in this autoreceptor would mean that release of noradrenaline would not be damped down by presynaptic inhibition and individuals with such a deficiency would experience larger than normal surges in noradrenaline and sympathetic nervous system activation in response to a perceived threat. A further example of a biological influence on the extent to which a perceived threat produces an increase in body sensations comes from the literature on hyperventilation. As already mentioned, in some patients the bodily sensations which occur in a panic attack are partly a result of hyperventilation and the effects of hyperventilation vary with resting levels of pCO_2 which in turn vary with phase in the menstrual cycle (Damos-Mora, Davies, Taylor and Jenner, 1980).

Finally, the extent to which bodily sensations which accompany anxiety are interpreted in a catastrophic fashion will largely be determined by psychological factors. However, biological factors may also have a role to play in this aspect of the vicious circle. For example, the hypothesized deficiency in central α_2-adrenergic autoreceptors would mean that individuals would be more likely to experience sudden surges in sympathetic activity and surges in activity may be more likely to be interpreted in a catastrophic fashion than gradual build-ups.

(7) Effects of pharmacological treatment

Within the model shown in Fig. 1, there are several ways in which drugs could be effective in reducing the frequency of panic attacks. Blockade of, or exposure to the bodily sensations which accompany anxiety, and a reduction in the frequency of bodily fluctuations which can trigger panic could all have short term effects on panic. However, if patients' tendency to interpret bodily sensations in a catastrophic fashion is not changed, discontinuation of drug treatment should be associated with a high rate of relapse.

So far, three drugs (propranolol, diazepam and imipramine) have been investigated in controlled trials which include measures of panic. Propranolol appears to be ineffective, even when given in doses which are sufficient to effect β-blockade (Noyes, Anderson, Clancy, Crowe, Slymen, Ghoneim and Hinrichs, 1984; Griez and van den Hout, 1986). This is perhaps because β-blockade reduces the cardiovascular aspects of panic but appears to leave some of the other bodily sensations unaffected (Gorman, Levy, Liebowitz, McGrath, Appleby, Dillon, Davies and Klein, 1983). Noyes et al. (1984) found that high doses of diazepam (up to 30 mg) were effective in reducing panic frequency over a period of 2 weeks but they failed to provide data on the long-term effectiveness of diazepam. However, other studies (Catalan and Gath, 1985) have raised serious doubts about the long-term effectiveness of diazepam as a treatment for anxiety. In contrast to propranolol and diazepam, more positive results have been obtained with imipramine. Three controlled trials (Zitrin et al., 1980, 1983; McNair and Kahn, 1981) have found that imipramine is more effective than an inert placebo in reducing the frequency of panic attacks in agoraphobics with panic and a further trial (Telch, Agras, Taylor, Roth and Gallen, 1985) obtained a trend towards a significant difference between imipramine and placebo ($P < 0.1$). However, two further studies with agoraphobics (Marks et al., 1983; Mavissakalian and Michelson, 1986) failed to find differences between imipramine and placebo on measures of panic. In those studies in which imipramine has been more effective than placebo it has always been combined with graded exposure to feared situations. This raises the possibility that imipramine may not have direct anti-panic effects, but instead simply potentiates the effects of self-initiated and/or therapist-initiated graded exposure. Consistent with this suggestion, Telch et al. (1985) found that imipramine had no effect on panic when given in conjunction with counter-exposure instructions. However, in the only study to investigate the effects of imipramine in panic disorder (as opposed to agoraphobia with panic), Garakani, Zitrin and Klein (1984) found that imipramine without the addition of psychological treatment was associated with a marked reduction in panic attacks. This study was a case series and so did not include a placebo control group. Until a study is reported which includes such a group, it will remain unclear whether imipramine has a specific anti-panic effect in panic disorder.

SUMMARY AND PREDICTIONS

It has been suggested that panic attacks result from the catastrophic interpretation of certain bodily sensations. The sensations which are misinterpreted are mainly those which are involved in normal anxiety responses (e.g. palpitations, breathlessness, dizziness etc.) but also include some other sensations. The catastrophic misinterpretation involves perceiving these sensations as much more dangerous than they really are (e.g. perceiving palpitations as evidence of an impending heart attack). Encouragingly, a review of the literature indicates that the proposed model is consistent with the nature of the cognitive disturbance in panic patients, the perceived sequence of events in an attack, the occurrence of 'spontaneous' attacks, the role of hyperventilation in attacks, the effects of sodium lactate and the literature on psychological and pharmacological treatments. However, at this stage, no studies have been reported which provide a direct test of the cognitive model. Final evaluation of the model must therefore await studies which test its central predictions. These predictions are:

(1) Compared to other anxious patients and normal controls, patients who suffer from panic attacks will be more likely to interpret certain bodily sensations in a catastrophic fashion.*

(2) Pharmacological agents which provoke panic (such as sodium lactate) do so only when the somatic sensations produced by the agent are interpreted in a catastrophic fashion, and the panic-inducing effects of these agents can be blocked by instructional manipulations.

(3) Treatments which fail to change patients tendency to interpret bodily sensations in a catastrophic fashion will have higher rates of relapse than treatments which succeed in changing interpretations.

Acknowledgements—The author is grateful to the Medical Research Council of the U.K. for its support. In addition, he would like to thank Aaron T. Beck, Michael Gelder, Ruth Greenberg, Eric Griez, Elizabeth Knox, David Nutt, Jack Rachman, John Rush, Paul Salkovskis and Marcel van den Hout for helpful discussions.

REFERENCES

APA; American Psychiatric Association (1980) *Diagnostic and Statistical Manual of Mental Disorders*, 3rd edn. APA, Washington, D.C.

Appleby I. L., Klein D. F., Sachar E. J. and Levitt M. (1981) Biochemical indices of lactate-induced panic: a preliminary report. In *Anxiety: New Research and Changing Concepts* (Edited by Klein D. F. and Rabkin J.). Raven Press, New York.

Beck A. T., Emery G. and Greenberg R. L. (1985) *Anxiety Disorders and Phobias: a Cognitive Perspective*. Basic Books, New York.

Catalan J. and Gath D. H. (1985) Benzodiazepines in general practice: time for a decision. *Br. med. J.* **290**, 1374–1376.

Charney D. S., Beninger G. R. and Breier A. (1984) Noradrenergic function in panic anxiety: effects of yohimbine in healthy subjects and patients with agoraphobia and panic disorder. *Archs gen. Psychiat.* **41**, 751–763.

Charney D. S., Beninger G. R. and Jatlow P. I. (1985) Increased anxiogenic effects of caffeine in panic disorders. *Archs gen. Psychiat.* **42**, 233–243.

Chouinard G., Annabie L., Fontaine R. and Solyom L. (1982) Alprazolam in the treatment of generalised anxiety and panic disorders: a double-blind placebo-controlled study. *Psychopharmacology* **77**, 229–233.

Clark D. M. (1979) Therapeutic aspects of increasing pCO_2 by behavioural means. Unpublished M. Phil. Thesis, Univ. of London.

Clark D. M. (1986) Cognitive therapy for anxiety. *Behavl Psychother.* In press.

Clark D. M. and Hemsley D. R. (1982) The effects of hyperventilation: individual variability and its relation to personality. *J. Behav. Ther. exp. Psychiat.* **13**, 41–47.

Clark D. M., Salkovskis P. M. and Chalkley A. J. (1985) Respiratory control as a treatment for panic attacks. *J. Behav. Ther. exp. Psychiat.* **16**, 23–30.

Damas-Mora J., Davies L., Taylor W. and Jenner F. A. (1980) Menstrual respiratory changes and symptoms. *Br. J. Psychiat.* **136**, 492–497.

Freud S. (1894) The justification for detaching from neurasthenia a particular syndrome: the anxiety-neurosis. Reprinted in: Freud S. (1940) *Collected Papers*, Vol. 1. Hogarth Press, London.

Freud S. (1895) Obsessions and phobias: their psychical mechanisms and their aetiology. Reprinted in: Freud S. (1940) *Collected Papers*, Vol. 1. Hogarth Press, London.

Garakani H., Zitrin C. M. and Klein D. F. (1984) Treatment of panic disorder with imipramine alone. *Am. J. Psychiat.* **141**, 446–448.

---

*In testing this prediction it may be important to distinguish between immediate and long-term threat. It is likely that interpretations of sensations which lead patients to believe they are in immediate danger of a catastrophy such as dying or going mad will be particularly characteristic of panic while interpretations which imply some distant danger may be more characteristic of hypochondriasis.

Gibson H. B. (1978) A form of behaviour therapy for some states diagnosed as "affective disorder". *Behav. Res. Ther.* **16,** 191–195.

Goldstein A. J. and Chambless D. L. (1978) A re-analysis of agoraphobia. *Behav. Ther.* **9,** 47–59.

Gorman J. M., Levy G. F., Liebowitz M. R., McGrath P., Appleby I. L., Dillon D. J., Davies S. O. and Klein D. F. (1983) Effect of β-adrenergic blockade on lactate induced panic. *Archs gen. Psychiat.* **40,** 1079–1082.

Griez E. and van den Hout M. A. (1983) Treatment of phobophobia by exposure to CO_2 induced anxiety symptoms. *J. nerv. ment. Dis.* **171,** 506–508.

Griez E. and van den Hout M. A. (1984) Carbon dioxide and anxiety: an experimental approach to a clinical claim. Unpublished Doctoral Dissertation, Rijksaniversiteit, Maastricht, The Netherlands.

Griez E. and van den Hout M. A. (1986) CO_2 inhalation in the treatment of panic attacks. *Behav. Res. Ther.* **24,** 145–150.

Hallam R. S. (1978) Agoraphobia: a critical review of the concept. *Br. J. Psychiat.* **133,** 314–319.

Hibbert G. A. (1984a) Ideational components of anxiety: their origin and content. *Br. J. Psychiat.* **144,** 618–624.

Hibbert G. A. (1984b) Hyperventilation as a cause of panic attacks. *Br. med. J.* **288,** 263–264.

Hibbert G. A. (1986) Ambulatory monitoring of transcutaneous pCO_2. In *Proceedings of the 15th European Conference on Psychosomatic Research* (Edited by Lacey L. and Sturgeon J.). Libby, London.

van den Hout M. A. and Griez E. (1982) Cognitive factors in carbon dioxide therapy. *J. psychosom. Res.* **26,** 209–214.

van den Hout M. A. and Griez E. (1984) Panic symptoms after inhalation of carbon dioxide. *Br. J. Psychiat.* **144,** 503–507.

van den Hout M. A. and Griez E. (1985) Peripheral panic symptoms occur during changes in alveolar carbon dioxide. *Compreh. Psychiat.* **26,** 381–387.

Kerr W. J., Dalton J. W. and Gliebe P. A. (1937) Some physical phenomena associated with anxiety states and their relation to hyperventilation. *Ann. intern. Med.* **11,** 961–992.

Klein D. F. (1964) Delineation of two-drug responsive anxiety syndromes. *Psychopharmacologiea* **5,** 397–408.

Klein D. F. (1981) Anxiety reconceptualised. In *Anxiety: New Research and Changing Concepts* (Edited by Klein D. F. and Rabkin J.). Raven Press, New York.

Lewis B. I. (1954) Chronic hyperventilation syndrome. *J. Am. med. Ass.* **31,** 1204–1208.

Ley R. (1985) Agoraphobia, the panic attack and the hyperventilation syndrome. *Behav. Res. Ther.* **23,** 79–82.

Liebowitz M. R., Fyer A. J., Gorman J. M., Dillon D., Appleby I. L., Levy G., Anderson S., Levitt M., Palij M., Davies S. O. and Klein D. F. (1984) Lactate provocation of panic attacks: I. Clinical and behavioural findings. *Archs gen. Psychiat.* **41,** 764–770.

Liebowitz M. R., Abby J. F., Gorman J. M., Dillon D., Davies S., Stein J. M., Cohen B. S. and Klein D. F. (1985a) Specificity of lactate infusions in social phobia versus panic disorders. *Am. J. Psychiat.* **142,** 947–950.

Liebowitz M. R., Gorman J. M., Abby J. F., Levitt M., Dillon D., Gail L., Appleby I. L., Anderson S., Palij M., Davies S. O. and Klein D. F. (1985b) Lactate provocation of panic attacks: II. Biochemical and physiological findings. *Archs gen. Psychiat.* **42,** 709–719.

Lum L. C. (1976) The syndrome of habitual chronic hyperventilation. In *Modern Trends in Psychosomatic Medicine,* Vol. 3 (Edited by Hill O. W.). Butterworths, London.

McNair D. M. and Kahn R. J. (1981) Imipramine compared with a benzodiazepine for agoraphobia. In *Anxiety: New Research and Changing Concepts* (Edited by Klein D. F. and Rabkin J.). Raven Press, New York.

Marks I. M., Grey S., Cohen S. D., Hill R., Mawson D., Ramm E. M. and Stern R. S. (1983) Imipramine and brief therapist-aided exposure in agoraphobics having self exposure homework: a controlled trial. *Archs gen. Psychiat.* **40,** 153–162.

Mathews A. M., Gelder M. G. and Johnston D. W. (1981) *Agorophobia: Nature and Treatment.* Guildford Press, New York.

Mavissakalian M. and Michelson L. (1986) Agoraphobia: relative and combined effectiveness of therapist-assisted *in vivo* exposure and imipramine. *J. clin. Psychol.* In press.

Michelson L., Marchione K. and Mavissakalian M. (1985) Cognitive and behavioural treatments of agoraphobia: clinical, behavioural and psychophysiological outcome. *J. consult. clin. Psychol.* **53,** 913–926.

Nesse R. M., Cameron O. G., Curtis G. C., McCann D. S. and Huber-Smith M. J. (1984) Adrenergic function in patients with panic anxiety. *Archs gen. Psychiat.* **41,** 771–776.

Noyes R., Anderson D. J., Clancy J., Crowe R. R., Slymen D. J., Ghoneim M. M. and Hinrichs J. V. (1984) Diazepam and propranolol in panic disorder and agoraphobia. *Archs gen. Psychiat.* **41,** 287–292.

Pennebaker J. W. (1982) *The Psychology of Physical Symptoms.* Springer, New York. Verlag.

Rainey J. M., Pohl R. B., Williams M., Knitter E., Freedman R. R. and Ettedgui E. (1984) A comparison of lactate and isoproterenol anxiety states. *Psychopathology* **17,** 74–82.

Salkovskis P. M., Clark D. M. and Jones D. R. O. (1986a) A psychosomatic mechanism in anxiety attacks: the role of hyperventilation in social anxiety and cardiac neurosis. In *Proceedings of the 15th European Conference on Psychosomatic Medicine* (Edited by Lacey H. and Sturgeon J.). Libby, London.

Salkovskis P. M., Jones D. R. O. and Clark D. M. (1986b) Respiratory control in the treatment of panic attacks: replication and extension with concurrent measurement of behaviour and pCO_2. *Br. J. Psychiat.* In press.

Salkovskis P. M., Warwick H. M. C., Clark D. M. and Wessels D. J. (1986c) A demonstration of acute hyperventilation during naturally occurring panic attacks. *Behav. Res. Ther.* **24,** 91–94.

Svebak S. and Grossman P. (1986) How aversive is hyperventilation? Submitted for publication.

Telch M. J., Agras W. S., Taylor C. B., Roth W. T. and Gallen C. C. (1985) Combined pharmacological and behavioural treatment for agoraphobia. *Behav. Res. Ther.* **23,** 325–336.

Westphal C. (1872) Die Agoraphobie: eine neuropathische Erscheinung. *Arch Psychiat. NervKrankh.* **3,** 138–171.

Wolpe J. (1973) *The Practice of Behaviour Therapy,* 2nd edn. Pergamon Press, New York.

Zitrin C. M. (1983) Differential treatment of phobias: use of imipramine for panic attacks. *J. Behav. Ther. exp. Psychiat.* **14,** 11–18.

Zitrin C. M., Klein D. F. and Woerner M. G. (1980) Treatment of agoraphobia with group exposure *in vivo* and imipramine. *Archs gen. Psychiat.* **37,** 63–72.

Zitrin C. M., Woerner M. G. and Klein D. F. (1981) Differentiation of panic anxiety from anticipatory anxiety and avoidance behaviour. In *Anxiety: New Research and Changing Concepts.* (Edited by Klein D. F. and Rabkin J.). Raven Press, New York.

Zitrin C. M., Klein D. F., Woerner M. G. and Ross D. C. (1983) Treatment of phobias. I. Comparison of imipramine hydrochloride and placebo. *Archs gen. Psychiat.* **40,** 125–133.

OBSESSIONAL–COMPULSIVE PROBLEMS:
A COGNITIVE–BEHAVIOURAL ANALYSIS

Paul M. Salkovskis

Department of Clinical Psychology, Leeds General Infirmary, Great George St, Leeds LS1 3EX, England

(*Received* 20 *February* 1985)

Summary—Cognitive–behavioural approaches have made no impact on research and treatment in obsessional–compulsive disorder, despite the obvious link between thinking and psychopathology that characterizes this disorder. A close examination of cognitive and behavioural models leads to the suggestion that intrusive thoughts are best regarded as cognitive stimuli rather than responses. Cognitive responses (negative automatic thoughts) to these stimuli are typically linked to beliefs concerning responsibility or blame for harm to self or others. A cognitive–behavioural model based on this view is outlined and illustrated by clinical material derived from a case series. The model is used to explain a wide range of phenomena observed clinically, and a number of specific predictions are made. Implications for cognitive approaches to therapy are discussed.

The recent explosion of cognitive–behavioural approaches to clinical conditions has been matched by an increasing interest in the experimental validation of the underlying theoretical formulations. Teasdale (1982) has suggested that clinically useful strategies tend to arise from the availability of new paradigms, that is, well-elaborated sources of potential hypotheses and methodology. In these terms, cognitive models of emotional disorders have attained paradigmatic status and are beginning to make major contributions to the development of empirically based psychological therapies. In particular, Beck's cognitive model (Beck, 1967, 1976) has provided a coherent theoretical explanation of the basis of a variety of clinical conditions and normal mood states with important implications for treatment. It is particularly important that this model has also served to generate a considerable amount of experimental work testing predictions regarding, for instance, depression (Clark and Teasdale, 1982) and anxiety (Butler and Mathews, 1983).

Although the cognitive model has provided useful information on the nature and treatment of depression and anxiety disorders in general, it has so far failed to offer a comprehensive approach to the understanding and treatment of obsessional disorders. This is particularly surprising as it could be argued that obsessional thinking is the archetypal example of a cognitive disorder in the neuroses. A cognitive explanation of obsessional–compulsive problems is proposed by Beck (1976). However, this account of obsessional thoughts appears to be based solely on the view that the content of obsessions is related to thoughts of danger in the form of doubt or warning. There is no discussion of the difference between these and the thoughts of danger or risk subsequently shown to be specific to anxiety (e.g. Sewitch and Kirsch, 1984), although one might expect this distinction to be necessary for any cognitive view specific to the psychopathology of obsessions. Indeed, a number of the examples identified by Beck (1976, Chap. 7) as being anxiety- and fear-related cognitions appear to involve major elements of doubt or warning.

A differently orientated attempt at a cognitive–behavioural conceptualization of obsessive–compulsive disorder was made by McFall and Wollersheim (1979). However, this is directed at 'bridging the gap' between behavioural and psychoanalytic theory, and carries with it many of the problems associated with such an enterprise (Yates, 1983). Throughout there is a heavy dependence on the presence of preconscious and unconscious cognitions, which, compared to the psychoanalytic formulation, are said to be 'closer to the individual's awareness' as unacceptable ideas and feelings. No serious attempt is made to elaborate the processes involved in the direct cognitive and behavioural manifestations of these processes, other than mention of an undue belief in 'magical rituals'. Drawing heavily on Carr (1974) the main mediating processes are considered to be 'deficits' in primary and secondary appraisal—unfortunately, they are unable to distinguish between inaccuracies of cognitively mediated threat appraisals in obsessional patients and those in other patients. This lack of specificity must surely be a key issue and one which will probably only be resolved by a careful analysis of the *psychological processes* involved in intrusive phenomena rather than description of the characteristics of individuals experiencing obsessions. Furthermore, it is hard to see what benefits will arise from adopting psychodynamic concepts in an area where so much effort has been directed towards psychoanalytic treatment with such conspicuously poor outcome (Cawley, 1974), irrespective of the elaborate theoretical basis of this approach.

Previous attempts at cognitive *intervention* have concentrated on largely atheoretical techniques such as thought-stopping (e.g. Stern, Lipsedge and Marks, 1973) and have been mostly unsuccessful. Rachman and Hodgson (1980) have discussed distraction and dismissal procedures; however, convincing empirical evidence of the utility of such approaches has yet to be reported. It is important to consider the possibility that such procedures may be counter therapeutic, either by virtue of becoming 'neutralizing' in themselves, or by interfering with functional CS exposure (Borkovec, 1982).

Clearly, any attempt to conceptualize obsessions in cognitive terms must, as a first step, specify the position of obsessions within an hypothesized framework of cognitive phenomena such as that proposed by Beck (Beck, Epstein and Harrison, 1983). The relationship between 'negative automatic thoughts' and obsessions initially appears promising. Certainly, both can be regarded as subsets of Rachman's (1981) group of unpleasant intrusive cognitions. However, Beck (1976) clearly states that automatic thoughts are

"not the typical repetitive thoughts reported by patients with obsessional neurosis"
(p. 37),

although he does not go on to discuss what the important differences are. There are three major reasons why it is important to clarify the relationship between automatic and obsessional thoughts and hence place intrusions firmly within the context of cognitive theory:

1. The integration of the concept of unpleasant intrusive cognitions with cognitive theory seems particularly important now that there is evidence supporting the view that such intrusions or obesssions are part of "normal experience" (Rachman and de Silva, 1978; Salkovskis and Harrison, 1984). It is now possible to entertain the view that obsessional thoughts, previously regarded as pathological, may be on a continuum with normality, in the same fashion as mood states such as anxiety and depression, together with their associated cognitions.

2. It has been suggested by workers such as Rachman (1983a) that the link between depressed mood states and clinical worsening of obsessions (as well as resistance to behavioural treatments) could be accounted for in terms of the growing evidence of increased accessibility of negatively valenced cognitions in depressed mood states (Teasdale, 1983). For such an account to be fully useful, obsessional phenomena need to be integrated into cognitive theory so that more specific predictions about the putative mechanism of this interaction can be made with confidence, allowing the direct testing of propositions from both areas of work.

3. The development of specific cognitive techniques for the treatment of obsessional–compulsive problems could augment behavioural treatments in general and perhaps allow new approaches to 'treatment failures' as descibed by Foa (1979), Foa, Steketee, Grayson and Doppelt (1983) and Rachman (1983b) in whom cognitive factors (especially depressed mood and overvalued ideation) appear to be crucial.

Interesting comparisons may be made between the separate literatures on obsessions (including unwanted intrusive thoughts) and negative automatic thoughts. Rachman (1981, p. 89) defines intrusive unwanted thoughts as

"repetitive thoughts, images or impulses that are unacceptable and/or unwanted"

and goes on to specify the necessary and sufficient conditions for identification of a thought, image

Table 1. Comparison of obsessional thoughts (Rachman and Hodgson, 1980) and automatic thoughts described by Beck (1976)

Characteristic	Obsessional thoughts	Negative automatic thoughts
Relationship to 'stream of consciousness'	Intrude into	Run parallel to
Accessibility	Very easy	Can be difficult even with training
Perceived intrusiveness (irrelevance of interruption)	High	Low
Perceived rationality	Irrational	Rational
Relation to belief system	Inconsistent (ego dystonic)	Consistent (ego syntonic)
Relationship to external stimuli	Partial	Partial
Attributed source	Internal	Internal
Modalities affected	Linguistic, images and impulses	Linguistic and images
Content	Idiosyncratic	Idiosyncratic

or impulse as intrusive as

> "the subjective report that it is interrupting an ongoing activity; the thought, image or impulse is attributed to an internal origin, and is difficult to control."

Negative automatic thoughts, on the other hand, are defined by Beck, *et al.* (1983) as

> "elicited by stimuli (actual external events *or* thoughts about events)"

and

> "*plausible* or reasonable, although they may have seemed far-fetched to somebody else. The patients accepted their validity without question and without testing out their reality or logic." (Beck, 1974, p. 36)

Further careful examination of the literature allows us to derive the comparison illustrated in Table 1. The major differences between these negative automatic thoughts and obsessions seem to lie in the perceived intrusiveness, immediate accessibility to consciousness and the extent to which they are seen as being consistent with the individual's belief system. This last difference is particularly important, insofar as Beck's view of cognitions producing affective disturbance rests on their perceived *realistic* and *plausible* nature, and their acceptance by the individual experiencing them. By contrast, obsessions are unacceptable, irrational and implausible. Obsessions are incongruent with the individuals belief system, unlike negative automatic thoughts which are an expression of it.

If we are not able to regard obsessions as being a type of negative automatic thought, where do they fit into a cognitive model of psychopathology? Rachman (1971, 1976) has suggested that obsessional thoughts are noxious conditioned stimuli which have failed to habituate, and which are maintained by the mechanisms involved in two-process learning. Adopting this view and attempting to consider obsessional problems from a cognitive standpoint, I would like to argue that obsessional thoughts function as stimuli which may provoke a particular type of automatic thought. The evidence is that disturbing *intrusions* occur frequently in normal individuals without leading to serious disturbance of mood or coping. It seems likely that they may become a persistent source of mood disturbance only when they result in negative automatic thoughts through interaction between the unacceptable intrusions and the individuals belief system, i.e. in some kind of adverse evaluation ('this is a bad thing to be thinking'). This process is very similar to one frequently considered to produce affective disturbance in depressed patients when making global judgements of self in relation to behaviour, viz. 'if I get angry with the children that means I'm a bad mother'; 'if I have thoughts like this that means that I'm an evil person', 'thinking this is as bad as doing it' (Fennell, 1984). The intrusions will only be expected to produce distress when they have some (idiosyncratic) meaning or salience to the individual experiencing them (i.e. strong adverse personal implications). This is consistent with the findings of Parkinson and Rachman (1981), who report finding that, for normal Ss, intrusions high on unacceptability were 'worse in all respects' than intrusions of low acceptability, i.e. less dismissable, controllable, produced more discomfort, anxiety, stress, resistance and were of longer duration. In terms of Beck's model intrusions may, for some individuals on some occasions, activate pre-existing dysfunctional schemata and hence result in unpleasant automatic thoughts. Such automatic thoughts in response to intrusions appear to relate specifically to ideas of being responsible for damage or harm coming to oneself or to others, or associated imagery of a similar nature (see below and Table 4). That is, obsession-provoked automatic thoughts or images revolve around personal responsibility, the possibility that if things go wrong it might well be the persons' own fault. Such responsibility may be indirect as well as direct, so that the possibility of preventing harm caused by external agents is equally potent. Clearly, such ideas of responsibility would lead to self-condemnation in vulnerable individuals to the extent that such responsibility (or failure to avoid culpability) is abhorrent to them. Such ideas of responsibility can extend to having had the thought itself; that is, if the person believes that they are responsible for their own thoughts (Borkovec, Robinson, Pruzinsky and DePree, 1983; Borkovec, 1984), the content of which is abhorrent to them, then they presumably regard themselves as being responsible for being a bad or evil person unless they take steps to ensure their blamelessness. The affective disturbance usually described as arising from the obsession or intrusion actually arises from such automatic thoughts about the intrusion rather than from the intrusion itself. As depression primes concepts of self-blame this may be used to account for the increased distress experienced by obsessionals when depressed.

The prominence of a clearly identifiable and extremely obvious cognition (i.e. the intrusion) has probably served to prevent the closer examination of cognitions associated with obsessions, despite the adoption of Lang's (1970) three-systems model. The doubting described by Beck as typical of the ideation of obsessionals appears to be characteristic of the initial intrusion. The ideation from which the emotional disturbance arises is a cognitive response to this, and relates to responsibility or possibility of blame for some kind of personally salient harm (cf. Turner, Steketee and Foa, 1979). Impulses are similarly not particularly disturbing unless there is some belief in the possibility that they might be carried through, and blame being likely to fall on the individual as a result of failing to control the impulse.

Neutralization, either as compulsive behaviour or cognitive strategies (e.g. thinking a 'good thought' after having a 'bad thought') can be understood easily in this context as attempts to put things right, and avert the possibility of being blamed by self or others. Active attempts at such rectification are more likely against the background of thoughts of direct responsibility for harm, especially amongst those described by Rachman as being of 'tender conscience'. Clearly, if it is possible to rectify something that one may be responsible for, then any possible consequences cease to be a worry. The persistent seeking after reassurance, particularly from those in authority, displayed by many obsessionals also makes much more sense when viewed in this context and can be seen as a way of spreading the responsibility. Thus, the patient who has thoughts of harming others may somewhat diminish their feelings of responsibility by making sure that others know, often in great detail, the content of their worries or even carry out actions for them. So, if the doctor, psychologist or relative knows that the patient has touched a potential source of disease and then something likely to be touched by others, then they share the responsibility to some extent. This may also help account for the differences in the ability of different individuals to provide 'valid' reassurance. [See Foa (1979, p. 173) for a particularly interesting illustration of the power of reassurance in obsessionals with 'overvalued ideas'.] Some clinicians regard such reassurance seeking as a form of neutralization, but often the connection is unclear; for instance, in contamination fears where washing is the usual form of neutralization involved, but in addition reassurance is persistently (and often irritatingly) sought. Assessment and formulation based on ideas of responsibility or blame for disaster related to the effects of contamination and not washing may have greater explanatory value in the functional analysis of individual patients than fears of contamination *per se*. The implications for treatment are also important. Whereas some writers (Marks, 1981, p. 84) have stressed the importance of not providing reassurance during treatment, more often this important topic is given little prominence in descriptions of behavioural treatments. Where it is discussed, reassurance is, at best, defined very narrowly indeed, usually in terms of direct verbal requests. Frequently, reassurance seeking adopts subtle guises, and may not be recognized as a form of neutralization by patient or therapist. At worst, active provision of reassurance is recommended as a way of decreasing discomfort and improving compliance, with little regard for potential detrimental effects (Warwick and Salkovskis 1985). These authors highlight the important difference between effective transmission of new information relevant to the patient's problems as opposed to repetitive provision of old information as a way of producing a temporary reduction in anxiety in response to doubts (i.e. intrusive thoughts) expressed by the patient. A further important implication is for the *way* in which treatment is carried out. That is, therapist-directed exposure could, under some circumstances, act to provide inappropriate reassurance and hence unwittingly lead to failure of response prevention. Examples of this include repeated unnecessary therapist modelling and excessive use of specific instructions without a shift in the emphasis towards self-directed exposure. In such circumstances, a careful analysis of the individual case with such a possibility in mind could be coupled with a strong emphasis on homework and self-programmed generalization. For the same reason, care also needs to be exercised in the use of spouse as therapist. In cases where there is a failure to generalize outside therapist-directed sessions, careful examination of this possibility is indicated, and programmed exposure to responsibility for their own programme is often useful. Some evidence for this view is provided by Roper and Rachman (1976), who demonstrated that it is difficult to elicit urges to check in the presence of the experimenter, and that urges to check elicited in the absence of the experimenter were significantly stronger than if the experimenter were present. In fact, they account for this phenomenon in terms of the transfer of responsibility to the experimenter or therapist, although they do not explain why this should have such an effect.

Neutralization can therefore be regarded as attempts to avoid or reduce the possibility of being responsible for harm to oneself or others. Frequently, the effort required for neutralization is slight when compared to the awful consequences of failure to neutralize, at least in the early stages of the disorder. Certainty of blamelessness is extremely difficult to achieve, however, and if the consequences of being to blame are particularly unpalatable to the individual concerned then the availability heuristic might be expected to come into operation, in a similar way to that suggested in anxiety by Butler and Mathews (1983). It is possible to go on to argue that the cognitive distortion involved in obsessional–compulsive problems relates to an inflated belief in the probability of *being the cause* of serious harm to others or self, or failing to avert harm where this may have been possible rather than an increased belief in the probability of harm *per se*. Related to this is Rachman's (1983) view that close clinical and theoretical attention needs to be paid to cognitions in which the informational content is "recent representative, personally salient (and) vivid" (p. 76). Frequently occurring *thoughts* regarding unacceptable actions (or possible failures to 'put right' where this may have been possible) may seem to the patient to be representative of the actions (or failure to act) themselves, in the light of their beliefs regarding the connection between thought and action (Borkovec et al., 1983). This could equally apply to thoughts of having made a mistake. Clearly such thoughts are likely to be salient both in terms of their implications for possible unpleasant outcomes such as blame or criticism by others (Turner et al., 1979), and in terms of their implications for action (neutralizing).

This view allows the explanation of a previously problematic clinical observation, the occurrence of intrusions without consequent discomfort. The presence or absence of dysphoric mood or salient belief appears to be an important determinant of whether discomfort follows such intrusions or not. Beck (1976) argues that negative automatic thoughts become more prominent when disturbed mood is present; thus, the intrustions are likely to cause more affective disturbance in the dysphoric individual due to the increased accessibility of *specific types* of negative automatic thoughts (Teasdale, 1983). This is not to say that pre-existing dysphoria is necessary for such affective disturbance; clearly, a particularly salient or vivid intrusion could provoke discomfort in the absence of generalized disturbed mood state rather in the way that failure experiences can provoke depressed mood whatever the initial state, but are more likely to when there is a pre-existing mood disturbance. Themes of danger (as in anxiety) and loss (as in depression) are both frequently present in the content of obsessional compulsive ideation, so that, for instance, it could appear very likely (dangerous) that something terrible (constituting a loss) *will* happen, and the individual concerned be responsible to some degree for this. Some degree of responsibility is assumed by the obsessional as similar to being fully responsible. This model would predict that increased accessibility of such concerns (as occurs in heightened anxiety and depression) would result in clinical worsening of obsessions.

The formulation outlined above was arrived at as a result of careful consideration of a large number of obsessional patients, and is illustrated below by two examples of quite different patients. Both patients were interviewed about the content of their intrusive thoughts, and then asked to try and focus on any thoughts subsequent to the intrusions as they occurred, particularly if these were associated with discomfort.

Case 1

Patient J.F. had recently qualified as a medical doctor, and was referred just prior to starting her house jobs and getting married. She was displaying compulsive behaviour related to ideas that she might become contaminated by substances such as cosmetics which could have become transformed by sunlight or heat into carcinogens; also that she might catch warts from her fiancee. She was well aware of the extremely unlikely nature of her intrusion, but was disturbed by the possibility to the extent that she spent most of the day protecting cosmetics, soap powders and the like from sunlight and heat, and avoided contact with anything which might be contaminated by such combinations. She avoided any consumer goods which might be 'different' or 'untested' for carcinogens, to the point of dismantling enormous shop displays to find an unflawed packet. She reported intrusions regarding the possibility of things having become carcinogenic, and the safety standards used ("have they tested handcream with this particular brand of toothpaste *and* when it has all been in the sun?"). She reported that when discomfort was provoked by these stimuli, it was accompanied by a vivid image of herself with her face disfigured by skin cancer, or the thought that if she did get cancer that her fiancee would certainly be so revolted that he would abandon her. Also, she reported that the thing that made it worst of all was the idea that *it would all be her fault because she had not done enough to prevent such an occurrence.* When she experienced intrusions which were not accompanied by these throughts and images and the idea of blame, they did not particularly upset her and compulsive behaviour did not follow. Table 2 shows the intrusions and associated automatic thoughts for this patient.

Table 2. Intrusions and automatic thoughts for patient J.F.: health concerns

Intrusion	Automatic thought	Consequence
This hand cream may be contaminated as a result of mixing with sunlight, and some chemical interaction	I'll get cancer and it'll be my own fault (plus image of her face horribly disfigured by a growth)	Seeks reassurance, refuses to use cosmetics
Some contaminated handcream may still be on my hands	No-one will want to know me not even my fiance, because I'll have made myself rot away	Rinses hands repeatedly
This damaged packet of food might have become contaminated by some (unknown) chemical and have become carcinogenic	If I don't find a perfect packet I'll have been responsible for Peter and myself getting cancer	Asks assistant, doesn't buy it, tries to find a packet without any flaws

This patient clearly illustrates thoughts of being responsible for physical harm, mainly to herself. The second example is quite different, insofar as the range of intrusions is much more varied, and the ideation is related to social-evaluative concerns.

Case 2

Patient E.C. was a 50-yr-old schoolteacher, and had been referred as a result of an acute worsening of long-standing problems. At the time of referral he was checking excessively, showing clear depressive symptoms which he attributed to the severity of the obsessional symptoms. His obsessions took the form of 'unfinished business', in that he could not leave the topics concerned alone until he was sure that he had not been "responsible for something resulting in terrible disgrace" (his words). He was convinced of the stupidity of the checking, but had no doubts about the certainty of disgrace if the intrusion were true. Table 3 shows the intrusions and ideation for this patient.

A series of patients seen by the author were reviewed prior to detailing the specific model outlined above, and the results of these investigations (based on interviews) are given in Table 4.

Table 3. Intrusions and automatic thoughts for patient E.C.: social evaluative

Intrusion	Automatic thought	Consequence
(When closing a building) I might not have switched the light off	I'll get into dreadful trouble; I'll be disgraced or lose my job because of this carelessness on my part	Checks light repeatedly
(Shakes hands having touched an unidentified substance on a desk) I've given this girl a disease, perhaps poisoned her	I'll have caused terrible harm to her, might even have caused her death	Makes sure she isn't ill
(Made an unwitting comment to class about headmaster) someone will tell him I was rude about him	My thoughtlessness will result in my getting the sack, or at least into terrible trouble	Tells class he didn't mean what he said in that way
(Took some drawing pins from work to use at church) someone will find out about this	I'll be described as a thief, I'll be in terrible disgrace because of what I have done	Hides drawing pins

Table 4. Obsessions and their associated ideation

Sex	Duration (yr)	Type of intrusion	Ideation	Behaviour
F	5	Blasphemous thoughts	I won't be forgiven for these thoughts; I have sinned by having them	Avoids churches, prays
F	7	Thoughts of having picked up someone's money, or set fire or made them lose their purse	I might have done something which will make me a thief; the thought might mean I want to be a thief	Asks if people have their purse, seeks reassurance, avoids tills, purses
F	14	Thoughts of harming her children; images of strangling them, them dead by her hand	This means that I want to do these things; having such thoughts means I am evil; having the picture may make it happen	Avoids being on her own with children, tries to think good thoughts
F	2	Thoughts of having contaminated others, especially her children by touching them	I will have caused people/my children to get cancer, they'll get sick because of me	Avoids touching anything which others may touch, washes, checks reassurance
M	6	Thoughts of having made a serious mistake at work (architect) of having missed some vital detail out	I'll be blamed for having made an expensive or injurious mistake through carelessness; I'll lose my job	Checks work repeatedly, asks others for advice, avoids finishing work
F	8	Thoughts of things being out of place, untidy	People will regard me as a bad wife/person because of my behaviour	Cleans, reassurance
F	4	Thoughts of harm coming to her dog	It'll be me that hurt the dog	Tries to think good thoughts
F	7	Doubts about having turned off the gas, etc.	My flat will explode, my neighbours will die because I didn't check	Repeated checking
M	13	Thoughts of getting a sexually transmitted disease, of leaving the gas (and other things) turned on	I'll be ill because I neglected my health, things will go wrong because I was neglectful	Checks genitals, seeks reassurance, checks gas
F	3	Thoughts of wishing harm on friends and family	Having these thoughts might make these things happen, I'll have harmed people I love	Tries to think of people alive and well
F	4	Thoughts of being very overweight, thoughts of ghosts coming into the house (as she does things, e.g. closing door)	If I do things while having such awful thoughts, these things might happen because of this	Thinks of herself as underweight, pictures an angel as she repeats
M	8	Thoughts of having herpes or other disease	I may transmit disease to my family; if I don't show the doctor, he'll not make the right diagnosis	Avoids contact with family, goes repeatedly to clinic
F	2	Thoughts of harming others by contamination, carelessness, fire and other things	If I cause harm to other people then I will not go to heaven	Checks, washes, gets other to do things for her
M	10	Thoughts about not having locked the door; ruminating about 'floaters' in his eyes	If I don't get rid of these thoughts I won't be able to enjoy myself	Checks, deliberately distracts himself

A COMPREHENSIVE COGNITIVE–BEHAVIOURAL MODEL OF OBSESSIONS

The account of obsessions described here clearly owes much to the previous 'anatomy of obsessions' proposed by Rachman (1978), and makes many of the same assumptions, specifically that obsessional symptoms should be conceptualized along the lines of a three-systems model, and that intrusions *per se* are a normal phenomenon.

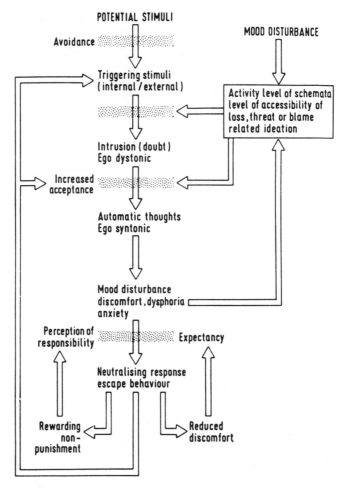

Fig. 1. Mechanisms and modulating influences in obsessional thoughts and behaviour.

Figure 1 illustrates the main elements of the proposed model, including the mechanisms by which resonating responses are maintained, and the gating mechanisms affecting the probability of particular sequences. The environment is full of a wide range of potential triggering stimuli for intrusive thoughts. However, most obsessional patients will take steps to avoid encountering such stimuli as much as possible (Robertson, Wendiggenson and Kaplan 1983). This avoidance may be overt or covert—that is, it may involve keeping out of particular environments and not allowing contact with particular stimuli, or may involve attempts to steer their thoughts off particular topics. This type of behaviour will be indistinguishable from that seen in phobics, with the intention being identical. Clearly such strategies may fail (or even be counter-productive, so that the avoidance behaviour itself begins to trigger the thoughts it is intended to prevent), in which case triggering stimuli are encountered. Such stimuli may be external (e.g. the sight of sharp knives), or may be other thoughts related or unrelated to the obsession. It seems likely that they may include the performance or even the satisfactory termination of a neutralizing response. There is no reason to believe that the processes governing the triggering of unpleasant intrusive thoughts are different from those involved in any other type of thought.

The intrusive thought triggered at this stage is, by definition, ego dystonic—that is, the content is experienced as inconsistent with the individual's belief system, and is perceived as objectively irrational. The reaction of the individual experiencing this intrusion (stimulus) will therefore be determined by the extent to when its occurrence is salient for the person concerned. It they believe that odd thoughts with an unpleasant content can occur and have no further implications, then the sequence will terminate here. If, on the other hand, they believe that thoughts of this kind might have important implications, then automatic thoughts would be expected to arise as a function of the strength of the beliefs concerned, which in turn will be affected by pre-existing mood state

(Teasdale, 1983). The kinds of belief involved are probably best summarized in terms of Beck's (1976) concept of 'dysfunctional assumptions'. Dysfunctional assumptions most likely to interact with intrusive thoughts include:

(1) having a thought about an action is like performing the action;
(2) failing to prevent (or failing to try and prevent) harm to self or others is the same as having caused the harm in the first place;
(3) responsibility is not attenuated by other factors (e.g. low probability of occurrence);
(4) not neutralizing when an intrusion has occurred is similar or equivalent to seeking or wanting the harm involved in that intrusion to happen;
(5) one should (and can) exercise control over one's thoughts.

The assumptions involved in each case will vary considerably, but in each case an element of responsibility, blame or control will be involved in a way which interacts with the content of intrusive thoughts to produce automatic thoughts concerning some combination of blame, threat and loss. As already discussed, such automatic thoughts will, by definition, be ego syntonic.

Mood disturbance will result from the automatic thought, and this in turn is likely to lead to neutralizing responses. The likelihood of occurrence of neutralizing responses will depend on previous experience in terms of the extent to which relief is expected as a result of their performance (including schedule effects). Also important is the extent to which their non-performance is salient to the beliefs described above (i.e. perceived responsibility).

There are three main consequences of neutralizing, each of which have further implications for the process described. Firstly, neutralizing usually results in reduced discomfort (Hodgson and Rachman, 1972; Roper, Rachman and Hodgson, 1973) which allows the development of obsessional behaviour as a strategy for coping with stress. This not only increases the probability of subsequent neutralizing, but may also result in generalization of this strategy for anxiety reduction to other circumstances (see below). Secondly, neutralization will be consistently followed by non-punishment. Rewarding non-punishment is a powerful reinforcement in its own right (Gray, 1975) and will also be expected to have an effect on the perceived validity of the beliefs described above. These would act along the lines of 'I acted on my belief and felt better, therefore the belief must have some basis in truth' and 'the disaster I attempted to forestall has not come about, which may mean that my neutralization was a reasonable and effective thing to do'. Finally, the performance or completion of neutralizing will be, in itself a powerful and unavoidable triggering stimulus.

Pre-existing mood disturbance, although not central to the model proposed, can act at several levels. It could, for example, lead to resonation of the system in the absence of specific triggering stimuli if it were strong enough, insofar as in predisposed individuals specific cognitions relating to responsibility would become available as a result of severe dysphoria (Teasdale, 1983). Mood disturbance would widen the range of stimuli which provoke intrusions in the first place, the range of intrusions which lead to negative automatic thoughts, and the activity level of pre-existing dysfunctional schemata. If the intrusion serves as a stimulus resulting in a negative automatic thought, then the consequent mood disturbance will feed back to increase accessibility of further negative automatic thoughts. Specifically it can be predicted that increases in anxiety will result in more frequent intrusions, while depression will result in an increased probability of negative automatic thoughts and hence discomfort.

Clearly, if the automatic thoughts arising from the intrusion do not include the possibility of being in some way responsible (either actively or passively), then neutralizing is very unlikely to take place, and the result is likely to be heightened anxiety or depression rather than an obsessional problem. It could also be added that rapid extinction of affective responses would also be predicted in these circumstances, as in the stress-induced intrusions reported by Horowitz (1975). Thus, for the obsessional patient threat and loss are to be avoided, but responsibility more so.

For the model to be useful, a number of important observations need to be encompassed within the framework offered here, leading to specific modifications in particular circumstances. It should be added that these observations are problematic for most current theoretical models of obsessive–compulsive disorder, and the ways in which this model deals with them are, in the main part, not markedly different from other related formulations such as that proposed by Rachman (1978).

(1) Clinically, compulsions which appear to be fundamentally 'senseless' and not specifically related to thoughts of blame or responsibility may be encountered (de Silva, 1984). It is even possible to encounter individuals who actually find the performance of rituals pleasurable, although such individuals seldom present for treatment entirely of their own accord.

The key to this issue appears to be the presence of extremely well-elaborated and above all, effective, neutralization. This can be in the form of covert or overt compulsive behaviour. In each of the cases drawn to my attention, the compulsion has assumed considerable stereotypy, and most commonly has been present for a considerable period of time. For instance, a colleague allowed me to interview a girl (who had been referred for a psychosomatic condition), who found rearranging objects in exact lines, sometimes for many hours, a relaxing and pleasurable activity. She also reported strong urges to perform such activity during times of stress. When interviewed, she was able to date the onset of this behaviour to her early teens, at which time she recalled feeling that if she did not line things up harm would come to her parents. She did not recall these thoughts having diminished, but was emphatic that they had not been present for some years. It would appear that completely effective avoidance may lead to the disappearance of the automatic thoughts (and anxiety) in a way similar to that described by Solomon (Rescorla and Solomon, 1967). In avoidance experiments, dogs learned to shuttle so effectively that they did not encounter any aversive stimuli. They also ceased to show any signs of fear, although preventing the avoidance response resulted in the reinstatement of fear responses. It is interesting to note that Beck (1976) makes a similar observation, noting that consistent avoidance in phobics is related to lack of awareness of 'maladaptive ideation' (i.e. negative automatic thoughts), adding that being forced into the avoided situation leads to activation of such ideation, and consequent easy identification. In obsessions, this situation would be expected to occur in individuals for whom the neutralization is fully effective and can be carried out on every occasion. In such cases, the obsession would cease to elicit the negative automatic thoughts, as the thoughts of blame would not apply if 'putting things right' were immediately and consistently possible. It is also possible that the neutralizing response would come to have the kind of reinforcing properties associated with a strong safety signal (Rachman, 1984), and may occur independently of intrusions, as described in the case above. In cognitive terms, the neutralizing response could come to elicit *positive* automatic thoughts, although this need not necessarily happen. From this analysis, a number of testable predictions can be made about obsessions for which no thoughts of blame or responsibility can be found: (i) a highly effective neutralizing response will always be present; (ii) thoughts of blame or responsibility will have been present at the onset of the obsession; (iii) the obsession will tend to be of very long duration or of early onset; (iv) little or no resistance to the obsession will be present for most of the time; (v) little or no subjective or psychophysiological disturbance will accompany the performance of the neutralizing behaviour, although response prevention will tend to produce both; and (vi) the neutralizing response will tend to be very stereotyped. Such patients are relatively rare, but these predictions have been borne out in the five such cases the author has been able to interview.

(2) Thoughts of blame or responsibility are not prominent in many 'normal' obsessions, in the absence of compulsive behaviour.

In a sense, this may well be a key strength of the present formulation. It does appear that thoughts of blame and responsibility are not present in some normal Ss. This is particularly the case for individuals who report that they do not engage in any neutralizing activity. The explanation for this can be found in the previously described distinction between automatic thoughts and intrusions. Normal Ss experiencing intrusions with weak or no negative automatic thoughts of blame are almost certain not to attempt neutralizing, as this would clearly serve no function whatsoever. Parkinson and Rachman (1980) report, in a study of habituation of 'normal' obsessional thoughts, that eliciting the thought stimulated the urge to neutralize in only 1 of 60 Ss. This is in very marked contrast with studies on clinical obsessions, in which the urge to neutralize is consistently elicited in such circumstances. This, then, appears to be a major difference between 'normal' and clinical obsessions, and can be easily explained within the framework offered here. Hence, it is argued that 'normal' obsessions, in most circumstances, do not elicit negative automatic thoughts of blame. They may not elicit any response at all, or they may elicit negative automatic thoughts unrelated to blame or responsibility (such as thoughts related to threat or loss), produce discomfort without neutralizing, and simply habituate with repetition. Predictions from this aspect of the model would be: (i) there will be a strong association between neutralization and thoughts of blame in normal obsessions; (ii) normal and abnormal obsessions will differ in terms of the likelihood of thoughts of blame being present; (iii) when thoughts of blame are present in normal obsessions, the belief in such thoughts will be considerably less than in a clinical population even when the effect of frequency of intrusive thoughts is partialled out; (iv) the content of intrusive thoughts is likely to be more variable over time in a normal compared to a clinical sample; and (v) when neutralization takes place frequently in a normal obsession, the scope of this will closely parallel clinical obsessions.

(3) While the relationship between mood and obsessions is easily explained where obsessions increase as a result of mood disturbance, there is a small identifiable subsample ('losers') for whom depression results in a decrease and sometimes complete remission of obsessional symptoms (Gittelson, 1966). Such individuals show a return of obsessional symptoms once the depression lifts. The explanation for this phenomenon may be found in the content of the cognitions involved in these patients when they become depressed. In depression two relatively distinct sets of cognitions may be involved; self-blame and guilt feelings as opposed to overwhelming feelings of helplessness and hopelessness. The belief that things are going (or have gone) wrong as a result of the patients own actions as opposed to the belief that nothing one does makes any difference at all, now or ever, would have quite different effects on the assumptions described as underlying obsessional problems. Ideas of self-blame and guilt should amplify any pre-existing obsessional thoughts ('gainers'), while hopelessness and helplessness would invalidate those already present ('losers'). Predictions from this would be: (i) 'gaining' and 'losing' should relate to the interactions between obsessional beliefs and depressive beliefs such that hopelessness specific to obsessional content will inversely correlate with worsening of obsessions; (ii) 'losing' should be confined to depression (particularly retarded depression), and should not be seen in anxiety states without severe depression or hopelessness; and (iii) for such patients the intrusive thoughts will still occur in depression but will be regarded as 'not mattering'.

The therapeutic implications of this model are largely consistent with those of the behavioural model, with some particular additions. It would be predicted that attempts at cognitive modification of obsessions should concentrate not on modification of intrusions, which would be unlikely to have other than a transient effect on the belief system of the individual, but on the automatic thoughts consequent on the intrusions, and the beliefs which give rise to these. Clearly, exposure and response prevention are vital in the context of this model in terms of their effect on the resonating circuits in the later stages of the sequence described here. These procedures, together with related techniques such as modelling, would also function in the same way as the behavioural experiments currently employed in cognitive therapy for depression and anxiety (Beck, Rush, Shaw and Emery, 1979; Beck and Emery, 1979). Such an approach provides the opportunity to challenge automatic thoughts by thinking and behaving differently, in ways which may often be more effective than purely cognitive manoeuvres alone (Rachman, 1983a). If some modification of the occurrence, nature or impact of automatic thoughts concerning responsibility were possible in tandem with such procedures, then the subjective discomfort and psychophysiological disturbance could be reduced as well (de Silva and Rachman, 1981) with important implications for compliance. Likewise, if it were possible to alter the assumptions associated with the obsession, presumably the possibility of any resonance being set up would be removed and habituation enhanced accordingly. Another major application of cognitive techniques would be with individuals who may present difficulties in exposure, such as those who fear contamination by stimuli which it would be unwise to allow direct exposure (e.g. poisons) or in whom the predicted disasters arising from failure to perform the obsessions are remote in time, such as fears of contamination by potential carcinogens.

It is important to stress that attempts to act on the intrusion itself by means of direct argument would probably be unsuccessful between sessions and would, at worst, be most akin to providing reassurance and hence serve to strengthen the dysfunctional schemata. If the intrusion is regarded as the stimulus resulting in particular automatic thoughts rather than the cognitive basis of the discomfort itself this is clearer; reassurance is simply providing a further means of avoiding the stimulus. Another possibility for therapy relates to the use of cognitive intervention in depressed obsessionals, for whom there is now considerable evidence or failure to respond to behavioural treatments (Rachman, 1983b; Foa, 1979). If a cognitive approach is employed with such patients, then particular attention would need to be paid to dealing with thoughts of guilt or overwhelming responsibility; within-session habituation to exposure would then be expected to proceed, this probably being a necessary condition for clinical improvement (Foa, 1979).

Clearly, further validation of the view expounded here is required, and a study to provide this is under way. Preliminary single-case experiments evaluating the value of an approach of this kind with a variety of problems are also being carried out (Salkovskis and Warwick, 1985b). A case study which raises further questions of the type discussed here and illustrates the use of a cognitive intervention in a depressed obsessional who developed overvalued ideation has been completed (Salkovskis and Warwick, 1985a). Ultimately, the utility of such a model must rest on its ability to make a contribution to the clinical assessment and treatment of obsessional patients.

Acknowledgements—The author is grateful to a number of people for help with the ideas discussed here. In particular, I would like to thank Ivy Blackburn, Tom Borkovec, David M. Clark, Melanie Fennell, Edna Foa and Hilary Warwick for useful discussions; also David A. Clark, David M. Clark, Padmal de Silva, Melanie Fennell and Hilary Warwick for substantial comments on earlier versions of this paper.

REFERENCES

Beck A. T. (1967) *Depression: Clinical, Experimental and Theoretical Aspects.* (Republished as *Depression: Causes and Treatment.* Univ. of Pennsylvania Press, Philadelphia, Penn., 1972.)

Beck A. T. (1976) *Cognitive Therapy and the Emotional Disorders.* International Univ. Press, New York.

Beck A. T. and Emery G. (1979) Cognitive therapy of anxiety and the phobic disorders. Unpublished manuscript, Center for Cognitive Therapy, Univ. of Pennsylvania, Philadelphia, Penn.

Beck A. T., Rush A. J., Shaw B. F. and Emery G. (1979) *Cognitive Therapy of Depression.* Guilford Press, New York.

Beck A. T., Epstein N. and Harrison R. (1983) Cognitions, attitudes and personality dimensions in depression. *Br. J. cog. Psychother.* **1**, 1–16.

Borkovec T. G. (1982) Facilitation and inhibition of functional CS exposure in the treatment of phobias. In *Learning Theory Approaches to Psychiatry* (Edited by Boulougouris J.), pp. 95–102. Wiley, New York.

Borkovec T. G. (1984) Worry: physiological and cognitive processes. Paper presented at the *14th A. Congr. European Association for Behaviour Therapy*, Brussels.

Borkovec T. D., Robinson E., Pruzinsky T. and DePree J. A. (1983) Preliminary exploration of worry: some characteristics and processes. *Behav. Res. Ther.* **21**, 9–16.

Butler G. and Mathews A. (1983) Cognitive processes in anxiety. *Adv. Behav. Res. Ther.* **5**, 51–62.

Carr A. T. (1974) Compulsive neurosis: a review of the literature. *Psychol. Bull.* **81**, 311–318.

Cawley R. (1974) Psychotherapy and obsessional disorders. In *Obsessional States* (Edited by Beech H. R.), pp. 259–290. Methuen, London.

Clark D. M. and Teasdale J. D. (1982) Diurnal variation in clinical depression and accessibility of memories of positive and negative experiences. *J. abnorm. Psychol.* **91**, 87–95.

Fennell M. J. V. (1984) Personal communication.

Foa E. B. (1979) Failures in treating obsessive–compulsives. *Behav. Res. Ther.* **17**, 169–176.

Foa E. B., Steketee G., Grayson J. B. and Doppelt H. G. (1983) Treatment of obsessive–compulsives: when do we fail? In *Failures in Behaviour Therapy* (Edited by Foa E. B. and Emmelkamp P. M. G.), pp. 10–34. Wiley, New York.

Gittelson N. (1966) The fate of obsessions in depressive psychosis. *Br. J. Psychiat.* **112**, 705–708.

Gray J. A. (1975) *Elements of a Two-process Theory of Learning.* Academic Press, London.

Hodgson R. J. and Rachman S. J. (1972) The effects of contamination and washing in obsessional patients. *Behav. Res. Ther.* **10**, 111–117.

Horowitz M. (1975) Intrusive and repetitive thoughts after experimental stress. *Archs gen. Psychiat.* **32**, 1457–1463.

Lang P. J. (1970) Stimulus control, response control and the desensitization of fear. In *Learning Approaches to Therapeutic Behaviour* (Edited by Levis D. J.). Aldine, Chicago, Ill.

Marks I. M. (1981) *Cure and Care of Neurosis.* Wiley, New York.

McFall M. E. and Wollersheim J. P. (1979) Obsessive–compulsive neurosis: a cognitive–behavioural formulation and approach to treatment. *Cog. Ther. Res.* **3**, 333–348.

Parkinson L. and Rachman S. J. (1980) Are intrusive thoughts subject to habituation? *Behav. Res. Ther.* **18**, 409–418.

Parkinson L. and Rachman S. J. (1981) The nature of intrusive thoughts. *Adv. Behav. Res. Ther.* **3**, 101–110.

Rachman S. J. (1971) Obsessional ruminations. *Behav. Res. Ther.* **9**, 229–235.

Rachman S. J. (1974) Some similarities and differences between obsessional ruminations and morbid preoccupations. *Can. psychol. Ass. J.* **18**, 71–73.

Rachman S. J. (1976) The modification of obsessions: a new formulation. *Behav. Res. Ther.* **14**, 437–444.

Rachman S. J. (1978) An anatomy of obsessions. *Behav. Analysis Modif.* **2**, 253–278.

Rachman S. J. (1981) Special issue on unwanted intrusive cognitions. *Adv. Behav. Ther.* **3**, 87–123.

Rachman S. J. (1983a) Irrational thinking with special reference to cognitive therapy. *Adv. Behav. Res. Ther.* **5**, 63–88.

Rachman S. J. (1983b) Obstacles to the successful treatment of obsessions. In *Failures in Behaviour Therapy* (Edited by Foa E. B. and Emmelkamp P. M. G.), pp. 35–57. Wiley, New York.

Rachman S. J. (1984) Agoraphobia—a safety-signal perspective. *Behav. Res. Ther.* **22**, 59–70.

Rachman S. J. and Hodgson R. J. (1980) *Obsessions and Compulsions.* Prentice-Hall, Englewood Cliffs, N.J.

Rachman S. J. and de Silva P. (1978) Abnormal and normal obsessions. *Behav. Res. Ther.* **16**, 233–248.

Rescorla R. A. and Solomon R. L. (1967) Two process learning theory: relationships between Pavlovian conditioning and instrumental learning. *Psychol. Rev.* **74**, 151–182.

Robertson J., Wendiggenson P. and Kaplan I. (1983) Towards a comprehensive treatment of obsessional thoughts. *Behav. Res. Ther.* **21**, 347–356.

Roper G. and Rachman S. J. (1976) Obsessional–compulsive checking: experimental replication and development. *Behav. Res. Ther.* **14**, 25–32.

Roper G., Rachman S. J. and Hodgson R. (1973) An experiment on obsessional checking. *Behav. Res. Ther.* **11**, 271–277.

Salkovskis P. M. and Harrison J. (1984) Abnormal and normal obsessions: a replication. *Behav. Res. Ther.* **22**, 549–552.

Salkovskis P. M. and Warwick H. M. C. (1985a) Cognitive therapy of obsessional–compulsive disorder: treating treatment failures. *Behav. Psychother.* **13**. In press.

Salkovskis P. M. and Warwick H. M. C. (1985b) Morbid pre-occupations, health anxiety and reassurance. Submitted for publication.

Sewitch T. S. and Kirsch I. (1984) The cognitive content of anxiety: naturalistic evidence for the predominance of threat-related thoughts. *Cog. Ther. Res.* **8**, 49–58.

de Silva P. (1984) Personal communication.

de Silva P. and Rachman S. J. (1981) Is exposure a necessary condition for fear reduction? *Behav. Res. Ther.* **19**, 227–232.

Stern R. S., Lipsedge M. S. and Marks I. M. (1973) Obsessive ruminations: a controlled trial of thought-stopping. *Behav. Res. Ther.* **11**, 659–662.

Teasdale J. D. (1982) What kind of theory will improve psychological treatment? In *Learning Theory Approaches to Psychiatry* (Edited by Boulougouris J.), pp. 57–66. Wiley, New York.

Teasdale J. D. (1983) Negative thinking in depression: cause, effect or reciprocal relationship? *Adv. Behav. Res. Ther.* **5**, 3–25.

Turner S. M., Steketee G. and Foa E. B. (1979) Fear of criticism in washers, checkers and phobics. *Behav. Res. Ther.* **17**, 79–80.

Warwick H. M. C. and Salkovskis P. M. (1985) Reassurance. *Br. med. J.* **290**, 1028.

Yates A. J. (1983) Behaviour therapy and psychodynamic psychotherapy: basic conflict or reconciliation and integration? *Br. J. clin. Psychol.* **22**, 107–126.

EMOTIONAL PROCESSING

S. RACHMAN

Institute of Psychiatry, Department of Psychology, De Crespigny Park,
Denmark Hill, London, SE5 8AF, U.K.

(Received 16 July 1979)

Summary—A working definition of the concept of emotional processing is presented, with the aim of integrating a set of clinical and experimental observations. If successful, the concept may help to unify such apparently unrelated events as obsessions, the return of fear, abnormal grief reactions, nightmares, treatment failures, and so on.

Factors that may facilitate or impede emotional processing are presented, and some circumstances that may give rise to initial difficulties in processing are mentioned. A number of theoretical problems are posed, and some methodological innovations offered.

In one of his early papers, Freud (1910) said that hysterical patients suffer from 'reminiscences'. He suggested that "their symptoms are the remnants and the memory symbols of certain traumatic experiences" (Freud, 1910, p. 8). These ideas were richly illustrated by references to the famous case of Anna O., a patient treated by Breuer. According to Freud and Breuer this patient's problems "originated at the time when she was caring for her sick father, and her symptoms could only be regarded as memory symbols of his sickness and death. They corresponded to mourning, and a fixation on thoughts of the dead so short a time after death is certainly not pathological, but rather corresponds to normal emotional behaviour" (p. 8). While caring for her father, Breuer's patient had to "suppress a strong excitement instead of giving vent to it by appropriate words and deeds". As a result of this failure to express the appropriate emotions, she was later handicapped by a range of neurotic symptoms. According to the account given by Breuer, and subsequently related by Freud in various versions, Anna O. derived considerable if transient benefit from talking to Breuer about her symptoms and their origin—the famous 'talking cure'.

This notion that emotional experiences can reverberate for a considerable length of time and may continue to disrupt one's behaviour for many years after the event, is not a new one, but ideas of this kind are once more becoming a subject of interest. For the most part, disturbing emotional experiences are satisfactorily absorbed. Even in these cases however it is not uncommon to find that they return, at least in part, after an absence—sometimes to the surprise of the person experiencing the return.

THE CONCEPT

Several sets of apparently disconnected findings and observations can be brought into the same framework by using the concept of emotional processing. As a start, emotional processing is regarded as a process whereby emotional disturbances are absorbed, and decline to the extent that other experiences and behaviour can proceed without disruption. Anna O. finally overcame most of the disturbing features described by Breuer and resumed a fruitful way of life. If an emotional disturbance is *not* absorbed satisfactorily, some signs become evident. These signs are likely to recur intermittently, and may be direct and obvious, or indirect and subtle. The central, indispensable index of unsatisfactory emotional processing is the persistence or return of intrusive signs of emotional activity (such as obsessions, nightmares, pressure of talk, phobias, inappropriate expressions of emotion that are out of context or out of proportion, or simply out of time). Indirect signs may include an inability to concentrate on the task at hand, excessive restlessness, irritability. As all this suggests, it is far easier to come to grips with *failures* of emotional processing than with successes. Broadly, successful processing can be gauged from the person's ability to talk about, see, listen to or be reminded of the emotional events without experiencing distress or disruptions (see below, the discussion of test probes).

Before setting out a full analysis of emotional processing, it is necessary to give some indication of the sort of phenomena which the concept is designed to deal with. If emotional processing provides a useful framework, then an apparently unrelated set of events should begin to hang together: obsessions, the return of fear, incubation of fear, abnormal grief reactions, failures to respond to fear-reducing procedures, nightmares. Whatever their dissimilarities, and there are many, all of these phenomena can be regarded as indices of incomplete emotional processing.

Some of the impetus for the concept of emotional processing comes from the need to integrate the findings of behaviour therapists, and a more immediate prompt was provided by Lang's (1977) stimulating analysis of fear imagery. The need to establish unifying concepts that can incorporate the accumulated findings on the effects of behaviour therapy is nowhere clearer than it is in the fact that different fear-reduction procedures (notably desensitization, flooding, and modelling) are capable of producing comparable successes (Rachman, 1978a). The alternative possibility, that all three methods are mediated by separate processes, is improbable and not parsimonious. Moreover, these three methods appear to be capable of producing comparable reductions in other forms of neurotic disorder, especially obsessional-compulsive problems (Rachman and Hodgson, 1979). Adhering to the goal of parsimony, one might strive to connect these three behavioural methods, and at the same time link fear with obsessional-compulsive problems.

WHY CHOOSE EMOTIONAL PROCESSING?

Freud attributed Anna's continuing problems with reminiscences to the fact that when she was required to care for her ailing father, she had been unable to express her disturbed emotions. He implied that had Anna O. been able to express the appropriate emotions at the time of her father's illness, she would not have suffered from these troublesome reminiscences. In modern terms, we might redescribe these events as an example of discordance (Rachman and Hodgson, 1974). The strong social demands prevailing during her father's illness inhibited Anna O's expression of her emotional feelings, and if Freud was correct, this enforced discordance prepared the ground for later problems. It is not too far-fetched to quote in this connection a recent statement by a pioneer of behaviour therapy, Wolpe (1978, p. 235), who has observed that systematic desensitization (using imagination) does not succeed in helping that "considerable number of people" who "do not have fear when they imagine the things they fear". The implication is that the fear must be experienced before it can be reduced or eliminated—it requires processing perhaps.

An even closer analogy to the phenomenon described by Freud comes from some of the fear-reduction experiments carried out by Lang et al. Lang (1977) reported that subjects who had minimal heart-rate responses showed little improvement with desensitization. He concluded from these results, which contrasted with the concordance observed in the successfully treated subjects, that psychophysiological reactions to imagined scenes "may be a key to the emotional processing which the therapy is designed to accomplish" (Lang, 1977, p. 863). In the same paper he asserts that "the critical requirement ... is that at least partial response components of the affective state must be present if an emotional image is to be modified" (p. 874).

FACILITATION

The idea that fear-reduction techniques may proceed more satisfactorily if the stimulus material provokes at least some sign of reaction received partial support from a study of speech anxious subjects conducted by Borkovec and Sides (1979). On the other hand, an indirect attempt by Grey et al. (1979) to confirm Lang's observation of a relationship between heart rate responsiveness and the outcome of a fear-reduction technique, was not successful. Nevertheless the interest attaching to Lang's work is not thereby diminished (Grey *et al.* used an *in vivo* method of presentation, and Lang was referring to processing of *imagery*).

In his careful review of the psychophysiological literature, Mathews (1971) postulated that "one of the effects of relaxation may be to increase the vividness of imagery experienced during desensitization" and moreover, stronger physiological responses to phobic imagery may thus be produced, (p. 88). This view was recently supported in the experiment by Borkovec and Sides referred to earlier.

If fear reduction, by desensitization or other means, is indeed facilitated by relaxation (see Rachman, 1968), and if relaxation increases the vividness of the phobic imagery, perhaps it is the vividness that mediates the therapeutic value of relaxation. Do these therapeutic steps facilitate emotional processing? Relaxation exercises improve the vividness of the imagery, the vividness enhances the physiological reactions, and this in turn improves the quality of the emotional processing.

Another recent piece of evidence which is consistent with this possibility comes from Borkovec's research on insomnia, in which it was observed that relaxation training reduces the latency of sleep onset and the number of interfering, intrusive thoughts. Evidence drawn from an indirect source indicates that the successful completion of a course of fear-reduction is followed by the decline in frightening, relevant ruminations (possible signs of incomplete processing). Bandura *et al.* (1977) found that the snake fearful subjects who successfully completed a course of fear-reduction training, reported "marked or moderate relief from aversive thoughts and recurrent nightmares about reptiles. They were no longer preoccupied with frightening ruminations concerning snakes ... evidence that mastery experiences fostered through performance accomplishments can eliminate distressing nightmares of long-standing is especially noteworthy" (p. 135). These diverse pieces of evidence indicate that the indices of emotional disturbance proposed in this analysis, decline with relaxation or other treatments.

It seems to be commonly believed, probably unwisely (Shackleton, 1978), that after experiencing a bereavement, all people need to complete what is described as 'grief work'. Sometimes this notion is used in a vague sense and is employed too frequently and loosely. Nevertheless deaths usually produce emotional disturbances and many of these persist for prolonged periods. The idea that for some people, abnormal grief reactions can be reduced by repeatedly thinking about and reacting to material associated with the dead person, has received a measure of support from Ramsay's (1975) original research. By adopting the unusual and extremely demanding method of repeated rehearsals of the upsetting material (in a way not unlike imaginal exposure treatment), Ramsay appears to have helped his subjects to absorb the disturbing material in a way that reduced its persisting and disruptive effects. Can we say that his method facilitates the emotional processing of grief material?

There will be little disagreement with the claim that successful fear-reduction methods, with their emphasis on repeated exposures to the fearful stimuli, can be viewed as a means of absorbing persistent, disruptive emotional reactions. If current research on the modification of obsessional thoughts by the method of habituation training proves to be successful (Rachman, 1978a), this approach may be added to the growing list of procedures that facilitate emotional processing. Once one adopts the view that the fear-reducing (and related) methods used by behaviour therapists can be seen as forms of emotional processing, it becomes feasible to carry out an analysis of the kind presented below.

FAILURES

Some prominent examples of the failure of emotional processing include many forms of what are classed as neurotic symptoms—e.g. excessive and/or inappropriate fears, obsessions, sleep disturbances. At present we know most about fear, and hence I will concentrate on this phenomenon. Three aspects of abnormal fear are worth considering in terms of unsatisfactory emotional processing: the undue persistence of a fear, the unprovoked return of fear, and the incubation of fear. This is perhaps the point at which to recall that the overwhelming number of fear-provoking experiences are satisfactorily processed. Examples drawn from war-time observations include the following, and others are described in Rachman (1978a).

In a study of veteran combat airmen, the "interesting finding is that flyers who were wounded or injured indicated that they were as willing to return to combat as those who had not been wounded or injured" (Flanagan, p. 233). A second example of the apparent absorption of presumably disturbing experiences [which is equally surprising in terms of the 2-stage theory of fear and avoidance (see Rachman, 1977)] comes from surveys of civilian air-raid casualties. Apparently, the (surprisingly few) air-raid fears were no greater among those people who had been wounded or injured than they were among the luckier survivors (Janis, 1951).

What if anything is to be gained by regarding those minority instances of persisting, excessive fear, as failures of emotional processing? First, it offers a possible connection with related emotional phenomena. Second, it can be linked with the processes of habituation and extinction, and for purposes of analysing fear-reduction, it incorporates both of them under one concept. Thirdly, it opens a door for the development of new methods of reducing fears—the main therapeutic aim now being redefined as one of *facilitating the desired emotional processing*.

Although the undue persistence of fear can be accounted for in several ways (e.g. insufficient extinction trials, preservation of avoidance behaviour, etc.), the unprovoked return of fear presents some problems for traditional theories. The return of fear, literally the re-appearance of some degree of a fear that had undergone diminution, was encountered in an early experiment by Rachman (1966) and again by Grey *et al.* (1978), and points to the need for a concept such as emotional processing. The return of fear after an interval during which the new learning of fear is unlikely to have taken place, implies that at least some of the fear-reduction originally accomplished, must have been transient and in that sense, incompletely processed. So the return of fear presents a useful test-bed for analysing the degree and duration of emotional processing. Under experimental conditions, we should be able to *predict* the recurrence of fear from our knowledge of the type and degree of emotional processing accomplished during the experimental treatment periods. If the return of fear is to be regarded as an index of incomplete processing, it is essential to avoid circularity of argument; this can be done by making precise predictions and by using the test-probe method described below. At present, the emotional processing viewpoint does little to advance our understanding of the incubation of fear (Eysenck, 1979). Such incubation can be taken not merely as evidence of uncompleted emotional processing, but also as signifying the influence of as yet unidentified sensitizing factors (in addition to intense, brief exposures).

WORKING DEFINITION

Returning to the working definition of emotional processing (a return to undisrupted behaviour after an emotional disturbance has waned) three conditions must be met before the term can be applied. Firstly, there must be evidence of an emotional disturbance; secondly, there must be evidence that the disturbance has declined; and thirdly, we need evidence of a return to normal, undisrupted (routine) behaviour. If the first condition is met (i.e. an emotional disturbance occurs), but conditions two or three (declining disturbance, and a return of routine behaviour) are not met, then the emotional processing is incomplete.

This definition presents some problems. For example, a person may suffer from 'reminiscences'; signs of incomplete processing (disrupted behaviour and/or signs of emotional disturbance) reappear some time after the original disturbance has waned. Fear may return, grief may be delayed, and so on. How and when can we be confident that the emotional processing is complete? How long a period of tranquil, routine behaviour is required before we can be confident of our judgement? As it is unlikely that a suitable time scale can be developed for this purpose, one turns instead to use of test *probes*. After

Table 1. Indices of satisfactory emotional processing

1. Test probes fail to elicit disturbances
2. Decline of subjective distress
3. Decline of disturbed behaviour
4. Return of 'routine' behaviour (e.g. concentration)

an emotional disturbance has subsided, the extent of emotional processing can be estimated by presenting relevant stimulus material in an attempt to re-evoke the emotional reaction. The degree to which the test probes are successful in provoking the reaction provides *a measure of emotional processing*. For example, six months after successfully completing a fear-reducing training course, a subject is re-presented with the phobic stimulus. Or, a former griever may be reminded about or asked to speak about the dead person some time after he has ceased to show overt signs of grief. Test probes offer the most direct and best way of ascertaining the progress of emotional processing, but there are other signs that can be used alone or in combination. A list of signs that may index the satisfactory completion of emotional processing is given in Table 1. Even though the *test probe method* will probably prove to be the most useful one, there will be circumstances in which probes cannot be used. Then one can turn to the secondary signs as alternative or supplementary indices. The relations between indices, and their comparative value, will need to be determined.

As mentioned earlier, there are many more signs of *unsatisfactory* or incomplete emotional processing (see Table 2). Where an index has been derived directly, the source is referenced in the table. Running through all of these indices is the time factor. Emotional processing may reach completion but take an inordinate length of time, and hence be regarded as unsatisfactory. All of the signs listed in Table 2 can be regarded as falling within normal limits if they occur shortly after the emotional disturbance takes place. Their failure to subside, their undue persistence, constitutes unsatisfactory emotional processing. Some of the indices, especially if intense, may provide sufficient evidence in themselves of unsatisfactory emotional processing (e.g. repetitive nightmares, severe obsessions), but the indirect signs (such as restlessness) are of course insufficient.

Table 2. Indices of unsatisfactory emotional processing (N.B. time factor operates throughout)

(A) Direct signs
  1. Test probes elicit disturbances
  2. Obsessions (Rachman, 1978b)
  3. Disturbing dreams (Bandura *et al.*, 1977; Wickert, 1947)
  4. Unpleasant intrusive thoughts (Horowitz *et al.*, 1975)
  5. Inappropriate expressions of emotion (as to time/place)
  6. Behavioural disruptions/distress (e.g. crying)
  7. Pressure of talk
  8. Hallucinations (e.g. after bereavement)
  9. Return of fear (Rachman, 1978c)
(B) Indirect signs
  10. Subjective distress
  11. Fatigue
  12. Insomnia
  13. Anorexia
  14. Inability to direct constructive thoughts
  15. Pre-occupations
  16. Restlessness (Rachman, 1978a)
  17. Irritability (Rachman, 1978a)
  18. Resistance to distraction (Lang, 1977)

FACTORS THAT INITIATE DIFFICULTIES

As can be seen from Table 3 there are four groups of factors that might give rise to difficulties in emotional processing: state factors, personality factors, stimulus factors,

Table 3. Initiating factors giving rise to difficulty in processing

Factors causing difficulties	Factors avoiding difficulties
State factors	
Dysphoria	Relaxation
High arousal	
Illness	
Fatigue	
Disturbed dreams	
Sleeplessness	
Personality factors	
Neuroticism	Broad competence
Introversion	Self-efficacy
Inner-oriented (Jones, 1978)	Stability
Stimulus factors	
Sudden	Signalled
Intense (e.g. Horowitz, 1975)	Mild
Dangerous	Safe
Prepared	Unprepared
Uncontrollable	Controllable
Unpredictable	Predictable
Irregularity	Small chunks
Large chunks	Progressive
Associated activity factors	
Concurrent stressors (overload)	
Intense concentration on separate task	
Heat, noise (Broadbent, 1971)	
Need to suppress expression (Freud, 1910)	

and associated activity factors. It has been pointed out that most people successfully process the overwhelming majority of the disturbing events that occur in their lives. Among the state factors, it seems likely that a state of relaxation helps to ensure that future difficulties are avoided. On the personality side, it is to be expected that people who have broad competence and a high level of self-efficacy, should successfully process most emotional experiences. At present it is the stimulus factors about which most can be said. As can be seen from Table 3, the stimulus qualities that are least likely to give rise to processing difficulties include the following: signalled events, mild events, signals of safety, unprepared (Seligman's term) and controllable events, predictable events, stimuli in small chunks, and progressive incrementations. The associated activity factors that are likely to facilitate emotional processing are those which carry a moderate to high demand and which give one a sense of increased controllability.

It has to be said that at the present time we appear to have more clues about the factors which initiate *difficulties* in processing. The personality factors that are likely to be associated with difficulties in processing include a sense of incompetence, high levels of neuroticism, introversion. The state factors that are probably associated with difficulties in emotional processing are high arousal, dysphoria, illness, fatigue, disturbing dreams, sleeplessness and immaturity. The inclusion of disturbing dreams, itself an index of incomplete processing, is merited because there appear to be occasions on which obsessions are triggered by aversive dream material.

The stimulus factors that are likely to give rise to difficulties in processing include the following: sudden stimuli, intense stimulation [e.g. Horowitz (1975) found a positive correlation between the *degree* of stress experienced and the amount of intrusive thoughts experienced subsequently], signals of danger, prepared stimuli in Seligman's sense, uncontrollable stimuli, unpredictable stimuli, irregularity of presentation and large chunks of stimulation. The associated activities that might impede satisfactory processing include the presence of concurrent stressors (hence giving rise to an overload), intense concentration on a separate task, heat and/or noise, and possibly the need to suppress the appropriate emotional expression (Freud, 1910).

FACTORS THAT PROMOTE OR IMPEDE SATISFACTORY PROCESSING

Given that experiences, or certain kinds of material, are proving difficult to process, how might one set about overcoming the difficulty? In Table 4 a division has been made between factors that are likely to promote and factors that are likely to impede the process. The factors that are thought to promote satisfactory emotional processing will of course be familiar to behavioural therapists, and indeed most of them are drawn directly or indirectly from current methods. In sum, it is expected that the following factors will facilitate processing: engaged exposure to the disturbing material, habituation training, extinction trials, calm rehearsals (especially of coping behaviour), long presentations, repeated practice, proceeding from high to low provoking stimuli, the use of relaxation, vivid presentations of stimuli, the evocation of controlled autonomic reactions, a sense of perceived control, relevant conversation.

On the other side, it is possible to make an initial attempt at listing those factors which are likely to impede processing. They include: the avoidance of the disturbing stimuli or situation, a refusal or inability to talk about them, repeated exposures to disturbing material under uncontrolled conditions, poorly presented material, excessively brief presentations, few practice sessions, presentations that evoke no autonomic reactions, immobility, fatigue, irregularity of stimulation, and absence of perceived control.

This identification of the factors that facilitate or impede emotional processing is based on experimental and clinical observations, combined with logical probabilities, and must be regarded as the menu and not the meal. No doubt some of the factors are merely moderators, while others are at the core of emotional processing. Comparative experimental evaluations will help to extract the critical factors, but this enterprise may be difficult because of the complexity of the processes involved. For example, the introduction of a three-systems analysis raises the possibility that the major components of emotional responses are likely to be influenced by differing stimuli, at differing rates and to varying degrees—discordance and desynchrony are to be expected (Rachman, 1978a; Rachman and Hodgson, 1974). However, it is not unreasonable to hope that the major influences on emotional processing will act generally i.e. across systems, to at least some degree.

CONCLUSIONS AND QUESTIONS

The main goals of this theoretical framework are: to introduce some order, to unify some disparate findings, to identify new questions and invite new solutions.

The transformation or neutralization of emotion-provoking stimuli is facilitated by repeated presentations, by stimuli presented for certain minimal durations, by piecemeal presentations, by minimizing distractions, by inducing a low level of arousal. The transformation can be impeded by brief presentations, excessive stimulus intensities, unduly

Table 4. Factors that promote or impede emotional processing

Promote	Impede
Engaged exposures	Avoidance behaviour
Calm rehearsals (esp. of coping)	Agitated rehearsals (esp. of not coping)
Talk	Silence
Habituation training	Distractions
Extinction	Poorly presented material
No distractions	Excessively brief presentations
Catharsis	Inadequate practice
Vivid presentations	Excessively large 'chunks'
Long presentations	Immobility (Rachman, 1978a)
Repeated practice	Fatigue
Descending (?) presentations (Lang, 1970; Klorman, 1974; Grey, 1979)	Irregularity of stimulation (Rachman, 1978a)
Relaxation (Wolpe, 1958; Mathews, 1971)	Unresponsive autonomic reactions
Autonomic reactivity (Lang, 1977; Wolpe, 1978; Borkovec, 1979)	

complex, ambiguous or large stimulus inputs, excessively high levels of arousal. The accompanying or consequent signs of this process include heightened autonomic reactions, increased disturbances in dream activity, nightmares, intrusive thoughts, disturbances of concentration, tension and fatigue.

All of this leads to the speculation that the process of transformation is a matter of breaking down the incoming stimulation into manageable proportions and then absorbing it over an optimal period. The process of breakdown and absorption is facilitated by the factors listed above and impeded by excessively intense or complex stimulation.

Before introducing some of the new questions, it is worth noticing that successful emotional processing may well be followed by significant benefits for the person concerned. It is not merely a matter of surviving and then absorbing a succession of unpleasant experiences. For example Houston et al. (1978) reported that their subjects described increases in self-esteem after having gone through stressful experiences. Similarly, Hallam and Rachman (1979) found that bomb-disposal personnel who successfully completed stressful tours of duty felt that they had benefited from their experience.

This theoretical analysis gives rise to a number of questions, some of which are worth mentioning at this early stage. One of the first questions is whether or not emotional processing can occur multiply. That is to say, are we capable of processing different types of emotional material simultaneously? Or if not, is the processing done in serial and sequential form—and if so, what determines the order of precedence?

Next we can consider whether emotional processing varies with different modalities— are essentially the same processes involved regardless of whether the experience is predominantly visual or auditory? Closely related is the question of whether an emotional stimulus, such as a fearful object, is processed in the same way and at the same rate by different modalities? One might attempt to answer this question by presenting a noisy fearful object of unpleasant appearance and then determining the speed with which the visual and auditory components are processed. Naturally, questions of this kind lead on to speculations about the transfer of processing across modalities. How much transfer of training, or transfer of processing can we anticipate?

Along not dissimilar lines one might attempt to find out what effect, if any, simultaneously occurring processing of cognitive material has on the processing of emotional material. What happens for example if we present fearful stimuli to a person who is engaged in carrying out a vigilance or arithmetical task? Does this impede or facilitate the emotional processing, and does it facilitate or impede the cognitive processing? Are there circumstances in which work produces emotional comfort and relief? The early and substantial literature on the relationship between anxiety and learning (e.g. Eysenck, 1960) suggested that the Yerkes–Dodson law operates to some extent. According to Jones (1960, p. 493), "much evidence indicates that at least for complex learning and avoidance motivation, a very high level of drive decreases efficiency and the overall relationship between these two variables is curvilinear rather than linear. Excellent empirical example of this relationship is provided by the classic Yerkes–Dodson experiment ... "efficiency of learning is a curvilinear function of drive strength, some intermediate level of drive being optimal. Optimal drive strength is an inverse function of the difficulty of a learning task". The complex relationships between stress and performance were analyzed with subtlety by Jones, who also concluded that personality factors such as introversion and neuroticism play a major part in determining the effects of stress on performance. A re-examination of this interesting and substantial body of knowledge, within the framework of emotional processing, might be fruitful but it is not the main proposal. Instead a new or at least slightly different question is being posed: are people capable of simultaneously processing emotional and intellectual material, and what are the inter-relationships between these two processes? Will answers to these questions prove to be of practical and even therapeutic value?

The intimate but poorly understood relationship between depression and obsessions gives the clearest possible indication of the importance of mood factors on emotional processing. This aspect of emotional processing is one of the most tempting and will certainly absorb a great deal of attention, while promising considerable rewards. In the course of discussing the relationship between depression and obsession, Rachman and Hodgson (1979) devoted some attention to the role of habituation processes. Among other possibilities, they suggested that the presence of disturbed mood, specifically the presence of depression, may retard habituation processes. If this prediction is confirmed, one would need to know how and why this retarding influence operates. Given that such confirmation is forthcoming, it raises further questions about the relationship between mood disturbances and emotional processing in general.

In addition to the use of test-probes, and the methods implied by the suggestions contained in this concluding section, emotional processing can be studied by two other methods. It follows from the general argument that if the processing that is initiated after the occurrence of an emotional experience is interrupted (blocked or prevented by competing events or demands), then we should detect at a later stage the persisting signs of incomplete processing (e.g. ruminations, nightmares, etc.). This sequence of events, and the predictions that can be extracted, is open to direct experimental manipulation. So too is the next stage in the sequence—the persisting signs of incomplete processing observed after blocking events have taken place, can be reduced by providing those conditions that facilitate processing, e.g. relaxation, clear and graduated presentations of material. The full sequence can be sketched: emotional experience → processing begins → interruption → signs of incomplete processing persist → corrective facilitatory factors introduced → decline in signs of incomplete processing.

Another avenue into the subject, one which focuses on the temporal qualities of processing, can be illustrated by Rachman et al.'s (1976) study of the spontaneous decay of compulsive urges. In this study the spontaneous decline of subjective discomfort and compulsive urges were tracked after exposing obsessional patients to provoking stimulation. Their method enabled Rachman et al. to observe the nature and time course of processing of a discrete, controlled emotional experience (most of the processing was completed within 1 h). The effect of repeated instances of such discrete acts of processing is now under investigation, and should allow us to draw some conclusions about the cumulative effects of repeated processing, and the time course of discrete and cumulative instances of processing. The method can be extended in order to study the relation between facilitative/impeding factors and the time course of processing, e.g. it is to be expected that intense experiments will take longer to be processed.

These are some of the possible lines of development that can be drawn out from the concept of emotional processing. Lang (in press) is exploring the deeper nature of processing by intensively studying a narrower seam, emotional imagery, and it is to be hoped that the two approaches will yield complementary information and some enlightenment.

Acknowledgements—I wish to thank P. de Silva, R. Hallam, C. Philips and G. Sartory for their helpful advice.

REFERENCES

BANDURA A., ADAMS N. and BEYER J. (1977) Cognitive processes mediating behavioral change. *J. Person. soc. Psychol.* **35**, 125–139.

BORKOVEC T. (1979) Pseudo (experimental) Insomnia and idiopathic (objective) insomnia. *Adv. Behav. Res. Ther.* **2**, 27–55.

BORKOVEC T. and SIDES J. (1979) The contribution of relaxation and expectancy to fear reduction. *Behav. Res. Ther.* **17**, 529–540.

BROADBENT D. (1971) *Decision and Stress.* Academic Press, New York.

EYSENCK H. J. (Editor) (1960) *Handbook of Abnormal Psychology.* Pitmans, London.

EYSENCK H. J. (1979) The conditioning model of neurosis. *Behav. Brain Sci.* **1** (in press).

FLANAGAN J. (Editor) (1948) The Aviation Psychology Program Report No. 1. U.S. Govt. Printing Office, Washington.

FREUD S. (1910) The origin of psychoanalysis. Reprinted in *A General Selection from The Works of Freud.* (Edited by J. Rickman). Hogarth Press, London.

GREY S., SARTORY G. and RACHMAN S. (1979) Synchronous and desynchronous changes during fear reduction. *Behav. Res. Ther.* **17**, 137–148.

HALLAM R. and RACHMAN S. (1979) Unpublished report.

HOROWITZ M. (1975) Intrusive and repetitive thoughts after stress. *Arch. Gen. Psychiat.* **32**, 1457–1463.

HOUSTON B., BLOOM L., BURISH T. and CUMMINGS E. (1978) Positive evaluation of stressful experiences. *J. Person.* **46**, 205–214.

JANIS I. (1951) *Air War and Emotional Stress.* McGraw-Hill, New York.

JONES H. G. (1960) Learning and abnormal behaviour. In *Handbook of Abnormal Psychology* (edited by H. J. Eysenck). Pitmans, London.

JONES R. (1978) *The New Psychology of Dreaming.* Penguin Books, Middlesex.

KLORMAN R. (1974) Habituation of fear. *Psychophysiology* **11**, 15–26.

LANG P. (1977) Imagery and therapy. *Behavior Therapy* **8**, 862–886.

LANG P. A bio-informational theory of emotional imagery (In press).

LANG P., MELAMED B. and HART J. (1970) A psychophysiological analysis of fear modification. *J. Abnorm. Psychol.* **76**, 220–234.

MATHEWS A. (1971) Psychophysiological approaches to the investigation of desensitization. *Psychol. Bulletin* **76**, 73–83.

RACHMAN S. (1966) Studies in desensitization—III. Speed of generalization. *Behav. Res. Ther.* **4**, 7–15.

RACHMAN S. (1968) The role of muscular relaxation in desensitization. *Behav. Res. Ther.* **6**, 159–165.

RACHMAN S. (1976) The passing of the two-stage theory of fear and avoidance. *Behav. Res. Ther.* **14**, 125–131.

RACHMAN S. (1978a) *Fear and Courage.* W. H. Freeman, San Francisco.

RACHMAN S. (1978b) An anatomy of obsessions. *Behav. Anal. Mod.* **2**, 253–278.

RACHMAN S. (1978c) The return of fear. *Behav. Res. Ther.* **17**, 164–165.

RACHMAN S., DE SILVA P. and ROPER G. (1976) The spontaneous decay of compulsive urges. *Behav. Res. Ther.* **14**, 445–453.

RACHMAN S. and HODGSON R. (1974) Synchrony and desynchrony in fear and avoidance. *Behav. Res. Ther.* **12**, 311–318.

RACHMAN S. and HODGSON R. (1979) *Obsessions and Compulsions.* Prentice Hall, New Jersey.

RAMSAY R. (1975) Behaviour therapy and bereavement. in *Progress in Behavior Therapy.* (Edited by J. BRENGELMANN). Springer, Berlin.

SHACKLETON H. (1978) Review of grief work. Unpublished Ms.

WICKERT F. (Editor) (1947) *Psychological Research on Problems of Redistribution,* USAAF Report No. 14. U.S. Govt. Printing Office, Washington.

WOLPE J. (1958) *Psychotherapy by Reciprocal Inhibition.* Stanford University Press, Stanford.

WOLPE J. (1978) Self-efficacy theory and psychotherapeutic change. In *Perceived Self-efficacy* (Edited by S. Rachman), *Adv. Behav. Res. Ther.* **1**, 231–236.

PSYCHOLOGICAL TREATMENTS FOR DEPRESSION: HOW DO THEY WORK?*

JOHN D. TEASDALE

Department of Psychiatry, University of Oxford, The Warneford Hospital, Oxford OX3 7JX, England

(Received 26 July 1984)

Summary—There is good evidence that psychological treatments can be effective in reducing depression. However, effective treatments often differ considerably in the procedures they include and in their underlying rationales. Thus, the nature of their central effective therapeutic processes is unclear. It is proposed that 'depression about depression', arising from a reciprocal relationship between cognitive processing and the depressed state, is frequently an important factor maintaining depression. It is suggested that effective treatments operate, at least in part, by modifying this factor. Evidence from a trial of cognitive therapy consistent with this hypothesis is presented.

INTRODUCTION

The effectiveness of certain forms of psychological treatment for depression is now well-established [e.g. see reviews by Whitehead, (1979), De Rubeis and Hollon (1981), Rush (1982), Lewinsohn, Teri and Hoberman (1983), Rehm and Kaslow (1984)]. While the more traditional forms of psychotherapy do not appear particularly effective in producing symptomatic improvement in clinically depressed patients (Whitehead, 1979, p. 505; De Rubeis and Hollon, 1981, p. 110), a number of recently developed structured psychological treatments have been shown to produce clinically useful improvements. Cognitive therapy, for example, has been shown to reduce the symptoms of patients with major depressive disorder to an extent equal to or greater than anti-depressant medication in at least four clinical trials (Rush, Beck, Kovacs and Hollon, 1977; Blackburn, Bishop, Glen, Whalley, and Christie, 1981; Hollon, De Rubeis and Evans, 1983; Murphy, Simons, Wetzel and Lustmann, 1984). While cognitive therapy for depression probably has the most consistent evidence for its effectiveness with clinical populations (De Rubeis and Hollon, 1981, p. 111), it does not stand clearly apart from alternative approaches. A range of structured psychological treatments, often based on different underlying theories and emphasizing different specific therapeutic components, has been shown to be effective (Lewinsohn et al., 1983). The diversity of techniques and rationales is considerable and includes, among others, those that emphasize correction of negative distorted cognitions (Beck, Rush, Shaw and Emery, 1979), training in behavioural coping skills (McLean and Hakstian, 1979), training in social skills (Zeiss, Lewinsohn, and Muñoz, 1979) and training in self-control skills (Kornblith, Rehm, O'Hara and Lamparski, 1983), and there is even promising evidence for the effectiveness of aerobic exercise (Doyne, Chambless and Beutler, 1983). As yet, none of these treatments has been shown to be consistently more effective than the others. Although general features shared by effective treatments have been suggested (Zeiss et al., 1979, p. 437; Kornblith et al., 1983, p. 525), the effectiveness of specific therapeutic procedures or processes has not yet been demonstrated.

If it is assumed that psychological treatments operate through relatively specific therapeutic processes, and that further improvement in the effectiveness and efficiency of psychological treatments for depression is likely to depend on the identification of these processes, the present situation poses a puzzle and a challenge: How do such apparently diverse treatments have their effects? This paper attempts to answer this question by presenting, first, a working hypothesis related to the maintenance of clinical depression, and, second, a working hypothesis that attempts to account for the effectiveness of existing treatments and to indicate what should be included in further developments of treatment.

---

*This paper is based on one presented to the *A. Conf. of the British Psychological Society*, University of Warwick, England. 31 March 1984.

THE MAINTENANCE OF DEPRESSION—A WORKING HYPOTHESIHS

The onset of clinical depression may occur for a variety of reasons, not all of which we fully understand. However, as far as treatment is concerned, our best strategy is likely to be to concentrate on the factors that maintain depression after onset; treatment usually starts with someone who has already been depressed for some time so that changing the factors maintaining the depression is likely to be the first aim of treatment. It is assumed that depression in mild and transient forms is common, and that its normal course is one of remission and recovery. It follows that in looking at the maintenance of clinically significant depression we concentrate on the factors that impede the recovery that might otherwise occur.

A Depression–Cognition Vicious Circle

A number of vicious circles that may act to maintain depression can be identified. I wish to concentrate on one of these, which is illustrated in Fig. 1.

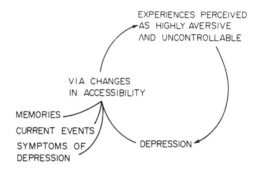

Fig. 1. The reciprocal relationship between depression and negative cognitive processing may set up a vicious circle which will act to maintain depression.

This draws heavily on 'cognitive' models of depression such as that of Beck (Beck *et al.*, 1979) and the learned-helplessness model of depression (Seligman, 1975; Abramson, Seligman and Teasdale, 1978), although it differs from each of these in certain respects. It suggests that *experiences* interpreted in particular negative ways can produce symptoms of depression, or intensify already existing symptoms. Symptoms of depression can also be produced by activation of the representations in memory of events or interpretations of events previously associated with depression. Two dimensions of experience are seen as critical in determining effects on depression: (1) aversiveness and (2) perceived controllability. It is hypothesized that:

> *depression is a response to current experiences perceived as highly aversive and uncontrollable* (or the activation in memory of representations of such experiences).

The way in which experiences are interpreted is a joint function of the nature of the experience and the state of the person's information-processing system. The latter will determine, for example, the type of information that is selected for attention, and the nature of the interpretative concepts that are highly primed and most likely to be used to interpret experience. Similarly, the type of information from memory that is processed will be a function both of what is available in memory and what is most accessible at a given time. The state of the information-processing system is affected by emotional state. In the depressed state, as illustrated in Fig. 1, there is a shift in the relative accessibility, or activation, of positive and negative cognitions. Negative interpretative concepts become more activated and likely to be used to interpret experience, while positive interpretative concepts become less activated and likely to be used. Memories of negative experiences become more accessible and likely to come to mind, whereas the reverse is true for positive memories. More specifically, it has been proposed (Bower, 1981; Teasdale, 1983a) that activation of cognitions shows a form of state dependency: the memories and concepts activated in a current depressed state or mood are those that have previously been activated in or associated with depressed states in the past. At least some of these depressed states will have been produced by experiences which were perceived as aversive and uncontrollable, involving the activation of cognitions associated with aversiveness and uncontrollability. It follows that activation of such cognitions will have been selectively associated with depressed mood, so that these cognitions are likely to be selectively reactivated in subsequent periods of depressed mood. As a result of this selective activation of cognitions related to aversiveness and uncontrollability, environmental stimuli that could be interpreted in ways that will produce further depression are more likely to be interpreted in that way once a person is depressed than when their mood is normal. Similarly, once depressed, the increased activation of memories of previous depressing experiences makes it more likely that they will come to mind. In this way, a vicious circle based on a reciprocal relationship between depression and cognition can be set up: experiences perceived as highly aversive and uncontrollable will intensify depression and, once depressed, experiences will be more likely to be interpreted as highly aversive and uncontrollable, so producing further depression. In the depressed person this vicious circle may perpetuate and intensify the already existing depression and prevent the recovery that might otherwise occur (Fig. 1).

This vicious circle model has been described in detail elsewhere (Teasdale, 1983a,b). Considerable evidence supports the suggestion that the depressed state, whether of clinical severity or mild normal depressed mood, is characterized by a shift in the relative accessibility of positive and negative cognitions (e.g. Bower, 1981; Teasdale, 1983a). Two examples are particularly relevant to the proposal that, once in a depressed state or mood, experiences are more likely to be interpreted in terms of concepts related to increased aversiveness and decreased controllability. Ikhlef (1982) examined the effects of inducing depressed mood on attribution. Normal Ss were seen in neutral mood state and experienced either success or failure on a task. They were then put into a depressed or elated mood and, once in the mood state, asked to make attributions for their previous successes or failures. In depressed mood, Ss were more likely to attribute their failures to their own lack of ability [an internal, stable, global attribution (Abramson et al., 1978)] than when in elated mood. For success, the opposite pattern was true, Ss in elated mood being more likely to attribute success to their own ability than those in depressed mood. If depressed mood makes it more likely that failures will be attributed to internal, stable and global factors then clearly this will act to increase the aversiveness and decrease the perceived controllability of failure (Abramson et al., 1978).

Kavanagh and Bower (1984) examined the effects of inducing mood states on Ss perceived efficacy, that is, their expectation that they would successfully be able to achieve various goals. They found that, compared to neutral or happy moods, sad mood reduced efficacy expectations across a wide range of behaviour. As a result of this effect of the depressed state on thinking, the perceived controllability of a range of aversive outcomes is likely to be reduced once a person is depressed.

Figure 1 summarizes the effects which may act to maintain depression through experiences perceived as highly aversive and uncontrollable:

(1) continuing major life difficulties or stressors, which would be interpreted as highly aversive and uncontrollable even in the non-depressed state;

(2) minor life difficulties and stressors, such as marital arguments or difficulties in child management, which, in the absence of depression would not be perceived as highly aversive and uncontrollable but which, as a result of the increased accessibility of negative cognitions, are seen in this way by the depressed person;

(3) memories of past depressing experiences which come easily to mind as depressive ruminations if the depressed person's attention is not otherwise occupied (Fennell and Teasdale, 1984); and

(4) the depressed state itself.

While psychological treatments may need to modify each of these effects, I would like for the moment to concentrate on the last of these: the way in which symptoms of depression may constitute experiences which, perceived as highly aversive and uncontrollable, contribute to the maintenance of depression. An important aspect of the current working hypothesis is that such 'depression about depression' may often be a factor in the maintenance of depression.

Depression about Depression

Many of the symptoms of depression are inherently aversive, for example, dysphoric mood, loss of pleasure, irritability, loss of energy, fatigue, difficulties in concentration, indecisiveness and guilt. Such symptoms may not be easy to control. The biasing effects of the depressed state on cognitive processing, in combination with lack of knowledge about depression as a psychological state, are likely to increase the inherent aversiveness of the depressed state and make patients more hopeless about controlling it. It is not uncommon for depressed patients to misinterpret symptoms of depression as signs of irremediable personal inadequacy: for example, the lack of energy, irritability or loss of interest and affection that characterize depression are seen as signs of selfishness, weakness or as evidence that the person is a poor wife or mother. Such interpretations, as well as making the symptoms more aversive, imply that they are going to be very difficult to control. Further, the general reduction in efficacy expectations occurring in the depressed state (Kavanagh and Bower, 1984) means that patients will be relatively pessimistic about the success of attempts to cope with symptoms of depression or the problem situations that produce them. As a result, patients will fail either to initiate or to persist with attempts at coping, reinforcing further their perception of depression as uncontrollable. It is suggested that *anyone who experienced the highly aversive symptoms and effects of depression, who saw these as evidence of personal inadequacy, and who felt quite hopeless that their situation would improve, either through their own efforts or otherwise, would experience depression about depression.* In some cases, this may be the major factor preventing the recovery of the depression that might otherwise occur.

THE TREATMENT OF DEPRESSION—A WORKING HYPOTHESIS

The working hypothesis that has been outlined to account for the maintenance of depression has clear implications for treatment which are summarized in Table 1: major and minor life difficulties interpreted as highly aversive and uncontrollable should be identified and modified by active problem-solving strategies, and/or reappraisal to counteract the effects of the depressed state negatively biasing the processing of information; the opportunity for depressive ruminations should be reduced, and the content of recurrent ruminations reappraised; depression about depression should be reduced.

The hypothesis that will be developed here is that, in addition to any effects that structured psychological treatments may have on other factors contributing to the maintenance of depression, an important aspect of the effects shared by potent treatments is the reduction of depression about depression.

How is depression about depression to be reduced? In principle, this would be achieved by reducing the aversiveness of the symptoms and effects of depression, and increasing their perceived controllability. In practice, the aversiveness of depression could be reduced by providing information and guidance to help patients to view symptoms of depression as regular features of a well-known psychological state, which is a natural reaction to certain circumstances, and which many people experience, rather than as evidence of personal inadequacy. Information that this psychological state affects many areas of function (behavioural, cognitive, affective and

Table 1. Treatment implications of the working hypothesis proposed to account for the maintenance of depression

Maintaining factors	Treatment approaches
Major and minor life stressors and difficulties	Active problem solving strategies; reappraisal to counteract depressive thinking.
Memories of previous depressing experiences	Distraction/activity to reduce frequency of ruminations; reappraisal of content of ruminations.
Depression—its symptoms and effects	Give information about: —depression itself —its effects Provide rationale that indicates counterdepressive coping responses Provide structured framework for: —learning and executing coping responses —monitoring and progress feedback

physiological) could also be helpful in reducing the total aversiveness of depression by leading patients to see its varied symptoms and effects as manifestations of one underlying problem, rather than as a multitude of unconnected problem areas: 'I am depressed' replaces 'my life is a total mess'.

The most effective way to change the perceived controllability of depression is likely to be to provide patients with the opportunity to learn that their actions can affect aspects of the depressed state, and, to maintain this perception of controllability, to ensure that they persist with such actions. Perceived controllability could be increased by:

(1) providing a credible rationale which indicates that the execution of certain coping responses (which should actually have a noticeable effect on psychological state) will reduce depression;

(2) providing a highly structured framework within which patients can learn and execute these responses; and

(3) ensuring, by monitoring and progress feedback, that patients recognize the effects of their coping actions and persist with their use.

In other words, depression about depression is best attacked by helping patients to view it as a problem to be solved, rather than evidence of personal inadequacy, by encouraging expectations that their actions can affect the problem, and by providing them with a structure to test out and repeatedly confirm the effectiveness of their problem-solving actions, thereby facilitating and maintaining a sense of control.

To suggest that the most effective way to change the perceived controllability of depression is for patients to learn that they can reduce it by executing certain coping responses is saying more than that procedures that reduce depression will reduce depression! The main reason for executing specific anti-depressive coping responses is not so much that the effects of these will progressively nibble away the depression bit by bit, but, rather, as a way of producing a change in the perceived controllability of depression, and of maintaining this perceived controllability or sense of efficacy in dealing with depression. It is possible that the same end can be achieved without necessarily teaching specific coping skills, but these are most likely to provide one of the most powerful means of changing perceptions of controllability.

It is interesting to compare these suggestions for changing depression about depression with the features which other workers have suggested are shared by effective psychological treatments for depression.

Zeiss et al. (1979, p. 437) proposed:

"Any treatment that meets the following criteria should be effective in overcoming depression:

1. Therapy should begin with an elaborate, well-planned rationale. This rationale should provide initial structure that guides the patient to the belief that he or she can control his or her own behavior and, thereby, his or her depression.

2. Therapy should provide training in skills that the patient can utilize to feel more effective in handling his or her daily life. These skills must be of some significance to the patient and must fit with the rationale that has been presented.

3. Therapy should emphasize the independent use of these skills by the patient outside of the therapy context and must provide enough structure so that the attainment of independent skill is possible for the patient.

4. Therapy should encourage the patient's attribution that improvement in mood is caused by the patient's increased skillfulness, not by the therapist's skillfulness."

Similarly, Kornblith et al. (1983, p. 525):

"Looking across cognitive and behavioral therapy procedures for treating depression generally, it is apparent that these packages have at least three important characteristics in common. First, they each present a concrete rationale. This rationale includes a vocabulary for describing and defining the problems of depression in ways that may be very new to participants. Rationales also provide a vocabulary for describing the mechanisms of change. Second, all of these therapy programs are highly structured. They provide clear plans for producing change in a logical sequence of steps. Third, all of these programs provide feedback and support so that participants can clearly see changes in their own behavior and are reinforced for these changes."

Clearly, these authors have identified as important features very similar to those included in the methods proposed for reducing depression about depression. It is suggested that one aspect of the effectiveness shared by structured psychological treatments, often based on varying underlying rationales, is that they break into the part of the vicious circle perpetuating depression that is maintained by depression about depression. They do this by reducing the perceived aversiveness of depression and by increasing the perceived control over its symptoms and effects. Once depression about depression is reduced, there is an increased probability that the processes leading to recovery and remission can operate.

For some patients, dealing with depression about depression may be sufficient. This is particularly likely in situations where the event provoking the depression, whether environmental or more biological, is no longer operative, but the person has become stuck in the kind of vicious circle that has been described. For other patients, in addition to 'depression about depression', there will be other factors contributing to the maintenance of the depression, such as continuing life problems and difficulties. In some of these patients, particularly those with good existing repertoires of coping skills, tackling 'depression about depression' may reduce levels of depression sufficiently for efficacy expectations, previously lowered by the effects of depression on cognitive processing, to rise to the point where patients will use their existing coping resources to deal with these problems. For others, further help directed at these problems may be required. This is particularly likely to be the case where the problems relate to situations which the patient has always had difficulties handling.

The working hypothesis that has been outlined may be summarized as follows:

> *effective psychological treatments for depression reduce 'depression about depression' by reducing its aversiveness and increasing its perceived controllability. For patients with few persisting life difficulties, and existing repertoires of coping skills, this may be sufficient.*

EVIDENCE FOR THE HYPOTHESIS

The features which, it has been suggested, characterize effective psychological treatments for depression (see above) are consistent with the working hypothesis that has been presented. So is the fact that such treatments appear to be more effective in patients with good existing repertoires of skills for coping with unpleasant thoughts and feelings, as measured by Rosenbaum's (1980) measure of learned resourcefulness (Rehm, 1982; Murphy *et al.*, 1984).

We were able to look for more specific evidence to examine this hypothesis in a detailed examination of the results of a trial of cognitive therapy for depression, for which initial outcome has already been reported (Teasdale, Fennell, Hibbert and Amies, 1984) and of which the detailed course and follow-up is the subject of another report (Fennell and Teasdale, 1985). In this trial, patients with major depressive disorder were randomly allocated either to continue with treatment-as-usual (TAU; which in most cases included anti-depressant medication) or to receive, in addition, sessions of cognitive therapy (CT). The addition of CT significantly and substantially accelerated the recovery of these patients. The detailed analysis of this trial that follows is necessarily *post hoc*, with all the interpretative difficulties that it inevitably entails. Nonetheless, it provides an interesting opportunity to examine the working hypothesis that has been proposed.

Presence of Depression about Depression

The first question to ask is, of course, does depression about depression actually exist in patients receiving psychological treatments? Clinical impression strongly suggests that it does, and in the present trial we also had a measure related to it. Patients completed the Cognitions Questionnaire (CQ; Fennell and Campbell, 1984), an instrument designed to measure aspects of depressive thinking in response to a series of hypothetical scenarios. One of the scenarios was specifically designed to examine negative thinking in relation to a situation that could be interpreted as a symptom of depression, waking early one morning. Responses to this item were used as an indicator of the extent of depression about depression. These responses did indeed show considerable evidence of depression about depression among patients entering the trial: patients predominantly chose response options such as: 'what's the matter with me—I should pull myself together and stop being pathetic'; 'this is the start of another black mood—when will it ever end?'; 'it is always the same—I never seem to feel any different from this'; and instead of choosing the coping responses of getting up and doing something about the situation they chose the relatively helpless and indecisive responses such as 'I can't decide whether to get up or stay in bed'.

Course of Response to Psychological Treatment

If a major component of the process by which structured psychological treatments have their effects is to change the perception of depression so that it is less aversive and more controllable, then one might expect that initial response to such treatments could be relatively rapid, certainly more rapid than if the treatments depended on unscrambling complex problematic life situations, slowly training new skills or gradually whittling depression away little by little. Figure 2 shows the

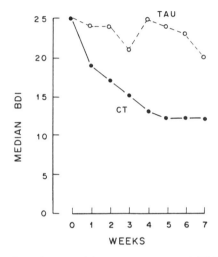

Fig. 2. Response to treatment in patients receiving treatment-as-usual (TAU) or, in addition, cognitive therapy (CT) as indicated by median BDI scores over the first 7 weeks of treatment.

response to treatment over the first few weeks of the trial for TAU and CT patients. Differences between the two conditions did, indeed, emerge very early and beneficial effects of CT were apparent after only two or three sessions, on average. Nonetheless, there was considerable variation in response to CT over this period. Patients in this group were dichotomized on the basis of their reduction in depression over the first three sessions of cognitive therapy to form a group of 'rapid' responders, whose Beck Depression Inventory (BDI) scores all dropped by 50% or more, and a group of 'slow' responders, whose BDI scores changed very little, on average, over this period. These differences in response in the very early stages of treatment were associated with significantly better outcome for the 'rapid' responders both at the end of treatment, and at 1 yr follow-up (Fennell and Teasdale, 1985).

In the next section, we shall examine the hypothesis that the 'rapid' responders are patients with high levels of depression about depression, which is dealt with rapidly by the first few sessions of CT. In order to do this, it is necessary first to demonstrate that the rapid improvement shown by the 'rapid' responders, compared to the 'slow' responders, is a relatively specific response to a structured psychological treatment and not merely an indicator of a general tendency to improve rapidly with any treatment, or, indeed, without treatment. The following suggests that this is, in fact, the case: if the patients continuing to receive TAU are dichotomized on the same basis as the CT patients to form groups of 'rapid' and 'slow' early improvers, then:

(i) 'rapid' improvers in the CT group show significantly greater reduction in BDI scores over the first 3 weeks of treatment than 'rapid' improvers in the TAU group; and

(ii) within the TAU group, there is no difference in outcome either at post-treatment or 1 yr follow-up assessments, between 'rapid' and 'slow' improvers.

Characteristics of Rapid Early Responders to CT

The hypothesis that much of the response to structured psychological treatments, particularly early response, is to do with reducing depression about depression predicts that early response to such treatments will be greatest in those who have high levels of depression about depression at the start of treatment. We investigated this prediction by examining the association between a pretreatment measure of depression about depression (the total score on the depression item of the CQ, referred to above) and reduction in scores on the BDI over the first three sessions of CT. Consistent with prediction, a significant, positive correlation was obtained ($r = 0.54$, df 15, $P < 0.05$). This could not be accounted for by the relationship between the depression about depression measure and pretreatment depression level (as measured by the BDI) as this was non-significant ($r = -0.05$). Interestingly, in the TAU condition, the correlation between the pretreatment measure of depression about depression and early response to treatment was in the opposite direction ($r = -0.53$, df 12, $P < 0.05$). This suggests that high levels of depression about depression are indeed characteristic specifically of people who responded rapidly to a structured psychological treatment, rather than a characteristic of good responders in general.

The evidence from this trial that is consistent with the working hypothesis that has been proposed, may be summarized:

(1) depression about depression, in the sense of the predicted perceptions of depression as something for which patients blamed themselves but felt helpless to do much about, was present in patients entering the trial;

(2) on average, the psychological treatment produced beneficial effects rapidly; and

(3) patients who showed the highest levels of depression about depression showed the greatest response to the first three sessions of psychological treatment.

As indicated above, these conclusions were based on *post hoc* analyses and must, therefore, be treated with caution. Nonetheless, they provide preliminary support for the hypothesis that has been advanced.

Comparison with Alternative Proposals

Zeiss *et al.* (1979), in attempting to explain the finding that different forms of structured psychological treatments appeared to be comparably effective, suggested hypotheses somewhat similar to that advanced here. They suggested:

"The effectiveness of the treatments may, in this view, be unrelated to the specific skills trained in each module. Instead, by various routes, all patients began to have positive experiences in their daily lives, which they attributed to their increased self-efficacy" (p. 437)

and drew a parallel with Frank's (1974) suggestion that the purpose of therapy was not to train special skills but to restore morale. The main difference between this and the present position, apart from the latter's derivation from a hypothesis concerning the maintenance of depression, is the specificity of the processes involved. Zeiss *et al.* (1979) appear to suggest that the specific skills taught may not matter too much so long as they restore a general sense of self-efficacy:

"Therapy should provide training in skills that the patient can utilize to feel more effective in handling his or her daily life. These skills must be of some significance to the patient and must fit with the rationale that has been presented." (p. 438)

By contrast, the present position emphasizes more specific requirments for effective treatments: in addition to any problem-solving activity directed at ongoing life problems, treatments should provide information to reduce the aversiveness of depression and, most importantly, train skills (or mobilize existing skills) that have a noticeable effect in reducing symptoms of depression. That is, rather than facilitating a general sense of self-efficacy in handling daily life, treatment should focus specifically on training skills to give a sense of efficacy in controlling depression. Clearly a number of behaviours can affect symptoms of depression, including engagement in mood-elevating behaviours (such as constructive or pleasant activity, exercise or positive social interaction) and modification of thought content. The present hypothesis suggests that the first phase of therapy should be directed to equipping patients with a repertoire of specific depression-management skills that can be used flexibly in a variety of situations. As a result, patients would acquire a relatively specific sense of efficacy in dealing with depression, which would thereby be perceived as controllable. This would break into that portion of the vicious circle maintained by depression about depression, allowing processes that would lead to recovery to occur. The subsequent reduction of depression might well lead to a more generalized improvement in expectations of efficacy, increasing the likelihood that previous repertoires of problem-solving skills would be employed. If this were not sufficient to deal with any ongoing problems producing aversive experiences perceived as uncontrollable, attention would then be directed to these areas. This might take the form of training general problem-solving skills, providing more specific assistance such as marital therapy, or remedying relatively persistent deficiencies or maladaptive patterns in other areas of function.

Acknowledgements—This work was supported by the Medical Research Council of the United Kingdom. I am grateful to June Dent for helpful comments on an earlier version of this paper.

REFERENCES

Abramson L. Y., Seligman M. E. P. and Teasdale J. D. (1978) Learned helplessness in humans: critique and reformulation. *J. abnorm. Psychol.* **87**, 49–74.

Beck A. T., Rush A. J., Shaw B. F. and Emery G. (1979) *Cognitive Therapy of Depression.* Guilford Press, New York.

Blackburn I. M., Bishop S., Glen A. I. M., Whalley J. J. and Christie J. E. (1981) The efficacy of cognitive therapy in depression: a treatment trial using cognitive therapy and pharmacotherapy, each alone and in combination. *Br. J. Psychiat.* **139**, 181–189.

Bower G. H. (1981) Mood and memory. *Am. Psychol.* **36**, 129–148.

De Rubeis R. J. and Hollon S. D. (1981) Behavioral treatment of the affective disorders. In *Future Perspectives in Behavior Therapy* (edited by Michelson L., Hersen M. and Turner S. M.). Plenum Press, New York.

Doyne E. J., Chambless D. L. and Beutler L. E. (1983) Aerobic exercise as a treatment for depression in women. *Behav. Ther.* **14**, 434–440.

Fennell M. J. V. and Campbell E. A. (1984) The Cognitions Questionnaire: specific thinking errors in depression. *Br. J. clin. Psychol.* **23**, 81–92.

Fennell M. J. V. and Teasdale J. D. (1984) Effects of distraction on thinking and affect in depressed patients. *Br. J. clin. Psychol.* **23**, 65–66.

Fennell M. J. V. and Teasdale J. D. (1985) Cognitive therapy for depression: individual differences and the process of change. Submitted for publication.

Frank J. D. (1974) *Persuasion and Healing.* Schocken, New York.

Hollon S. D., De Rubeis R. J. and Evans M. D. (1983) Final report of the cognitive–pharmacotherapy trial: outcome, prophylaxis, prognosis, process and mechanism. Papers presented to the *Wld Congr. on Behavior Therapy,* Washington D.C., 10 December.

Ikhlef A. (1982) Causal attribution and depression. Unpublished Ph.D. Thesis, Plymouth Polytechnic, Devon, U.K.

Kavanagh D.J. and Bower G. H. (1984) Mood and self-efficacy: impact of joy and sadness on perceived capabilities. *Cog. Ther. Res.* In press.

Kornblith S. J., Rehm L. P., O'Hara M. W. and Lamparski D. M. (1983) The contribution of self-reinforcement training and behavioral assignments to the efficacy of self-control therapy for depression. *Cog. Ther. Res.* **6**, 499–528.

Lewinsohn P., Teri L. and Hoberman H. M. (1983) Depression: a perspective on etiology, treatment, and life span issues. In *Perspectives on Behavior Therapy in the Eighties* (Edited by Rosenbaum M., Franks C. M. and Jaffe Y.). Springer, New York.

McLean P. D. and Hakstian A. R. (1979) Clinical depression: comparative efficacy of out-patient treatments. *J. consult. clin. Psychol.* **47**, 818–836.

Murphy G. E., Simons A. D., Wetzel R. D. and Lustmann P. J. (1984) Cognitive therapy and pharmacotherapy singly and together in the treatment of depression. *Archs gen. Psychiat.* **41**, 33–41.

Rehm L. P. (1982) Outcome of self-control therapy for depression with sub-populations. Paper presented at the *A. Meet. of the American Psychological Association,* Washington, D. C., 23 August.

Rehm L. P. and Kaslow N. J. (1984) Behavioral approaches to depression: research results and clinical recommendations. *Child Fam. Behav. Ther.* In press.

Rosenbaum M. (1980) A schedule for assessing self-control behaviors: preliminary findings. *Behav. Ther.* **11**, 109–121.

Rush A. J. (1982) *Short-term Psychotherapies for Depression.* Wiley, Chichester, U.K.

Rush A. J., Beck A. T., Kovacs M. and Hollon S. D. (1977) Comparative efficacy of cognitive therapy and pharmacotherapy in the treatment of depressed out-patients. *Cog. Ther. Res.* **1**, 17–37.

Seligman M. E. P. (1975) *Helplessness: on Depression, Development and Death.* Freeman, San Francisco, Calif.

Teasdale J. D. (1983a) Negative thinking in depression: cause, effect or reciprocal relationship? *Adv. Behav. Res. Ther.* **5**, 3–26.

Teasdale J. D. (1983b) Change in cognition during depression: psychopathological implications. *J. R. Soc. Med.* **76**, 1038–1044.

Teasdale J. D., Fennell M. J. V., Hibbert G. A. and Amies P. L. (1984) Cognitive therapy for major depressive disorder in primary care. *Br. J. Psychiat.* **144**, 400–406.

Whitehead A. (1979) Psychological treatment of depression: a review. *Behav. Res. Ther.* **17**, 495–509.

Zeiss A. M., Lewinsohn P. M. and Munoz R. F. (1977) Non-specific improvement effects in depression using interpersonal skills training, pleasant activity schedules, or cognitive training. *J. consult. clin. Psychol.* **47**, 427–439.

A LABORATORY METHOD FOR DIAGNOSING PREDOMINANCE OF HOMO- OR HETERO- EROTIC INTEREST IN THE MALE

K. Freund*

Summary—(1) Results obtained with two modifications of a previously described test for sexual interest in the differential diagnosis between (a) homosexual and heterosexual orientation towards adults, and (b) between homosexual orientation towards adults and towards adolescents or children are submitted.

(2) An experiment with induced faking was carried out and signs for diagnosing simulation were determined. The results of this experiment uphold the usefulness of the method.

(3) Results in the diagnosis of 17 cases in which there was disagreement between objective and subjective history are also included.

INTRODUCTION AND METHOD

In an earlier paper the details of a laboratory method for the diagnosis of sexual deviations in men were described (Freund, 1957). This method consists in the continuous recording of volume changes of the male genital while the subject is viewing projected pictures of possible erotic objects, in our case pictures of nude men, women and children of both sexes. Only static stimuli were available so that it was not possible to make sufficient use of the erotic effect of movement and behaviour. In modification A (see Table 1) of this method, 40 colour pictures were used. They were divided according to the age of the photographic subjects into five groups (A–E) and the whole set of photographs was divided into two matched series of 20 pictures each. The order of presentation of the figures in each series was random. The series are denoted with odd and even numbers respectively.

Each patient was shown both series in continuous sequence, always projecting first the one which had been shown as the second to the previous person examined. Each picture was exposed for 13 seconds, with an interval of 19 seconds between pictures. If, after 11 seconds (signalled by a light invisible to the patient) the tracing was still falling or rising steeply or if it had moved some considerable distance from its original level, the commencement of the next exposure was postponed until the ink-writer again began to move at the original level, or very near to it.

The record of every patient was evaluated as follows: In every part of the tracing corresponding to the presentation of one picture, the highest positive or negative perpendicular deviation from the level of the point corresponding to the beginning of the exposure was measured (in mm.); in the rare cases in which a positive and a negative value appeared together, the negative value was subtracted from the positive. In every patient the sum of the reactions (as indicated by volume changes) was determined for every class of stimuli according to sex and age. (Five age groups of male and five of female figures, each group consisting of four pictures.) Among the five sums of reactions corresponding to the five age groups of figures of each sex, the two highest sums of reactions were selected and summed up. Homo- or heterosexuality was then diagnosed, according to which of these two new sums corresponding to the male or female figures respectively was higher.

* Reader in Psychiatry, Charles' University, Psychiatric Research Institute, Prague 8. The reported studies were carried out at the University Hospital (1953–1960).

TABLE 1. STIMULI USED IN MODIFICATION A: THIS TABLE INDICATES THE NATURE OF THE PHOTOGRAPHS USED AND THEIR ORDER OF PRESENTATION

Age groups	A				B					C			D					E		
♀ Age (years/months)	4/11	5	7	8	10/6	10/6	11/11	12/2	14/10	14/11	15/10	15/10	18	18	20	20	21	21	22	25
♀ Ordinal numbers of presentation	27	36	33	16	18	35	9	24	39	30	4	25	26	31	13	34	5	12	2	21
♂ Age (years/months)	4	4/7	7	7	9/11	10/6	11/1	12/6	14	14/6	16/3	16/3	18	18	21	22	24	26	30	30
♂ Ordinal numbers of presentation	22	29	8	41	38	11	6	17	14	7	10	23	20	3	19	40	32	37	28	15

TABLE 2. RESPONSES TO THE STIMULI WERE CLASSIFIED ACCORDING TO MAXIMUM VOLUME INCREASES (M.V.I.). THIS TABLE SHOWS THE RESPONSES MADE BY 58 HOMOSEXUAL AND 65 HETEROSEXUAL SUBJECTS

Class	Reaction to stimuli	Concordance (+) Discrepancy (−)	Homosexual (n = 58)			Heterosexual (n = 65)				
			Ad.	Adol.	Ch.	Ad.	Adol.	Ch.	S.	S.D.
I	marked	+	18	11	2	17	4	3	9	12
	MVI = 0·40 ml →	−	0	0	1	0	0	0	0	0
II	slightly marked	+	2	0	0	2	0	2	2	2
	MVI = 0·30−0·39 ml	−	1	0	2	0	0	0	0	0
III	almost flat	+	3	8	0	4	1	0	2	0
	MVI = 0·10−0·29 ml	−	0	2	1	0	0	0	0	0
IV	flat	+	1	2	1	1	0	0	3	1
	MVI = → 0·09 ml	−	1	2	0	0	0	0	0	0
Total			26	25	7	24	5	5	16	15

Modification A of the method was applied in collaboration with Diamant and Pinkava (1958) in 123 patients, 58 of whom, according to their history (see Table 2) were exclusively, or almost exclusively homosexual (Hom.), while the others were exclusively, or almost exclusively heterosexual (Het.). Among the homosexuals, 26 had an erotic preference for adults (Ad.), 25 for adolescents (Adol.) and 7 for children (Ch.). Among the heterosexual patients, 24 could be regarded as sexually normal, 5 had an erotic preference for adolescents and 5 for children. Sixteen heterosexual patients were sent for examination because of premature ejaculation or impaired potency (S.) and 15 for psychosexual deviations (S.D.) such as exhibitionism etc. The ages of the patients ranged from 16 to 60 years. There is no reason to assume that many of our patients attempted to conceal their real erotic tendencies or to simulate erotic reactions to normal stimuli. There were, however, certain peculiarities in the tracings of some patients who underwent the examination because they desired evidence of their homosexuality in order to be exempted from military service and also in the records of some men who denied the homosexual activities of which they were accused. In several such cases artifacts appeared, e.g. much faster oscillations of the tracing than would correspond to the normally recorded volume changes. These are caused by voluntary movements, by means of which some patients succeeded in producing volume changes. These artifacts can be recognized quite easily. They were excluded before the tracings from modification A were evaluated.

Before comparing the erotic preferences of the persons examined according to the case history and the tracings, it should be mentioned that the records were classified according to the maximum volume increase (MVI) attained—I. marked, II. slightly marked, III. almost flat, IV. flat. The mean of the sizes of the 8 reactions in the two erotically most powerful age-groups of the predominant sex (according to the tracings) served as the basis for this classification. Table 2 shows the values of the four classes of records described above.

RESULTS

Among 77 patients with marked tracings, in only one case was there a discrepancy between the result of the laboratory examination and the case history as far as the diagnosis of exclusive or almost exclusive homo- or heterosexuality is concerned. The slightly marked and almost flat tracings contained three discrepancies each and ten and eighteen cases of concordant results respectively.

In attempting to determine the erotic value of different degrees of physical maturity (i.e. to differentiate between erotic preference for adults, adolescents or children) the class IV tracings and the 7 records in which the result did not agree with the case history of the patient's sex-preference, were excluded.* Heterosexual perverts and patients with impaired potency were also excluded and this left a total of only 76 tracings.

For each of these, the proportion (A.P.) of the reactions to older age groups (i.e. to photographs of adults) of the preferred sex† was determined.

By arranging the records of homosexual patients with a preference for adults, adolescents or children according to this proportion (Table 3, sub-table a‡) it is found that these values in 16 homosexual persons with a predilection for adults are above the common median of the homosexual group; this is not the case in any of the patients with a predilection for adolescents or children. Only the values of three androphilic patients are below this median.

After arranging these values in only two groups (sub-table b)—one group with a preference for adults (Ad.) and the other with an erotic predilection for adolescents or children (AC.)—the binominal test shows that this difference is significant both in the first (Ad.) and in the second group ($P = 0.2\%$; $P < 0.1\%$). The Mann–Whitney test gave

TABLE 3. AGE PREFERENCES IN EROTIC INTERESTS: THE PROPORTION OF POSITIVE REACTIONS TO OLDER AGE GROUPS OF THE PREFERRED SEX IS DENOTED (A.P.) FOR HOMOSEXUAL AND HETEROSEXUAL SUBJECTS

	(A) Class I and II records Homosexuals						(B) Class I, II and III records Homosexuals				
	Ad.	Adol.	Ch.	Ad.	AC.		Ad.	Adol.	Ch.	Ad.	AC.
A.P. > median	16	0	0	16	0	A.P. > median	18	3	0	18	3
A.P. < median	3	11	2	3	13	A.P. < median	4	15	2	4	17
		a			b			c			d
	Heterosexuals						Heterosexuals				
A.P. > median	12	1	1	12	2	A.P. > median	15	1	0	15	1
A.P. < median	7	3	4	7	7	A.P. < median	8	4	4	8	8
		e			f			g			h

similar results: (AC.) $n_1 = 13$; (Ad.) $n_2 = 19$; $U = 10$, $P < 0.1\%$. In this survey, only records of Classes I and II have been taken into account. If the records of Class III are also included (sub-tables c and d), the results are basically the same (Mann–Whitney): (AC.) $n_1 = 20$; (Ad.) $n_2 = 23$; $U = 50$, $P < 0.1\%$.

* One of the homosexual patients was excluded as being too young to decide whether he actually preferred adults or adolescents.

† As indicated by the tracings.

‡ One patient, whose value is the median score, is omitted from sub-tables c, d, g, h.

Sub-tables e and f for the records of heterosexual patients of Classes I and II show similar conditions. The values of 12 patients with a preference for adults and one with a predilection for adolescents and one with a predilection for children are above the median, while those of seven patients with a preference for adults, three with a predilection for adolescents and four for children are below the median (sub-table e). Sub-table f shows the difference between the distribution of the values of the groups, (Ad.) and (Ch.), having been condensed in the same manner as in the case of the homosexuals. The Mann–Whitney test shows that the difference between the group of patients preferring adults as sexual objects and the group of those with a predilection for adolescents or children is significant (AC.) $n_1 = 9$; (Ad.) $n_2 = 19$, $U = 27$, $P < 1\%$. Sub-tables g and h for records of Classes I–III show similar results (Mann–Whitney: (AC.) $n_1 = 10$, (Ad.) $n_2 = 23$, $U = 29$, $P < 0.01\%$).

Using the records of the patients belonging to the groups mentioned above with whom the examination could be repeated (after an interval of 14 days approx.) and from two other groups—Kl and P.*—(Table 4†) we tried to ascertain whether there was a marked

TABLE 4. RETEST RELIABILITY: RESPONSES OBTAINED ON FIRST (A) AND SECOND (B) EXAMINATIONS COMPARED

Group		M.V.I. category				+ = cases in which diagnosis failed
		I	II	III	IV	
Hom.	A	12	1	3	1	(+IV)/II
Ad.	B	12	1	4	0	
Hom.	A	5	0	6	0	+III/III, +III/I, +III/+III, +III/+I, I/(+IV)
AC.	B	6	0	2	3	
Het.	A	12	1	1	0	0
Ad.	B	11	1	2	0	
Het.	A	3	2	1	0	0
AC.	B	4	2	0	0	
S.	A	2	1	0	1	0
	B	3	0	1	0	
S.D.	A	9	0	0	0	0
	B	8	0	0	1	
Kl.	A	12	1	3	0	+III/(+IV), +III/I, +III/I, I/+III
	B	10	2	2	2	
P.	A	3	0	4	1	(+IV)/III
	B	4	1	3	0	
Total	A	58	6	18	3	
	B	58	7	14	6	

* These two diagnostic groups have been discussed elsewhere (1959, 1962).
† The number of patients at the second examination was much smaller, as many failed to re-attend.

difference between the maximum volume increase in the first and second examinations, and whether it could be assumed that failure in the diagnosis of homo- and heterosexuality could be attributed to the flatness of the tracings. Table 4 shows that in patients who were examined twice, records of Class I and II occurred in 64 cases in the first examination (A) and in 65 in the second examination (B), while records of Class III and IV appeared in 21 and 20 cases respectively. There is, therefore, no striking difference between the maximum volume increase in the first and in the repeated examination.

A review of the cases in which the diagnosis failed (last column in Table 4) shows that this occurred six times in the first examination only, once both in the first and in the second and three times in the second only. There is, therefore, no reason to assume that the validity of differentiation between exclusively homo- or heterosexual persons was higher in the first than in the second examination. The above survey, however, indicates that failure of diagnosis could possibly be attributed to flatness of the tracing. In Class I and II records failure occurred only once, while in Class III and IV tracings it occurred ten times.

The diagnosis of predilection for adults, adolescents or children was established from the records of the second examination in the same way as in the first examination. From this investigation, two Class IV recordings together with one in which the diagnosis did not agree with the case history were excluded. Here again differentiation was made both in homosexual and heterosexual persons, between the group with preference for adults and the group with predilection for adolescents or children (using records of Classes I–III in both groups). According to the Mann–Whitney test, the difference between the two groups is significant both with the homosexual and the heterosexual persons. (Hom.: (AC.) $n_1=6$; (Ad.) $n_2 = 14$; $U = 19$, $P < 5\%$; Het.: (AC.) $n_1 = 6$; (Ad.) $n_2 = 14$; $U = 8$, $P < 1\%$.)

DIFFERENTIAL DIAGNOSIS

An attempt was made to increase the usefulness of the method in the differential diagnosis of homosexuality and heterosexuality by increasing the number of pictures in certain categories. The modification B differed from modification A by the use of 80 exposures, among other details.

Every picture previously used in modification A was now preceded by a picture of a woman aged 19 to 25 or man aged 19 to 30. Each of the 'preceding' pictures appeared twice in the course of the experiment. Each picture was exposed for 12 seconds. Two pictures were always projected in sequence with an interval of less than 2 seconds between them. A further pair of pictures was shown only after the plethysmographic tracing had returned approximately to the initial level and continued horizontally or oscillated—in the case of vivid tracings—with a minimal amplitude around the horizontal axis. The sequence of the projected pictures followed that used in an earlier study (Freund, 1961).

In order to focus the attention of the patient on the projected picture, flickering lights were used. These appeared on the screen at pseudo-irregular intervals. The subject was asked, before the beginning of the experiment, to press a button as soon as he saw a light and to keep the button pressed down as long as the light flickered. The appearance of these lights was signalled on the control panel next to the recording instrument and the response was automatically recorded on the paper. Flickering lights appeared between exposures and also during certain pictures (Freund, 1961) and the response of the subject had to be the same in both cases. This served as a check that the patient was really observing the picture.

On the day preceding this examination the patient was given 25 mg of *testosteronum propionicum* intramuscularly as it can be assumed that in most cases this would increase his sexual response (Beach, 1944; Kinsey *et al.*, 1953). Immediately before the experiment he was given 0·2 g of caffeine and 100–200 ml of wine. A certain degree of relaxation can possibly be achieved in this way. The subject is told in advance that he will be shown projected pictures of nudes and that the aim is to find out how quickly he will respond to flickering lights and whether or not he is excitable.

The response to the picture was measured by the difference in the height of the tracing at the beginning and at the end of the exposure. The activity degree (V) of each recording was established on the basis of the sum of heights of 'responses', both positive and negative (subtracted) to the first pictures of each pair which represent a person of the preferred sex as determined by the record. There are 20 such pairs. The characteristic (V) is the aforementioned sum divided by 20. Again a classification of records was made into flat, $V < 0.2$ ml; almost flat, from 0.2 to 0.3 ml; moderately vivid, from $V > 0.3$ to the average 1.1 ml; vivid with an average response over 1.1 ccm and very vivid with $V > 2.2$ ml. Flat tracings should probably not be considered as reliable.

Modification B of the test was applied to 31 neurotic patients hospitalized in the open ward of the University Psychiatric Hospital (six of whom were over 50), who according to their case records were entirely heterosexual and not suspected of preferring adolescents or children. In addition, 25 homosexual men (two of whom were over 50) interested in adult partners and 14 homosexual men interested in adolescents or children were tested.

In arriving at a differential diagnosis between homosexuality and heterosexuality, responses to the first picture of every pair are given greatest attention and the responses to the first and second viewing of the same picture were evaluated separately so that the differential diagnosis was arrived at twice (Diagnostic indicators I and II). In this process, every response to the picture of a woman was compared with the response to a picture of a man exposed at approximately the same time period. The sums of the pairs where the response was greater to the picture of the woman was compared with the sum of the pairs where the response was greater to the picture of the man and heterosexuality (Het.) or homosexuality (Hom.) was diagnosed in accordance with the greater sum. Value z, established according to a procedure used in Wilcoxon's test (Siegel, 1956) is used as an auxilliary index. If z is smaller than 0.1 the diagnostic indicator (I or II) is O, i.e. inconclusive.

The diagnosis arrived at by using indicators I and II was in all cases in agreement with the diagnosis from the case records. However, in the case of two patients the record could not be used for measurements. In these two cases, one of which was homosexual and the other heterosexual, ejaculation occurred in connexion with the exposure of pictures of appropriate partners and the investigation had to be interrupted. One of the patients was a neurotic and this occurrence helped to establish an important factor in the origin of his complaints. The earlier responses of both these subjects left no doubt as to their sexual orientation.

Modification B of the method has so far been used for the differential diagnosis of homosexuality or heterosexuality in 23 cases. In five cases the subjects were men accused of homosexual activities with adults, but who denied homosexual tendencies. D_1—age 56, attempted suicide because he was prosecuted, diagnostic indicators were: I = II = Hom. Presentation of the 10 pictures of women produced crude artifacts which indicated simulation. D_2—age 25, feeble-minded, diagnostic indicators: I = II = Hom. D_3—age 53, diagnostic indicators: I = II = Hom. This patient confessed after the test that he had been homosexual since sustaining a head injury six years previously. D_4—aged 61, bathing attendant, diagnostic indicators: I = II = Hom. D_5—age 35, diagnostic indicators: I = Hom. II = Het.

Two further subjects were not prosecuted but they were suspected of homosexuality. The first of them—D_6 (aged 33, police officer) arrived accompanied by his wife and both denied vehemently that he could be homosexual. He maintained that he had been sent to the test because a homosexual man had declared in the course of interrogation that there were also homosexual persons among police officers, but had refused to name such persons. He claimed that the suspicion had focused on him only because he had interrogated the homosexual immediately prior to this statement; diagnostic indicators: I = II = Het. The other—D_7 (aged 19 years) was brought by his father who suspected him of homosexuality. The boy was feminine and histrionic to a considerable degree. Prior to the test he denied homosexual tendencies (diagnostic indicators: I = Het., II = Hom.).

Patient D_8, a chronically depressive psychopath, observed for a number of years, was suspected by the physician because of lack of heterosexual interests. On the basis of his TAT, the psychologist believed that the patient was a masochist; diagnostic indicators: I = Het., II = Hom. The record is practically flat.

Two further subjects, youths aged 19 and 20 (D_9 and D_{10}) engaged in homosexual prostitution, claimed exclusively hetero-erotic motivation; diagnostic indicators: I=II=Het in both cases. Patient D_{11} referred to this examination because of *orgasmus deficiens*, was otherwise not suspected of homosexuality; diagnostic indicators: I = II = Het. One zoophilic patient (D_{12}) was examined because of *partialismus* concerning the male horse genital. There was no other suspicion of homosexuality (diagnostic indicators: I = II = Het.). A 34-year-old neurotic (D_{13}) was tested as a heterosexual control. Both diagnostic indicators however showed homosexuality. When asked after the test, he confirmed that he is practically exclusively homosexual.

Three of the following nine subjects who stated that they were homosexual, were not confirmed by the test (they were conscripts, due to start their military service). In the case of one of them there were crude artifacts in response to all the pictures of men so that we did not even attempt to measure the tracing. He admitted afterwards that he was heterosexual. In the second case, almost all his responses to pictures were negative and in the third case, the record (diagnostic indicators: I and II) showed heterosexuality without any doubt. In this case we thought that the diagnostic method had perhaps failed and hospitalized this subject for observation. Heterosexuality was proved by chance. The man was caught by the police while observing girl students undressing in their dormitories from a wall which he had climbed—the girls had called the officer.

A further patient (D_{17}) submitted to the examination was a transexualist who stated that he was attracted only by men; initially it was believed that he had made this assertion only to underline that he was actually a woman. The record confirmed his statement (I = II = Hom.).

Simulation

In order to investigate signs of dissimulation and simulation systematically the following experiment was carried out. Heterosexual patients were asked to imagine something very disagreeable when viewing the picture of a woman, and, when viewing the picture of a man, that they were having intercourse with a woman they liked. *Mutandis mutatis* the same was asked of the homosexual subjects.

Four groups were formed. The first consisted of 22 heterosexual men who were asked to simulate homosexuality and who had not been examined previously. The second group consisted of men who had seen the pictures once before without being asked to simulate (20 subjects). The third group, consisting of 9 subjects, and the fourth, consisting of 15 subjects, were made up of homosexual patients. The third group saw the pictures for the first time, the fourth group saw them for the second time.

Table 5 shows the influence of simulation on diagnostic indicators I and II. These results lead to the conclusion that disagreement between the diagnostic indicators I and II or a "O" indicate dissimulation or simulation or some other erotic orientation not covered by the test.

We believe that the modification B of the described method is of greater usefulness in detection of androphilia in the male than modification A. It is not, however, equally satisfactory in the diagnosis of sexual interest in adolescents or children. It seems that the subject is not given an adequate opportunity to manifest possible erotic orientation in this direction because of the small number of pictures of adolescents and children which would permit an evaluation of responses.

TABLE 5. THE EFFECT OF SIMULATION: TWO HETERO- AND TWO HOMOSEXUAL GROUPS OF SUBJECTS WERE ASKED TO SIMULATE CONTRASEXUAL INTERESTS. FALSE CLASSIFICATIONS ARE INDICATED IN ITALICS

Diagnosis		Subjects			
		Heterosexual		Homosexual	
I	II	P_1	P_2	P	P_2
Het.	Het.	16	15	*1*	5
Het.	Hom.	1	1		
Het.	O	1			
Hom.	Hom.	2	*3*	5	7
Hom.	Het.	1		*3*	*1*
Hom.	O	1			
O	Het.				1
O	Hom.		1		1
O	O				
n		22	20	9	15

The introduction of a further modification should therefore be contemplated which would resemble modification A but would include twice as many pictures. Flickering lights during intervals between the pictures and during the projection of some pictures should be used in the same way as in modification B.

REFERENCES

BEACH, F. A. (1944) Experimental studies of sexual behaviour in male mammals. *J. clin. Endocrin.* 4, 126–134.

FREUND, K. (1957) Diagnostika homosexuality u mužů. *Cs. Psychiat.* 53, 382–394.

FREUND, K. (1959) Die erotische Differenzierungsfähigkeit bei ander Klinefelteschen Störung leidenden Personen. *Z. Psychol.* 18, 207–218.

FREUND, K. (1961) Laboratory differential diagnosis of homo- and heterosexuality—An experiment with faking. *Rev. Czech. Med.* 7, 20–31.

FREUND, K. (1962) *Homosexualita u muže.* Stát. zdrav. nakl., Prague.

FREUND, K., DIAMANT, J. and PINKAVA, V. (1958) On the validity and reliability of the phaloplethysmographic diagnosis of some sexual deviations. *Rev. Czech. Med.* 4, 145–151.

KINSEY, A. C., POMEROY, V. B., MARTIN, C. E. and GEBHARD, P. H. (1953) *Sexual Behavior in the Human Female.* Saunders, Philadelphia.

SIEGEL, S. (1956) *Nonparametric Statistics for the Behavioral Sciences.* New York.

A LABORATORY TASK FOR INDUCTION OF MOOD STATES*

EMMETT VELTEN, JR.†

University of Southern California

(*Received* 15 *May* 1968)

Summary—One hundred female college students were administered the Harvard Group Scale of Hypnotic Susceptibility, Form A, to provide a measure of primary suggestibility. In a 2nd hr, each S was randomly assigned to one of five individual treatments of 20 Ss each. One group read and concentrated upon 60 self-referent statements intended to be elating; a second group read 60 statements intended to be depressing. A third group read 60 statements which were neither self-referent nor pertaining to mood. This group controlled for the effects of reading and experimental participation per se. Fourth and fifth groups received demand characteristics control treatments designed to produce simulated elation and simulated depression, respectively.

Two measures of pre-treatment mood level were obtained from each S at the beginning of her individual treatment. Following treatment, as criteria for elation and depression, seven behavioral task measures were obtained. Four of these distinguished significantly among the treatment groups. The comparative performance of Ss in the three control groups indicated that the obtained mood changes could not be attributed to artifactual effects. Moreover, post-experimental questionnaire data strongly supported the conclusion that Elation and Depression treatments had indeed respectively induced elation and depression.

INTRODUCTION

IN A FAMOUS review of the literature on the effects of psychotherapy, Eysenck (1961) concluded that only three studies offered even meagre evidence of psychotherapeutic efficacy. Two of these three were by "semantic" psychotherapists, Albert Ellis (1957) and E. Lakin Phillips (1957), whose methods were highly similar. The third was by Joseph Wolpe (1958), a leading exponent of behavior therapy. Since Eysenck's review, much work has been done and many hypotheses confirmed by investigators of behavior therapy. However, such research productivity has not been forthcoming from the Ellis-Phillips camp.

The theoretical goal of this experiment was to test the central tenet of "semantic" therapy, that the constructions or interpretations people place upon events determine their affective responses. Much evidence from the literature on the determinants of emotions suggests a model of emotion highly congruent with Ellis's (Mandler, 1962). Reviews of hypnosis and autosuggestion methods in psychotherapy (Ellis, 1963; Gordon, 1967; Schultz and Luthe, 1959; Sparks, 1962) lend indirect support to the tenets of the semantic psychotherapists.

* This study is based upon a Dissertation (Velten, 1967) submitted to the University of Southern California in partial fulfillment of the requirements for the PhD degree. Dr. L. Douglas DeNike served as Dissertation committee chairman and rendered invaluable service during the preparation of this article.

† Now at the Division of Psychological Services, Board of Education, Memphis City Schools, Memphis, Tennessee.

METHOD

Subjects

Ss were 100 unpaid volunteer undergraduate college women who signed up for an experiment in "the autosuggestion of mood states."

Physical arrangements

Subjects in the group section of the experiment sat at classroom desks. Each S in the individual treatment section of the experiment sat in a small room at a 36 × 40 in. table with S sitting at a longer side and E sitting at a shorter side to S's right.

Group assessment of primary suggestibility

A measure of primary suggestibility (Eysenck and Furneaux, 1945; Stukát, 1958; Weitzenhoffer, 1953) was obtained from each S to serve as a covariate in the analysis of treatment effects. The Harvard Group Scale of Hypnotic Susceptibility, (*HGS*), Form A, (Shor and Orne, 1962) provided the measure. All but 17 Ss received the hypnotic induction scale prior to the individual experimental treatment.

Individual experimental treatment

Pre-measures. Two variables were measured prior to experimental manipulations to assess pre-treatment mood level:

(1) *Decision Time* (DT). This pre-measure involved the use of five pairs of tins, each tin weighing about 1 oz, pre-arranged in parallel columns perpendicular to S's edge of the table. The tins in each pair were equal in weight. The E read aloud instructions which indicated that S was to pick up the weights in the first pair, decide which was the heavier and so indicate, then to go on to successive pairs.*

(2) *Perceptual Ambiguity* (PA). This pre-measure involved presenting S with a "vase and faces" ambiguous figure (Osgood, 1953, p. 220, Fig.A) which was drawn in black ink on a lineless index card. The instructions for this pre-measure required S to say "Now" whenever she perceived flutuations in the perspective of the ambiguous figure.

Mood induction and control group procedures

Immediately upon completion of the pre-measure *PA* task, each S was assigned randomly to one of five treatment groups. She read silently and then aloud either demand characteristics instructions or instructions which prepared her to receive mood or neutral statements. Instructions were in the first person, typed entirely in capitals on lineless index cards, and were placed before S by E one by one as S completed reading the previous card. Instructions for the mood (Elation and Depression) treatments emphasized that S should try to feel the mood suggested by the statements, that she could do this, that there was nothing to worry about, and so on. These instructions were read at S's own pace.

Identity and purpose of the five treatments

Immediately upon completion of their appropriate preparatory instructions, the Elation (*EL*), Depression (*DE*), and Neutral (*NU*) Ss read silently, then aloud, their appropriate mood induction statements. For *EL* and *DE* treatments, two sets of stimuli were used,

---

* Instructions and other original materials mentioned in this paper are available in Velten (1967).

each composed of 60 self-referent statements. The statements gradually progressed from relative mood neutrality to "elation" for the EL group, and from relative mood neutrality to "depression" for the DE group. In the NU group, they remained affectively neutral and were not self-referent. Subjects in the Elation Demand Characteristics (EDC) and Depression Demand Characteristics (DDC) treatments had no preparatory instructions, but proceeded directly from the pre-measures to the reading of instructions designed to induce simulated elation and depression, respectively. The mood statements, neutral statements, and demand characteristics instructions were all typed entirely in capitals on lineless index cards, and were presented individually to S by E. All these statements were exposed to S for 20 sec each, while the demand characteristics instructions were read at S's own pace.

Elation treatment. The tone of the statements exposed to Ss in the EL treatment was one of happiness, cheer, liveliness, efficiency, optimism, and expansiveness. Two sample EL statements were: "If your attitude is good, then things are good, and my attitude is good." "This is great—I really do feel good—I *am* elated about things."

Depression treatment. The tone of the statements exposed to Ss in the DE treatment was one of indecision, tiredness, slowness, unhappiness, inefficiency, and pessimism. Two sample DE statements were: "Every now and then I feel so tired and gloomy that I'd rather just sit than do anything." "I have too many bad things in my life."

Neutral treatment. The purpose of the NU treatment was to serve as a control for the possible effects of reading statements and experimental participation per se. Two sample NU statements were: "This book or any part thereof must not be reproduced in any form." "Utah is the Beehive State."

Elation demand characteristics and depression demand characteristics treatments. The purpose of the EDC and DDC treatments was to serve as controls for conscious role-playing or unconscious influence of Ss by the obvious demand characteristics (Orne, 1962) of the EL and DE treatments, respectively. Ss in both demand characteristics treatments read instructions which explained the procedure used with either the EL or DE treatment, were provided respectively with a few synonyms for elation or depression, and read instructions to "behave the way I (S) estimate other Ss behave who have been administered all sixty statements representing this mood of (elation) (depression)." They were then shown five samples of the EL or DE statements, and finally read instructions to "always remember to act as if I were (elated) (depressed)."

Critical measures

To assess the effects of the treatments on mood, seven criterial measures were taken in the following order:

Writing Speed (WS). Instructions required S to write out numbers in descending order from 100. Ss were stopped after 1 min.

Distance Approximation (DA). Instructions required S to close her eyes and to make certain specified estimations of distance by placing her hands those distances apart.

Decision Time (DT). Instructions and manner of presentation for this measure were the same as for pre-measure *DT*, although different pairs of weights were used.

Perceptual Ambiguity (PA). This measure consisted of another ambiguous figure (Osgood, 1953, p. 219, Fig. 81) similar to that of pre-measure *PA*, and presented in the same manner.

Word Association (WA). Instructions for this measure were typical of those employed in word association tests. There were 16 stimulus words.

Multiple Affect Adjective Check List, Today Form, (MAACL). Instructions required Ss to check adjectives which applied to them in a long list.

Spontaneous Verbalizations (SV). The score for this measure was obtained by E's making a record of the number of words uttered by S during the course of the criterial measures.

The general predictions made were that *EL* and *DE* Ss would differ significantly from each other on each criterial measure, and that the performance of *NU* Ss would fall between those of the two mood treatments. Performances of the two demand characteristics treatments were expected to be significantly different from the respective mood treatments for which they provided controls. Elation Ss were expected to write more numbers, have larger estimations of distances, to make decisions more quickly, to experience less perceptual ambiguity, to have briefer word association reaction times, to score lower on the *MAACL* "depression scale," and to make more spontaneous verbalizations than the *DE* Ss (Fisher and Marrow, 1934; Foulds, 1951; Johnson, 1937; Zuckerman, Lubin, and Robins, 1956).

Post-experimental questionnaire

Following the completion of the criterial measures, each S was required to fill out a questionnaire designed to indicate her awareness of effects induced by the treatment and her awareness of E's hypotheses regarding the criterial measures.

RESULTS

Pre-treatment equation of the experimental groups. To test for differences in mood level and primary suggestibility among treatment groups prior to treatments, one-way analyses of variance were performed on pre-measure *DT*, pre-measure *PA*, and the *HGS*. The results of the analyses indicated that there were no significant differences among groups prior to treatment.

Mood-relevant expressive behavior. On their post-experimental questionnaires, some *DE* Ss made such clear reports as the following: "Sad and lonesome, unhappy—I feel and felt like crying when I think hard about things" (S no. 9). "They (the mood-statements) made me feel upset at first because they held a lot of meaning for me. Later on though, I kind of gave up." And: "Everything kept making me think of crummy things and unwanted feelings" (no. 12). "Tired, lonely, unhappy, unloved, homesick, rejected, discontent, wistful, and loving" (no. 22). "When I came into the room, though I felt a bit worried about a coming exam, I was cheerful and rather contented. Apparently the statements did have a result, since I now feel tired and with little ambition to do anything" (no. 24). "Tired, depressed, worrying" (no. 35). Two *DE* Ss appeared to be close to tears.

On the questionnaire some *EL* Ss made such clear reports as the following: "They (the mood-statements) made me feel happier, wilder, more confident, more desirable, more capable of being a fascinating woman, sexier" (no. 30). "They made me feel very ambitious and I want to get right down to homework" (no. 34). "Good, alive, energetic, confident, more appealing, happier, more ready to get started, more able to work" (no. 77), "I feel more alive, more able to accomplish something today. I also feel more like seeing my friends and talking with them" (no. 89). "They made me feel more optimistic" (no. 90). "They amused me, pleased me, and gave me a confidence I didn't have when I first walked in" (no. 95).

In only a few cases did Ss in the two demand characteristics treatments appear elated or depressed, and in these cases their behavior was histrionic and easily identifiable as "faking." For example, of the two *DDC* Ss who engaged in attempts to portray depression, one pouted, shook her head woefully, pulled long faces, and said in response to an example of a *DE* mood-statement provided as part of the *DDC* instructions: "I don't have to read that one; I known that one by heart," in a quavering voice.

Behavior of the *NU* Ss tended to be typically neutral with regard to elation and depression, though several seemed initially to show non-verbal expressions of boredom or perplexity as they read their statements.

In sum then, the mood-relevant expressive behavior of Ss supported the contention that the mood treatments had induced elation and depression while the corresponding demand characteristics control treatments and the *NU* treatment had not been successful in inducing similar mood-like behavior. Behavior of the obviously role-playing demand characteristics Ss suggested that intentional role-playing by mood treatment Ss would have also been gross and easily identifiable.

Relation of primary suggestibility, pre-treatment mood level, and criterial performance. When correlations of primary suggestibility and pre-treatment mood level with criterial measure performance were calculated, performance on four criterial measures was found significantly related to primary suggestibility for both the *EL* and *DE* treatments. On these measures, the higher the primary suggestibility, the more the respective mood treatment affected S. Performance of Ss in other treatments was essentially unrelated to primary suggestibility, and pre-treatment mood level was essentially unrelated to any treatment S's criterial performance.

Primary suggestibility and pre-treatment mood level as covariates for the five treatments Double analyses of covariance were performed using as covariates primary suggestibility and pre-treatment mood level as measured by pre-measure *DT*, and using the seven criterial measures as experimental variables (see Table 1). These analyses revealed that the null hypothesis of equality of treatment group centroids after they had been adjusted for the contributions of the covariates could be rejected at the 0.001 level for four of the seven criterial measures: *WS*, *DT*, *WA*, and the *MAACL*. Thus, treatments produced significant differences among groups even after the control for possible confounding by primary suggestibility and pre-treatment mood level.

TABLE 1. SUMMARY OF ANALYSES OF COVARIANCE OF THE PERFORMANCE OF TREATMENT
GROUPS ON THE CRITERIAL MEASURES, USING THE GROUP SCALE AND PRE-MEASURE
DECISION TIME AS COVARIATES

	Source		Wilks' Lambda	d_f	F
Writing speed	Adjusted T	9.23	0.6125	4	14.71*
	Adjusted W	8.74		93	
Distance approximation	Adjusted T	9.13	0.9448	4	1.36
	Adjusted W	9.07		93	
Decision time	Adjusted T	11.12	0·7930	4	6.07*
	Adjusted W	10.89		93	
Perceptual ambiguity	Adjusted T	11.05	0.9255	4	1.87
	Adjusted W	10.97		93	
Word association	Adjusted T	10.28	0.8368	4	4.54*
	Adjusted W	10.10		93	
MAACL	Adjusted T	9.07	0.7088	4	9.55*
	Adjusted W	8.73		93	
Spontaneous verbalizations	Adjusted T	5.22	0.9300	4	1.75
	Adjusted W	5.14		93	

* $P < 0.001$.

Multiple comparisons among adjusted treatment means. To determine which of the differences between individual pairs of the five treatment means were significant after the means had been adjusted for the contributions of pre-treatment mood level and primary suggestibility, Tukey's multiple-range tests were performed (see Table 2).

The *MAACL* produced five significant differences in ten comparisons between pairs of means adjusted for the contributions of the covariates. On this criterial measure, DE Ss scored further in the predicted direction than all other groups. In addition, EL Ss scored as more elated than DDC Ss.

Writing Speed produced three significant differences. EL Ss wrote significantly more numbers in 1 min than did DE and EDC Ss. Depression Ss wrote significantly fewer numbers than did NU Ss. Thus, on this measure, the mood-relevant behavior of EL and DE Ss differed significantly and in the expected direction on an elation—depression continuum.

Decision Time produced three significant differences, with EL Ss taking significantly less time to make decisions than did Ss in DE, NU, and EDC treatments. Thus, according to prediction, the mood-relevant behavior of EL Ss was such as to indicate that they were more elated than all other treatment groups except, unexpectedly, the DDC treatment.

Word Association produced two significant differences. The reaction times of DE Ss were longer than those of EL and DDC Ss. Thus, on this measure, mood-relevant behavior of DE Ss differed in such a way as to indicate that they were more depressed than EL and DDC Ss.

Spontaneous Verbalizations produced only one significant difference, and this was between *EL* and *DE* treatment groups.

Distance Approximation produced only one significant difference. The distance approximations of *NU* Ss were significantly larger than those of *DE* Ss. Thus, on this measure, the mood-relevant behavior of *NU* and *DE* Ss differed in such a way as to indicate as predicted, that the latter were the more depressed.

TABLE 2. SUMMARY OF TUKEY'S MULTIPLE-RANGE TEST AS APPLIED TO INDIVIDUAL COMPARISONS BETWEEN ADJUSTED TREATMENT MEANS ON THE CRITERIAL MEASURES

Treatment groups	Means	E	D	N	EDC	DDC
			Writing speed			
E	50.19	..	11.88‡	4.42	10.84‡	6·25
D	38.31		..	7.46*	1.04	5.63
N	45.77			..	6.42	1.83
EDC	39.35				..	4·59
DDC	43.94					..
			Distance approximation			
E	54.90	..	8.40	2.09	3.00	0.34
D	46.49		..	10.50*	5.44	8.15
N	56.99			..	5.06	2.35
EDC	51.93				..	2.71
DDC	54.64					..
			Decision time			
E	37.83	..	24.10*	27.10*	21.70*	9.31
D	61.95		..	2.95	2.45	4.80
N	64.91			..	5.40	17.80
EDC	59.50				..	12.40
DDC	47.14					..
			Perceptual ambiguity			
E	31.87	..	5.28	10.99	11.18	7.78
D	37.15		..	16.27	16.46	13.06
N	20.88			..	0.17	3.21
EDC	20.69				..	3.40
DDC	24.09					..

TABLE 2. *Continued*

Treatment groups	Means	E	D	N	EDC	DDC
			Word association			
E	36.12	..	18.20†	6.62	7.64	6.33
D	54.32		..	11.58	10.56	11.87*
N	42.74			..	1.02	0.29
EDC	43.76				..	1.31
DDC	42.45					..
			MAACL			
E	10.55	..	14.00‡	3.23	2.05	7.65*
D	24.55		..	10.97‡	11.95‡	6.35*
N	13.78			..	1.18	4.42
EDC	12.60				..	5.60
DDC	18.20					..
			Spontaneous verbalizations			
E	1.74	..	1.15†	0.57	0.64	0.55
D	0.61		..	0.56	0.49	0.58
N	1.17			..	0.07	0.02
EDC	1.10				..	0.09
DDC	1.19					..

* $P < 0.05$.
† $P < 0.01$.
‡ $P < 0.001$.

Perceptual Ambiguity produced no significant differences.

Post-experimental questionnaire. Analysis of the questionnaire revealed that a preponderance of *EL* and *DE* Ss reported being signficantly affected in elated and depressed directions, respectively, by their experimental manipulations, while *NU*, *EDC*, and *DDC* Ss preponderantly failed to report any such effects. With very few exceptions, Ss in *EL*, *DE*, *EDC*, and *DDC* treatments did not report predicted effects on criterial measures significantly more than they reported nonpredicted effects.

DISCUSSION

The results of this experiment largely confirmed predictions made. Elation and *DE* treatments differed significantly from each other on five of seven criterial measures of mood-relevant behavior, and each difference was in the predicted direction. On every measure except *DA*, *NU* treatment means fell between those of *EL* and *DE* treatment groups, as was predicted. On two of seven measures, *EL* and *EDC* treatment groups differed significantly; and on two of seven, *DE* and *DDC* treatment groups differed significantly. In all cases *EDC* and *DDC* treatment means fell between *DE* and *EL* treatment means. On five criterial measures, means of both demand characteristics treatments were closer to the means of the opposite mood treatment than to the treatments for which they were intended to provide controls. The lack of significant correlations between primary suggestibility and the criterial measure performance of *EDC* and *DDC* Ss implies that Ss' willingness or ability to respond automatically to demand characteristics of the experiment was not related to primary suggestibility.

The post-experimental questionnaire data supported the conclusion from the behavioral measures that *EL* and *DE* treatments had been successful in inducing elation and depression, respectively, and that the *EL* treatment had been better retained than had the *DE* treatment. Neutral Ss did not report elation or depression. Elation Demand Characteristics and *DDC* treatments were generally unsuccessful in inducing apparent elation or depression. With a very few exceptions, Ss were unaware that they were performing on criterial measures in the directions predicted by E. Thus, the data consistently indicate that Ss did not simply respond to the demand characteristics of the experimental situation, that possession of correct hypotheses regarding criterial performance was not responsible for Ss' behavior, and that differential mood-relevant behavior had been induced.

Research use of the method. The present method appears to have potential for the experimental induction and study of elation, depression, and perhaps for other moods such as fear or sexual arousal. If appropriate lists of statements could be developed for the induction of these and other moods, the controlled laboratory investigation of mood might be greatly facilitated.

Statement-reading as a therapeutic specific. The generally positive results of this experiment suggest the possible value of lists of mood or other statements in psychotherapy. The T and the patient would develop appropriate statement lists after exploration of the patient's problems. This procedure would be somewhat analogous to the development of anxiety hierarchies in systematic desensitization. The patient would be instructed to practice appropriate lists at or near to the times he becomes aware of undesirable moods and behavior. According to conditioning theory, it might be expected that repeated use of a particular list of statements, particularly if the individual rehearsed them at times when he felt especially bad, would eventually lead to the conditioning of undesirable affect to the statements themselves. To counteract the possibility that the usefulness of the therapy-statements would be reduced either by this means or by simple habituation, alternate sets of statements could be constructed, and the patient could be instructed to begin his use of therapy-statements at the inception of the negative emotion, rather than waiting until it had become full-blown.

Implications for psychological inventories. The results of the present experiment are consistent with the finding that psychological inventories containing a preponderance of negative self-references are likely to be disturbing to those taking them. (Amrine, 1965). To the extent that such disturbance is attributable to depressive mood change as distinct from fear of self-disclosure, it might be possible to lessen objections to such inventories by increasing the number of neutral or positive items.

Relation to semantic psychotherapy. Insofar as the present experiment provided a test of the central tenet of rational-emotive and other semantic psychotherapies, and insofar as the results may be accepted, there is additional evidence that the claims of Ellis (1957; 1963) and Phillips (1957) regarding the efficacy of their therapies may be taken seriously.

REFERENCES

AMRINE M. (1965) The 1965 congressional inquiry into testing: A commentary. *Am. Psychol.* **20,** 859–871.
ELLIS A. (1957) Outcome of employing three techniques of psychotherapy. *J. Clin. Psychol.* **13,** 344–350.
ELLIS A. (1963) *Reason and Emotion in Psychotherapy.* Lyle Stuart, New York.
EYSENCK H. J. (1961) The effects of psychotherapy. In *Handbook of Abnormal Psychology* (Ed. H. J. EYSENCK). Basic Books, New York.
EYSENCK H. J. and FURNEAUX W. D. (1945) Primary and secondary suggestibility: An experimental and statistical study. *J. exp. Psychol.* **35,** 485–503.
FISHER V. E. and MARROW J. (1934) Experimental study of moods. *Character Person.* **2,** 201–208.
FOULDS G. A. (1951) Temperamental differences in maze performance. Part I: Characteristic differences among psychoneurotics. *Br. J. Psychol.* **42,** 209–217.
GORDON J. E. (Ed.) (1967) *Handbook of Clinical and Experimental Hypnosis.* Macmillan, New York.
JOHNSON W. B. (1937) Euphoric and depressed moods in normal subjects. *Character Person* **6,** 79–98.
MANDLER G. (1962) Emotion. In *New Directions in Psychology* (Ed. R. BROWN *et al.*). Holt, Rinehart & Winston, New York.
ORNE M. T. (1962) On the social psychology of the psychological experiment with particular reference to demand characteristics and their implications. *Am. Psychol.* **17,** 776–783.
PHILLIPS E. L. (1957) *Psychotherapy: A Modern Theory and Practice.* Prentice-Hall, Englewood Cliffs, New Jersey.
SCHULTZ J. H. and LUTHE W. (1959) *Autogenic Training.* Grune & Stratton, New York and London.
SHOR R. E. and ORNE M. T. (1962) *Harvard Group Scale of Hypnotic Susceptibility.* Consulting Psychologists Press, Palo Alto, California.
SPARKS L. (1962) *Self-Hypnosis: A Conditioned-Response Technique.* Grune & Stratton, New York.
STUKÁT K. -G. (1958) *Suggestibility: A Factorial and Experimental Analysis.* Almqvist & Wiksell, Stockholm.
VELTEN E. (1967) *The Induction of Elation and Depression through the Reading of Structured Sets of Mood-Statements.* (Doctoral Dissertation, University of Southern California) Ann Arbor, Michigan: University Microfilms, No. 67-13,045. *Diss. Abstr.* **28,** No. 4.
WEITZENHOFFER A. M. (1957) *Hypnotism: An Objective Study in Suggestibility.* John Wiley, New York.
WOLPE J. (1958) *Psychotherapy by Reciprocal Inhibition.* Stanford University Press, Stanford, California.
ZUCKERMAN M., LUBIN B. and ROBINS S. (1965) Validation of the Multiple Affect Adjective Check List in clinical situations. *J. Consult. Psychol.* **29,** 594.

THE MOBILITY INVENTORY FOR AGORAPHOBIA

Dianne L. Chambless, G. Craig Caputo, Susan E. Jasin,
Edward J. Gracely and Christine Williams

Department of Psychiatry, Temple University Medical School, Philadelphia, PA 19140, U.S.A.

(*Received* 14 *March* 1984)

Summary—The development of the Mobility Inventory for Agoraphobia (MI), a 27-item inventory for the measurement of self-reported agoraphobic avoidance behavior and frequency of panic attacks, is described. On this instrument, 26 situations are rated for avoidance both when clients are accompanied and when they are alone. These two conditions were found to be only moderately correlated and are thus analyzed separately, as is the item on frequency of panic attacks. Studies are reported which support the reliability and the concurrent and construct validity of these three measures, using comparison samples of agoraphobic, socially phobic and normal Ss. The MI appears to be a sound instrument, with which a broad range of situations troublesome to agoraphobic clients can be surveyed, and should prove useful for treatment planning and research.

INTRODUCTION

During the 1970s more effective treatments became available for the typically refractory problem of agoraphobia (see Chambless and Goldstein, 1980), followed by a rapid expansion of the number of treatment programs specifically designed for treating agoraphobics individually or in groups. While sophisticated assessment packages have been developed for some funded research projects (e.g. Barlow and Mavissakalian, 1981) including psychophysiological and *in vivo* cognitive and behavioral measures, little attention has been given to developing better paper-and-pencil measures of agoraphobia. This type of instrument is likely to be of more practical utility to the clinician, in addition meeting the researcher's need for a carefully developed self-report measure.

The best self-report measure to date has been the Fear Questionnaire (FQ; Marks and Mathews, 1979), which was derived from a series of factor analyses with phobic patients based on items from previous lengthy fear survey schedules. Designed for use with phobias of all types, the FQ has a 5-item Agoraphobia factor, which has been demonstrated to be reliable (test–retest) and sensitive to changes with treatment. There are two problems using this scale with agoraphobics, however. First, the Agoraphobia factor has so few items that it has limited utility for treatment planning, an important function for an assessment instrument. Second, the scale instructions do not provide a distinction between avoidance of and discomfort in situations when the agoraphobic person is alone vs when accompanied. Since having a companion is a critical factor in most agoraphobic clients' mobility (Marks, 1970), it is important to measure avoidance under both conditions when describing a treatment's effectiveness.

The purpose of this paper is to report the development of an inventory specifically designed to measure self-reported severity of agoraphobic avoidance behavior. Items for the original version of the scale were derived from: (a) items on the Fear Survey Schedule (FSS; Wolpe and Lang, 1964) rated highly by agoraphobic clients; (b) from interviews with agoraphobic clients about situations they avoid; or (c) from observations of avoidance behavior and reported anxiety during *in vivo* exposure sessions. Since the occurrence of panic attacks has been identified as a central feature of agoraphobia (e.g. Goldstein and Chambless, 1978), a final item was added, giving a definition of panic (which may be difficult to discriminate from high anxiety) and asking for a report of the number of such experiences during the prior week.

Although Watson and Marks (1971) devised a rating scale for panic which was determined to have good interrater reliability, their measure called for one rating incorporating the frequency, intensity and duration of attacks. We found our clients had difficulty collapsing these several dimensions, had little accurate sense of the duration of attacks and saw little difference in the intensity of various attacks (once panic was defined as different from just anxiety). Moreover, we wanted a scale that could be used in short-term therapy, but had found the 3-day interval on the Watson and Marks scale to be too brief. In one study (Chambless, Foa, Groves and Goldstein, 1979) the incidence of panic in a 3-day period was so low as to constitute a floor effect on measurement of panic. Consequently on the present panic frequency scale we extended the time period to 7 days. The scale, the Mobility Inventory for Agoraphobia (MI), was then tested in a series of validational studies which will now be described.

SAMPLE 1

Method

Subjects

Clinical sample *S*s were 159 clients applying for treatment at the Agoraphobia and Anxiety Program of Temple University Medical School, who were subsequently interviewed and diagnosed as agoraphobic according to the DSM-III criteria (American Psychiatric Association, 1980); 88% of these were women. The clients averaged 34.65 yr in age (SD = 9.45) and had been agoraphobic for a mean of 9.28 yr (SD = 8.68). All social classes were represented although 82% of the sample fell in the lower three categories of the Hollingshead (1957) index. Control sample *S*s were recruited through clients in treatment who were asked to indicate friends or acquaintances similar to them in demographic characteristics but who did not have anxiety problems. Of the 43 control *S*s who agreed to participate, 23 met the criteria for inclusion in a psychometrically defined normal control group. Control *S*s were similar to clients in age, sex and marital status, but tended to come from a higher socioeconomic class ($t = 2.48$, $df = 44$, $P < 0.02$).

Measures

Fear Questionnaire (FQ). Items concerning feared situations on this scale are rated on a 9-point Likert-type scale, where 0 indicates no avoidance and 8 total avoidance (Marks and Mathews, 1979). The 5-item Agoraphobia factor was used as a measure of convergent validity.

Mobility Inventory for Agoraphobia (MI). The 29 items on the scale were rated four times each on 5-point Likert-type scales. On the first page items were rated according to how much these situations were avoided, both if the clients were Alone (MI-AAL) and if Accompanied (MI-AAC). A rating of 1 indicated the situation was never avoided, and 5, always avoided. On p. 2, items were rated according to discomfort elicited, again when Alone (MI-DAL) and when Accompanied (MI-DAC) with 5 indicating severe discomfort. As previously described, the panic frequency (PF) measure involved a simple report of the number of panic attacks in the past 7 days.

Measures of psychopathology. Several widely used and well-validated measures of psychopathology were employed: the Beck Depression Inventory (BDI; Beck, Ward, Mendelson, Mock and Erbaugh, 1961), the Trait form of the State–Trait Anxiety Inventory (STAI; Spielberger, Gorsuch and Lushene, 1970) and the Eysenck Personality Questionnaire (EPQ) from which the Neuroticism (N) and Psychotocism (P) scores were extracted (Eysenck and Eysenck, 1975). The P factor was added in the 1975 version of the questionnaire. Although less extensively validated than the other factors, it has been found to be elevated in criminal and psychotic groups and to constitute a separate factor from N. Test–retest reliability has generally been in the 0.70–0.80 range. As a gross measure of other forms of emotional problems, the MiniMult (Kincannon, 1978), was used. Scale scores derived from this 71-item form of the MMPI correlate highly (*r*s range from 0.60 to 0.96) with scores based on the total inventory.

Socioeconomic status (SES). SES was calculated using the Hollingshead (1957) Two-factor Index of Social Position. This index combines educational attainment with occupation of the household head to yield a continuous measure ranging from 11–77 with the latter representing the lowest class, e.g. a grade-school educated person on public assistance.

Procedure

Upon telephoning for an interview, 85 clinical *S*s were mailed copies of the MI to complete immediately. A median 31 days later they reported to the clinic for intake, beginning with a standard set of assessment instruments including the FQ, BDI, EPQ and a second MI. A diagnostic psychological interview followed. Seventy-four additional clients participated in a 2-week intensive treatment program involving approx. 30 hr of *in vivo* exposure. Treatment Ss were administered the MI the first day of the 2-week program, a week subsequent to its completion, and 6 months posttreatment for follow-up.

Potential Ss for the control group were mailed all questionnaires described except the FQ with a consent form and an explanation of the study. Consent forms were returned separately to ensure anonymity. A normal classification for inclusion in the control group was psychometrically defined as requiring all of the following: a score below 10 on the BDI (normal range), a score of 13 (normal population mean) or below on the EPQ N and T-scores below 70 on all the clinical scales of the MiniMult. Also the Ss must not have been at the time, or at any time in the past, agoraphobic, according to the S's reading of an enclosed description.

Results

Scale characteristics

Items on the MI, except for PF, were averaged across situations yielding four global measures: MI-AAL (Avoidance Alone), MI-AAC (Avoidance Accompanied), MI-DAL (Discomfort Alone) MI-DAC (Discomfort Accompanied). All four measures were found to be normally distributed, very internally consistent, and highly reliable over the 31-day pretreatment test–retest interval. Individual item reliability was also high with rs ranging from 0.48 to 0.90 (median $r = 0.76$). Pearson product–moment correlations at pretreatment, posttreatment and follow-up indicated MI-AAL and MI-DAL ratings were highly correlated as were similar ratings for MI-AAC and MI-DAC; rs ranged from 0.87 to 0.94. Consequently only Avoidance scales ratings were considered in most subsequent analyses and are presented here (see Table 1). Data on the Discomfort scales are given in Tables A.1 and A.2. MI-AAL and MI-AAC were only moderately correlated ($r = 0.67$), indicating the importance of this distinction in measurement.

PF was found to be leptokurtic and positively skewed with a large standard deviation indicating considerable variation across Ss in this feature of agoraphobia. It may be seen (Table 1) that even with the increase in the reporting interval from 3 to 7 days, many agoraphobics continue to report a zero frequency of attacks. Since the distribution was not normal, reliability was calculated with a Kendall τ_b nonparametric statistic. The Pearson r is reported for comparison, as nonparametric analyses typically yield lower correlation coefficients. Test–retest reliability is rather low; however, this is not surprising in that the occurrence of panic is highly variable (Marks, 1970).

Validity analyses

Pearson product-moment correlations were computed among measures collected from the clinical sample, except for PF with which nonparametric analyses were conducted. Convergent validity of the MI Avoidance scales was confirmed by strong correlations with the FQ Agoraphobia factor (See Table 2). Assessing construct validity, we predicted that severity of avoidance and frequency of panic would be positively related to chronic anxiety and depression. In the latter case,

Table 1. Characteristics of MI measures

Variable	$\bar{X}$	n	SD	r	n	Cronbach's α	n
AAL							
Sample 1	3.35	94	1.06	0.89	85	0.96	76
Sample 2	3.30	83	0.99	0.90	36	0.94	71
AAC							
Sample 1	2.64	93	0.90	0.75	84	0.97	76
Sample 2	2.41	83	0.70	0.86	35	0.91	71
PF[a]							
Sample 1	2.72	87	2.77	0.62	72		
Mode	0			(0.49)			
Median	2.00						
Sample 2	3.21	65	3.98	0.56	34		
Mode	0			(0.60)			
Median	2.07						

[a]For this measure nonparametric τ_b correlations are reported in parentheses under the Pearson r-values.

Table 2. Correlations among measures before treatment

	AAL	AAC	PF	BDI	TA	AF
AAL						
AAC	0.67					
	n = 93					
	P < 0.001					
PF	0.15	0.23				
	n = 86	n = 85				
	P < 0.03	P < 0.003				
Depression BDI	0.44	0.51	0.31			
	n = 90	n = 89	n = 83			
	P < 0.001	P < 0.001	P < 0.001			
Trait anxiety (TA; STAI)	0.38	0.25	0.33	0.67		
	n = 86	n = 85	n = 79	n = 85		
	P < 0.001	P < 0.01	P < 0.001	P < 0.001		
Agoraphobia factor (FQ)	0.68	0.44	0.04	0.27	0.19	
	n = 42	n = 42	n = 41	n = 43	n = 39	
	P < 0.001	P < 0.002	P < 0.36	P < 0.36	P = 0.24	
P (EPQ)	−0.14	0.16	−0.18	0.06	−0.02	0.01
	n = 75	n = 75	n = 64	n = 61	n = 60	n = 75
	P < 0.11	P < 0.09	P < 0.03	P < 0.33	P < 0.43	P < 0.46

Pearson rs are used except for PF, the skewed distribution of which necessitates nonparametric analysis with Kendall τ_bs.

this hypothesis was based on demoralization, isolation and loss of pleasurable activities associated with severe agoraphobia. These predictions were supported.

Agoraphobia has been found to be related to so many variables (Chambless, 1982) it is difficult to conceive of variables which should be totally unrelated to agoraphobic severity. We did, however, predict that no positive relationship would emerge when the MI was correlated with the Eysenck P factor. High scorers on this factor were described by Eysenck and Eysenck (1975) as likely to be "solitary, not caring for people...often troublesome...cruel...hostile (p. 5)." We thought these descriptors were not particularly characteristic of agoraphobics and were unlikely to be associated with their avoidance behavior. The correlations in Table 2 are consistent with these predictions. A significant negative correlation was found between PF and P, while PF had positive correlations with the other measures. This would indicate that the tendency toward greater affiliative needs and lack of aggression may foster panic. However, it could be argued that the helplessness engendered by highly frequent panic attacks might increase needs for others' support and thus reduce aggression and disdain for social support. Overall, the MI correlations with indices of psychopathology are consistent with our understanding of agoraphobia.

By definition of agoraphobia, we expected that agoraphobic avoidance behavior would be reported as more marked when the S rated the Alone condition vs the Accompanied. Ratings on all individual items for the Alone and Accompanied conditions were compared using Wilcoxin matched-pairs signed-ranks tests. For the agoraphobic sample ($n = 74$) the MI-AAL ratings always significantly exceeded the MI-AAC ratings, all Ps $\leqslant 0.002$. For the normal sample ($n = 23$), however, significant differences were only found on a few items concerning social situations where it is customary for women to be accompanied (the theatre, restaurants, bars and parties, all Ps $\leqslant 0.01$) and on the item "Being on a boat", $P < 0.02$.

A valid measure should be sensitive to changes in clients' clinical status. Since in vivo exposure has been repeatedly shown to be an effective treatment by many criteria (Emmelkamp, 1982), we predicted the MI measures would reflect changes across treatment involving large amounts of in vivo exposure. The majority of Ss in the treatment sample were in weekly treatment for short periods of time from the time of their intake when they first took the MI and the administration of the MI on the first day of the 2-week intensive treatment program. Consequently only changes between the pretest measure given the first day of the treatment program and subsequent measurement points were considered. Data were available at all three points for 41 clients. From Table 3 it is clear that, as expected, all measures show significant improvement 1 week after the treatment program (posttest). During the 6-month follow-up period, 42% of the clients received some additional exposure treatment for an average of 8.20 (SD = 5.90) sessions. Continued significant change was observed during this period. Goldstein (1982) has provided data showing the instrument's continued sensitivity to change over a 1 yr period with a small subset of these clients.

Table 3. Changes with treatment by *in vivo* exposure on the MI for agoraphobic clients

Measure	Pretest $\bar{X}$	Pretest SD	Posttest $\bar{X}$	Posttest SD	6-Month follow-up $\bar{X}$	6-Month follow-up SD	Comparison	*Post hoc* tests
AAL	3.41	1.02	2.59	0.90	2.12	0.92	$F(2,80) = 64.04$†††	Pre vs post† Post vs FU†
AAC	2.37	0.89	1.81	0.73	1.53	0.60	$F(2,80) = 41.84$†††	Pre vs post† Post vs FU†
PF	2.38		2.08		1.54		$\chi^2(2) = 13.35$††	Pre vs post* Post vs FU**

Mean ranks and a Friedman ANOVA followed by Wilcoxon tests are reported for PF ($n = 37$), while repeated-measures ANOVAs and Newman–Keuls tests were used for AAL and AAC ($n = 41$).
*$P < 0.05$, one-tailed; **$P < 0.001$, one-tailed; †$P < 0.01$, two-tailed; ††$P < 0.001$, two-tailed; †††$P < 0.0001$, two-tailed.

The relationship of improvement on the MI to improvement on the FQ Agoraphobia factor was then tested as a further measure of convergent validity. For each of the 48 clients on whom both scales were available pre- and posttreatment, a ratio of improvement scores was computed. Scores on the MI-AAC and MI-AAL scales were summed before the ratio was computed to make the MI more comparable to the less specific Agoraphobia factor. A Pearson correlation of these two ratios of 0.47 ($P < 0.001$) was obtained, indicating significant agreement on improvement.

In a final test of construct validity, we hypothesized that scales purporting to measure agoraphobic symptoms should distinguish between an agoraphobic and nonagoraphobic sample. Biserial correlations on MI-AAL and MI-AAC total scores, as well as individual item scores, and a classification of agoraphobic vs normal control group membership were computed. Total scores biserials for AAL and AAC were 0.80 and 0.69, respectively ($P < 0.001$). Mean scores for the normal control group were 1.07 (SD = 0.08) for AAC and 1.25 (SD = 0.24) for AAL. All individual item biserials, which ranged from 0.31 to 0.73 (median = 0.53) were also significant at the 0.001 level. Since the clinical and normal samples were found to differ on SES, analyses of covariance were computed to ascertain whether these results would hold after statistically controlling for this confounding variable. With the exception of two items, all Fs were significant at the $\leqslant 0.003$ level. These two items, "Being in rooms with fluorescent lights' and "Going into bars", were dropped from the scale with no loss in α, leaving a scale of 27 items. A Kendall τ_b nonparametric correlation of 0.58 ($n = 60$, $P < 0.001$) between PF and classification group also supported the validity of that measure. Median PF for the normal group was 0.02.

SAMPLE 2

Since the MI discomfort scales were so highly correlated with avoidance, they were omitted when the scale was revised, as were the two items previously described. Additional minor changes were made in arrangement and wording (see the Appendix for the revised MI). Consequently it was desirable to replicate reliability analyses with a new sample. An additional 83 agoraphobic clients took the MI before treatment, 36 of whom completed the scale twice for stability computations in the same manner as for the first sample.

To allow comparisons between agoraphobics' responses on the MI to those of other clients with anxiety disorders, a sample of 18 socially-phobic clients were assessed in the same fashion. The socially-phobic clients were similar to the agoraphobic ones on age, but tended to be of a higher social class [$t(88) = 1.80$, $P < 0.08$] and were more likely to be male ($\chi^2 = 11.40$, $P < 0.01$).

Results

The means and standard deviations for the two agoraphobic samples are highly similar with the exception of PF (see Table 1). However, the mode and median are more appropriate measures of central tendency for this measure in light of its extreme skewedness. These measures are virtually identical for the two samples. Comparisons of means on MI-AAL and MI-AAC on the two versions yielded ts of 0.08 ($df = 70$) and 0.45 ($df = 70$), respectively (Ps > 0.65). A Mann–Whitney U on PF of 512.5 ($P = 0.72$) indicated no significant differences between the two versions of the inventory on this measure. Test–retest reliability over a median of 8 pretreatment days was as high or higher for all measures than in the previous sample. Once again, only a moderate ($r = 0.44$) correlation was obtained between MI-AAL and MI-AAC scores.

Socially-phobic clients were compared to the agoraphobic clients on each individual item of the inventory as well as on total scale scores. Mean scores for the former sample were 1.35 (SD = 0.27) on MI-AAC and 1.56 (SD = 0.41) on MI-AAL. Both MI-AAC and MI-AAL discriminated the two samples successfully, $r_{biserial} = 0.54$ and 0.59, respectively ($Ps < 0.001$). On individual item analyses we expected all items except those clearly social in nature ("Restaurants" and "Parties or social gatherings") would discriminate between the two groups. Mann–Whitney tests showed agoraphobics to score higher on all items (all $Ps < 0.05$) except for "Parties or social gatherings" on which the social phobics tended to have higher scores on AAC ($P < 0.10$). Thirteen clients with social phobia and 56 with agoraphobia responded to the question about PF with median reported frequencies of 1.33 and 2.66, respectively. This difference was significant on a Mann–Whitney test [$z = 1.94$, $P < 0.05$ (one-tailed)]. Because the two samples differed on some demographic variables, in a final set of analyses multiple-regression analyses were conducted for total scores on MI-AAL and MI-AAC. Sex and SES were forced to enter the equations first. Diagnostic category continued to account for a significant proportion of the variance for MI-AAC ($F = 34.21$, $P < 0.0001$) and MI-AAL ($F = 30.55$, $P < 0.0001$). Thus the MI proved to be a sensitive measure of agoraphobia *per se* rather than a reflection of anxiety disorders in general.

Additional data (means, reliability coefficients etc.) are provided in the Appendix.

DISCUSSION

The MI was found to be a stable and internally consistent scale that is sensitive to change with treatment. Test–retest reliability for the avoidance scales was high; that for panic frequency was somewhat low, but not suprisingly so given the episodic nature of panic. Tests of concurrent and construct validity were uniformly positive as well. Future research to investigate the relationship of MI scores to those obtained from different methods of measuring avoidance or behavioral avoidance tests would be desirable, although typically such correlations are low. The MI scales offer well-validated assessment measures of a broad range of agoraphobic avoidance behavior. This sample of items, wider than that of previous inventories, makes the scale more useful for planning behavioral treatment as well as a sensitive measure for research. Moreover, the scale provides an important distinction in measuring avoidance alone and accompanied. A considerable number of agoraphobics are quite mobile when accompanied but severely restricted when on their own.

Several suggestions may be offered for the use of the MI. The number of clients reporting a high frequency of panic pretreatment is low, and even among these clients, panic frequency is variable. Similar problems have been noted by Michelson and Mavissakalian (1983). The resulting measure, consequently, not only requires nonparametric statistics which are less powerful than parametric, but will also contain considerable S error. An investigator wishing to contrast treatment effects on panic would therefore do well to use a repeated-measures design and to have a larger n than would be necessary for studying avoidance behavior.

A second consideration is the use of individual items on the avoidance scales. The reliability and validity of most individual items is such that the clinician or researcher is warranted in interpreting scores and changes on all but a few items in their individual as well as total score form. Thus situations of particular concern to a client can be made focal. Means, standard deviations and item reliability correlations for individual items in Table A.1.

The last issue concerns the distinction between avoidance and discomfort on ratings of agoraphobia. Consistent with prior investigations (e.g. Marks and Mathews, 1979), these ratings were noted to be redundant on the MI, and the Discomfort scale was dropped. There are, however, a number of clients seeking treatment who report considerable situational anxiety, but allow themselves no avoidance. Data from the present study support the reliability and validity of modifying the MI to obtain discomfort ratings for use with such clients. Additional validity data on discomfort are available from the senior author.

Acknowledgements—The authors wish to thank the following for their contributions to the development of these scales: Priscilla Bright, Richard Gallagher, Sharon Graham, Wanda Hodges, Beth McAllister, Nancy McBrayer and Diane Zimmerman.

Reprint requests should be sent to Dianne L. Chambless, Department of Psychology, The American University, 4400 Massachusetts Avenue, N.W., Washington, DC 20016, U.S.A.

REFERENCES

American Psychiatric Association (1980) *Diagnostic and Statistical Manual of Mental Disorder*, 3rd edn. APA, Washington, D.C.

Barlow D. H. and Mavissakalian M. (1981) Directions in the assessment and treatment of phobia: the next decade. In *Phobia: Psychological and Pharmacological Treatment* (Edited by Mavassakalian M. and Barlow D. H.), pp. 199–245. Guilford Press, New York.

Beck A. T., Ward C. H., Mendelson M., Mock J. and Erbaugh J. (1961) An inventory for measuring depression. *Archs gen. Psychiat.* **4,** 561–571.

Chambless D. L. (1982) Characteristics of agoraphobics. In *Agoraphobia: Multiple Perspectives on Theory and Treatment* (Edited by Chambless D. L. and Goldstein A. J.), pp. 1–18. Wiley, New York.

Chambless D. L. and Goldstein A. J. (1980) Agoraphobia. In *Handbook of Behavioral Interventions* (Edited by Goldstein A. J. and Foa E. B.), pp. 322–415. Wiley, New York.

Chambless D. L., Foa E. B., Groves G. A. and Goldstein A. J. (1979) Brevital in flooding with agoraphobics. *Behav. Res. Ther.* **17,** 243–251.

Emmelkamp P. M. G. (1982) *In vivo* treatment of agoraphobia. In *Agoraphobia: Multiple Perspectives on Theory and Treatment* (Edited by Chambless D. L. and Goldstein A. J.), pp. 43–75. Wiley, New York.

Eysenck H. J. and Eysenck S. B. G. (1975) *Eysenck Personality Questionnaire*. EdITS, San Diego, Calif.

Goldstein A. J. (1982) Agoraphobia: treatment success, treatment failures, and theoretical implications. In *Agoraphobia: Multiple Perspectives on Theory and Treatment* (Edited by Chambless D. L. and Goldstein A. J.), pp. 183–213. Wiley, New York.

Goldstein A. J. and Chambless D. L. (1978) A reanalysis of agoraphobia. *Behav. Ther.* **9,** 47–59.

Hollingshead A. B. (1957) Two-factor index of social position. Unpublished manuscript. (Available from 1965 Yale Station, New Haven, Conn.)

Kincannon J. (1978) A brief form of the MMPI. *J. consult. clin. Psychol.* **32,** 319–325.

Marks I. M. (1970) Agoraphobic syndrome (phobic anxiety state). *Archs gen. Psychiat.* **23,** 538–553.

Marks I. M. and Mathews A. M. (1979) Brief standard self-rating for phobic patients. *Behav. Res. Ther.* **17,** 263–267.

Michelson L. M. and Mavissakalian M. (1983) Temporal stability of self-report measures in agoraphobia research. *Behav. Res. Ther.* **21,** 695–698.

Spielberger C., Gorsuch A. and Lushene R. (1970) *The State–Trait Anxiety Inventory*. Consulting Psychologists Press, Palo Alto, Calif.

Watson J. P. and Marks I. M. (1971) Relevant and irrelevant fear in flooding: a crossover study of phobic patients. *Behav. Ther.* **2,** 275–293.

Wolpe J. and Lang P. (1964) A fear survey schedule for use in behavior therapy. *Behav. Res. Ther.* **2,** 27–30.

APPENDIX

The Mobility Inventory for Agoraphobia (MI)

Name: _____ Date: _____

1. Please indicate the degree to which you avoid the following places or situations because of discomfort or anxiety. Rate your amount of avoidance when you are with a trusted companion and when you are alone. Do this by using the following scale.

    1, Never avoid
    2, Rarely avoid
    3, Avoid about half the time
    4, Avoid most of the time
    5, Always avoid

(You may use numbers half-way between those listed when you think it is appropriate. For example, $3\frac{1}{2}$ or $4\frac{1}{2}$).

Write your score in the blanks for each situation or place under both conditions: when accompanied, and, when alone. Leave blank those situations that do not apply to you.

Places	When accompanied	When alone
Theatres	_____	_____
Supermarkets	_____	_____
Classrooms	_____	_____
Department stores	_____	_____
Restaurants	_____	_____

Continued

Museums   _____   _____

Elevators   _____   _____

Auditoriums or
  stadiums   _____   _____

Parking garages   _____   _____

High places   _____   _____

  Tell how high _____   _____   _____

Enclosed spaces
  (e.g. tunnels)   _____   _____

Open spaces
(A) Outside (e.g. fields, wide
    streets, courtyards)   _____   _____

(B) Inside (e.g. large
    rooms, lobbies)   _____   _____

Riding In
Buses   _____   _____

Trains   _____   _____

Subways   _____   _____

Airplanes   _____   _____

Boats   _____   _____

Driving or riding in car
(A) At any time   _____   _____

(B) On expressways   _____   _____

Situations
Standing in lines   _____   _____

Crossing bridges   _____   _____

Parties or social
  gatherings   _____   _____

Walking on the street   _____   _____

Staying at home alone   NA   _____

Being far away
  from home   _____   _____

Other (specify)   _____   _____

We define a *panic attack* as:
    (1) a high level of anxiety accompanied by
    (2) strong body reactions (heart palpitations, sweating, muscle tremors, dizziness, nausea) with
    (3) the temporary loss of the ability to plan, think, or reason and
    (4) the intense desire to escape or flee the situation. (Note, this is different from high anxiety or fear alone.)
Please indicate the total number of panic attacks you have had in the last 7 days. _____ .

Table A.1. Individual items means, standard deviations and test–retest reliability coefficients for the MI Avoidance scales

Places	When accompanied			When alone		
	$\bar{X}$	SD	r	$\bar{X}$	SD	r
Theatres	2.17	1.06	0.72	3.89	1.49	0.87
Supermarkets	2.08	1.04	0.76	3.00	1.42	0.85
Classrooms	2.22	1.28	0.82	2.68	1.56	0.88
Department stores	2.27	1.04	0.63	3.30	1.38	0.79
Restaurants	2.39	1.23	0.70	3.52	1.48	0.75
Museums	2.18	1.33	0.68	3.75	1.66	0.77
Elevators	1.89	1.31	0.78	2.65	1.67	0.87
Auditoriums or stadiums	2.66	1.32	0.70	3.67	1.44	0.84
Parking garages	1.55	0.86	0.75	2.27	1.46	0.73
High places	3.06	1.49	0.72	3.61	1.52	0.83
Enclosed spaces (e.g. tunnels)	2.52	1.40	0.70	3.29	1.52	0.76
Open spaces						
(A) Outside (e.g. fields, wide streets, courtyards)	1.77	1.08	0.66	2.38	1.51	0.68
(B) Inside (e.g. large rooms, lobbies)	1.98	1.01	0.69	2.87	1.50	0.69
Riding in						
Buses	2.85	1.50	0.75	3.82	1.44	0.77
Trains	2.85	1.52	0.80	3.79	1.43	0.89
Subways	3.20	1.47	0.90	3.95	1.33	0.84
Airplanes	3.41	1.64	0.88	4.14	1.46	0.76
Boats	3.29	1.60	0.81	3.91	1.56	0.67
Driving or riding in car						
(A) At any time	1.97	1.08	0.48	2.87	1.51	0.71
(B) On expressways	2.46	1.32	0.54	3.59	1.56	0.71
Situations						
Standing in lines	2.46	1.18	0.78	3.24	1.31	0.87
Crossing bridges	2.15	1.35	0.57	3.00	1.69	0.79
Parties or social gatherings	2.25	1.21	0.80	3.03	1.48	0.83
Walking on the street street	1.90	1.02	0.61	2.62	1.45	0.82
Staying at home alone		NA		2.14	1.28	0.84
Being far away from home	2.78	1.22	0.58	3.98	1.33	0.68

Table A.2. Pearson product–moment correlations among scales on the MI for agoraphobic clients at pretest, posttest and 6-month follow-up

	DAC-PRE	DAC-POST	DAC-FU	DAL-PRE	DAL-POST	DAL-FU	AAC-PRE	AAC-POST	AAC-FU	AAL-PRE	AAL-POST	AAL-FU
DAC-PRE	(0.69) n = 67	0.59 n = 69 P = 0.001	0.27 n = 30 P = 0.147	0.38 n = 73 P = 0.001	0.25 n = 69 P = 0.038	0.46 n = 30 P = 0.010	0.91 n = 73 P = 0.001	0.62 n = 70 P = 0.001	0.54 n = 40 P = 0.001	0.41 n = 73 P = 0.001	0.26 n = 70 P = 0.031	0.35 n = 40 P = 0.026
DAC-POST			0.74 n = 31 P = 0.001	0.39 n = 69 P = 0.001	0.55 n = 72 P = 0.001	0.70 n = 31 P = 0.001	0.60 n = 69 P = 0.001	0.9 n = 79 P = 0.001	0.76 n = 39 P = 0.001	0.41 n = 72 P = 0.001	0.62 n = 72 P = 0.001	0.67 n = 39 P = 0.001
DAC-FU				0.41 n = 30 P = 0.023	0.62 n = 31 P = 0.001	0.85 n = 32 P = 0.001	0.50 n = 30 P = 0.005	0.72 n = 31 P = 0.001	0.94 n = 32 P = 0.001	0.24 n = 30 P = 0.208	0.52 n = 31 P = 0.003	0.76 n = 32 P = 0.001
DAL-PRE				(0.84) n = 68	0.73 n = 69 P = 0.001	0.41 n = 30 P = 0.023	0.38 n = 73 P = 0.001	0.28 n = 70 P = 0.018	0.23 n = 40 P = 0.155	0.94 n = 74 P = 0.001	0.76 n = 70 P = 0.001	0.67 n = 40 P = 0.001
DAL-POST						0.74 n = 31 P = 0.001	0.20 n = 69 P = 0.100	0.44 n = 72 P = 0.001	0.58 n = 39 P = 0.001	0.69 n = 69 P = 0.001	0.87 n = 72 P = 0.001	0.74 n = 39 P = 0.001
DAL-FU							0.44 n = 30 P = 0.016	0.68 n = 31 P = 0.001	0.82 n = 32 P = 0.001	0.41 n = 30 P = 0.023	0.67 n = 31 P = 0.001	0.93 n = 32 P = 0.001
AAC-PRE							(0.77) n = 71	0.7 n = 73 P = 0.001	0.54 n = 44 P = 0.001	0.37 n = 77 P = 0.001	0.23 n = 73 P = 0.049	0.32 n = 44 P = 0.037
AAC-POST									0.80 n = 43 P = 0.001	0.27 n = 73 P = 0.021	0.52 n = 76 P = 0.001	0.58 n = 43 P = 0.001
AAC-FU										0.20 n = 44 P = 0.191	0.49 n = 43 P = 0.001	0.64 n = 46 P = 0.001
AAL-PRE										(0.91) n = 72	0.78 n = 73 P = 0.001	0.65 n = 44 P = 0.001
AAL-POST												0.49 n = 43 P = 0.001
AAL-FU												

Table A.3. Means and standard deviations for the MI Discomfort Accompanied and Discomfort Alone scales across treatment for 29 agoraphobic clients

	Pretest		Posttest		6-Month follow-up	
	X̄	SD	X̄	SD	X̄	SD
Alone	3.18	0.91	2.43	0.73	1.84	0.71
Accompanied	2.41	0.82	1.87	0.55	1.45	0.49

Two weeks of intensive daily treatment were followed by varying amounts of treatment in the follow-up period; 42% clients had additional *in vivo* exposure sessions (an average of 8.20, SD = 5.90, each). Test-retest stability over an average pretreatment interval of 31 days of 39 clients showed no significant change without treatment, (t_{alone} = 1.01, P = 0.32; $t_{accompanied}$ = 0.05, P < 0.96). Differences between pretest, posttest and follow-up are all significant with the Newman–Keuls test (all Ps < 0.01).

MODIFICATION OF EXPECTATIONS IN CASES WITH OBSESSIONAL RITUALS

V. MEYER

Academic Department of Psychiatry Middlesex Hospital Medical School, London

(*Received 6 May* 1966)

Summary—Some theoretical issues in relation to the nature of obsessional rituals and the most commonly adopted method of behaviour therapy for this disorder are critically considered. On the basis of these considerations, a different method—"modification of expectations" or "reality testing" is put forward and its successful application to two patients described and discussed.

INTRODUCTION

THE LITERATURE on long-term follow-up investigations of obsessional neurosis appears to show that the prognosis for this illness is worse than that of any other neurotic disorder (Kringlen, 1965). Grimshaw (1965), surveying the effects of different types of treatment, concludes that "no elaborate type of therapy seems indicated" and there is little use for electroconvulsive treatment; supportive psychotherapy with or without simple sedation or stimulation is "probably the most practical of all".

As regards the efficacy of behaviour therapy for obsessional neurosis, no firm conclusion can be drawn since no adequate control trials have been reported. The three studies, in which more than a single case was treated, indicate a poor response of such patients to behaviour therapy. Thus Walton and Mather (1963) treated six patients, two of whom responded well. Cooper *et al.* (1965) included ten patients with obsessional rituals in their sample of neurotics and reported three as showing improvement. Amongst a large sample of neurotics treated by Wolpe (1958) there were nineteen patients with obsessions and compulsions. Unfortunately Wolpe did not give separate data on the results of therapy for these cases. It would appear, however, that he obtained better results than those reported by the other behaviour therapists. The chosen treatment method in these and other reports has been mainly systematic desensitization in imagination and/or in real life situations.

The purpose of this paper is to discuss some theoretical issues and to describe and consider a different method of treatment applied to two chronic patients with obsessional rituals, both of whom responded well.

THEORETICAL CONSIDERATIONS

In a theoretical paper, Metzner (1963) attempts to account for some features of obsessional neurosis in terms of learning principles. He draws on some relevant animal experimental studies which may be regarded as suggestive analogues of compulsive and ritualistic actions of obsessional patients. Such actions are conceived of as learned avoidance responses, originally evoked in traumatic situations. The well-known resistance to extinction of traumatic avoidance responses, under conditions of repeated occurrence of a conditional stimulus, is implicated to account for the persistence of the behaviour in obsessional cases where it is elicited by definable stimuli and reinforced by obvious rewards. For cases exhibiting "fixated" and apparently "senseless" ritualistic acts to relieve spontaneously recurring, internally-produced anxiety, he refers to five animal studies. It appears that a response may become "fixated" when it reduces an approach drive and the anxiety associated with the drive. Also, an avoidance response may be "fixated" if it becomes unsuccessful.

We need not concern ourselves with the validity of the cited studies as examples of the conditions under which behaviour becomes "fixated" (it may be noted that in some of these studies extinction, although prolonged, did take place). The main interest here lies in the paradigms of unsuccessful avoidance.

It seems to the author that Metzner's analysis is questionable. The animals were trained to succeed at avoiding punishment (UCS) and then these conditioned avoidance responses were rendered unsuccessful by the re-introduction of punishment, either following avoidance responses or randomly. Thus, "fixated" and increased rate of responding resulted from a failure to avoid the UCS. Metzner suggests that these experiments may be considered as equivalent to the compulsive and "senseless" ritualistic actions of obsessionals. This does not appear to be so because in the case of obsessionals the persistence of rituals is assumed by him to result from "unsuccessful avoidance" of conditioned stimuli and not unconditioned stimuli. If rituals are conceptualized as learned avoidance responses then they are successful in that they eliminate the original punishment and reduce the anxiety elicited by conditioned stimuli associated with the original punishment. Clinical evidence provides some support for this, i.e. patients report that performance of rituals does reduce anxiety and that if they are prevented from carrying them out increased anxiety is experienced.

In view of these considerations it seems justifiable to argue that the persistence of rituals may be accounted for in terms of traumatic avoidance responses, irrespective of the source of conditioned stimuli. Metzner's analysis is acceptable if "unsuccessful avoidance" merely means that the repeated occurrence of conditioned stimuli is not under the subject's control. Thus, if an external anxiety-producing stimulus occurs frequently and cannot be eliminated by the patient from his environment, repeated rituals may take place to reduce the evoked anxiety. Similarly, if the sources of anxiety are frequently recurring impulses or ideas which are not under the patient's voluntary control, repeated and apparently "senseless" ritualistic actions may ensue.

Wolpe (1958) distinguishes this type of obsessional behaviour—which he calls anxiety-reducing obsessions—from another type which he refers to as "anxiety-elevating obsessions". In the latter the immediate response to anxiety-provoking stimuli has secondary effects of increasing anxiety (e.g. an intrusive and persistent impulse to strike people). It may well be that in this case the impulse represents a socially unacceptable act which originally acquired immediate anxiety-reducing properties but the consequences of which eventually led to the development of conditioned anxiety. The impulse persists as a response to similar anxiety-producing situations probably because it momentarily reduces anxiety; but from the first moment of awareness of the impulse conditioned anxiety emerges and prevents the execution of the act. Whether this is the case or not, the important point is that in "anxiety-elevating obsessions" the frequent occurrence of conditioned stimuli is not under the patient's control.

It may well be that the main difference on the behavioural level between the phobic and the obsessional arises from the nature of the conditioned stimuli. The former, in contrast to the latter, can completely withdraw from anxiety-provoking stimuli (e.g. the housebound housewife). Furthermore, the phobic avoids phobic situations apparently because of the anticipation of unchecked anxiety. The obsessional executes rituals not only to check and to reduce the elicited anxiety, but also, at least in some cases, to deal with a fear that if these are not performed he or his family will be eventually afflicted by some disaster, e.g. illness or punishment in the after-life.

These differences may have important implication for treatment of the two conditions. Wolpe (1964) pointed out that deconditioning of neurotic anxiety in both anxiety-reducing and anxiety-elevating obsessions and in phobias is the crux of therapy. On theoretical grounds, systematic desensitization by reciprocal inhibition is the method of choice for behavioural disorders mediated by anxiety. So far this has been borne out by practice in relation to phobias but not to obsessional rituals. Some plausible reasons for the differential response to this method may be offered.

It is important for the outcome of treatment to put the symptom under control not only during specific treatment situations but also between them. Recurrence of the symptom between the treatment sessions is detrimental. Such control is relatively easy to achieve in phobics but extremely difficult, it not impossible, in patients with persistent symptoms like rituals (Meyer and Crisp, 1966).

Secondly, it has been customary to desensitize obsessionals to stimuli eliciting anxiety and rituals. This may not be sufficient, particularly in chronic patients. As Walton and Mather (1963) point out, and they provide some evidence for their view, "the extinction of both the initial autonomic conditioned responses and the motor reactions may be required".

Thirdly, the above-mentioned concern of some patients with eventual untoward consequences of not performing rituals may hamper the response to treatment and may be responsible for relapses.

The above points paved the way for a different approach to the treatment of obsessional rituals. Learning theories take into account the mediation of responses by goal expectancies, developed from previously reinforcing situations. When these expectations are not fulfilled, new expectancies may evolve which, in turn, may mediate new behaviour. Thus, if the obsessional is persuaded or forced to remain in feared situations and prevented from carrying out the rituals, he may discover that the feared consequences no longer take place. Such modification of expectations should result in the cessation of ritualistic behaviour.

A recent survey of the animal experimental literature furnishes some support for the plausibility of this formulation (Lomont, 1965). A number of studies indicate that preventing or delaying the escape from a feared conditioned stimulus hastens the extinction of that response. Also, some evidence suggests that such extinction may not be due to learning a new instrumental response which interfered, or was incompatible, with the original avoidance response. The final conclusion of Lomont's review is that it is still essentially an open question as to whether the concept of reciprocal inhibition or extinction is more appropriate for explaining "reciprocal inhibition therapy."

The above considerations appeared to justify the use of the "modification of expectations" method of treatment to two chronic patients with obsessional rituals, both of whom expressed a strong belief that the non-performance of rituals would lead to "disastrous consequences". One of these patients had previously failed to benefit from systematic desensitization.

DESCRIPTION OF PATIENTS

Case 1

A 33-yr-old, intelligent school-mistress, married with one child and with a 3-yr history of severely disabling washing and cleaning rituals, was admitted under the care of Professor D. Hill.

Some compulsive checking (doors, lights and marking of school papers) occurred 3 yr prior to the main complaint. A few months after the birth of her baby she began to over-wash the nappies so that no diaper rash would occur. After the birth of the child she started to worry about anything which might be "dirty". A wide range of objects and situations, e.g. door knobs, blankets, clothes, dustbins, meat, animals, men, sexual intercourse, were considered as "contaminated by dirt" and led to almost continuous washing and cleaning. It appeared that the reason for this behaviour was due to a fear of "dirt" which was grounded in the belief that any contact with it would result in her baby and/or her being "eventually afflicted by some disease due to contamination."

Prior to the first hospitalization the main symptoms of her illness were: she would only touch foreign objects with tissue paper; would not allow her daughter or her husband to touch any of the "contaminated objects"; unless the husband and the daughter were "clean" she would not permit them to touch her; stopped having sexual intercourse; became housebound because of the fear of "contamination"; touching any of the "contaminated objects" evoked excessive washing of hands; spent most of her time washing and rewashing clothes and scrubbing her house (used £3-10-0 a week worth of soap, detergents and disinfectants and developed a severe dermatitis on her hands).

Had three previous admissions to three different hospitals and attended psychiatric O.P.D. (given ECT, supportive psychotherapy, drugs and behaviour therapy).

During her last admission to this department (October, 1963) was submitted to a combination of systematic desensitization in imagination and in real-life situations to stimuli graded along a "contamination dimension". Her child was admitted with her and her husband was seen periodically in order to make him more assertive with his wife. She remained on tranquilizers throughout the treatment, the total time of which was 35 hr (WAIS Full Scale IQ-120; MPI-N34; E22).

Responded to treatment and at the time of discharge (January, 1964) was improved. Reported less anxiety in relation to the customary stimuli but her belief in the "affliction" remained virtually unchanged.

On discharge, home situation ("higher chances of contamination") produced a rapid deterioration; and a few treatment sessions at home did not prevent a complete relapse a month later.

Was readmitted in October 1964 to be considered for leucotomy. It was decided to postpone this and to try another method of behaviour therapy.

Case 2

A 47-yr-old school-mistress of superior intelligence, married with one daughter and with a history of 36-yr duration of compulsive thoughts and rituals, was admitted under the care of Professor D. Hill.

Recalls that at the age of 10, after hearing a passage from the Bible—"to blaspheme against the Holy Ghost is unforgivable"—became preoccupied with this thought. Shortly afterwards, words like "damn", "blast", "bloody" came to her mind despite all her attempts to resist them. These "blasphemous thoughts" elicited guilt and anxiety which she found could be alleviated by repeating any activity on hand a certain number of times. By the age of 13, these intrusive thoughts became of a direct sexual nature, centred on the sexual words and the idea of having sexual intercourse with the Holy Ghost. The associated anxiety continued to be allayed by performing repetitive acts, e.g. dressing and undressing, writing and rewriting, walking up and down staircases, retracing her steps.

At 29, attended a psychiatrist for 9 months with little improvement. At 31, deteriorated and was admitted for 3 months; had ECT and drugs and left unimproved. Soon after developed a compulsive urge to kill her husband and daughter and was leucotomized at the age of 32. Two years later embarked on psycho-analysis and remained in it for 11 years. At the end of the analysis was much worse. Now not only the intruding sex words and thoughts about the Holy Ghost evoked ritualistic behaviour, but also any activity with sexual meaning, e.g. shutting drawers, putting in plugs, cleaning a pipe, wiping tall receptacles, putting on stockings, eating oblong objects, doing things four times (association with four letter Anglo-Saxon words), stepping on patterns in the shape of sex organs, entering underground trains etc. Whenever possible avoided these activities, e.g. stopped eating bananas and sausages, and her life became a "misery". For instance, it took her hours to dress or to travel short distances. Attributes this change to the psycho-analysis since in it she learned about the extent of sexual symbolization. After 2 yr of supportive psychotherapy and drugs with another psychiatrist, was referred to the National Hospital to be considered for another leucotomy. This was decided against and was referred to this Department for behaviour therapy in March 1964.

On the ward appeared mildly depressed, constantly agitated and frequently engaged in avoidance and ritualistic behaviour. These were more pronounced when on her own. Said she felt constantly afraid waiting for the thoughts to "strike her". Symptoms appeared to subside when occupied with interesting and important tasks, e.g. writing children's stories. The illness did not prevent her from working as a part-time supply teacher of children. While teaching, to which she was dedicated, the symptoms did not trouble her. It was interesting that marital sexual intercourse was completely satisfactory and did not give rise to her ritualistic behaviour.

Regarded her rituals as "acts of repentance for being a sinner". Felt that non-performance of rituals would result in her family being eventually "afflicted by some disaster" and was convinced that she herself would face an "eternal damnation". Did not regard herself as excessively religious but had high moral standards (WAIS Full Scale IQ-134; MPI-N34, E28).

TREATMENT AND RESULTS

Case 1

At the outset the patient was withdrawn from all drugs and put under continuous supervision by nursing staff. In order to make the supervision easier and more effective, the taps in her room were turned off and a strict control over her cleansing agents exerted. Persuasion, reassurance and encouragement were used to prevent the patient from unnecessary and excessive washing and cleaning. The patient was instructed to report any avoidance behaviour and compulsion to engage in her rituals. The treatment sessions, carried out by the author, consisted of making the patient perform activities which persistently presented difficulties for her (e.g. touching door knobs, handling dust bins, her child's toys, milk bottles; using public transport; shopping).

After 4 weeks of this regime the supervision and restrictions were gradually withdrawn and she was allowed more and more freedom to do things on her own. Five weeks later she was permitted to go home for weekends and was discharged from the hospital after 3 additional weeks. Throughout this period she was required to report any difficulties encountered and these were dealt with, in the manner described above, by the author and nursing staff. She was also requested to keep a daily record of the number of unnecessary washings and avoidances (total stay in the hospital 12 weeks; total time of treatment carried out by the author 20 hr).

Response to treatment. The main object of the initial stage was achieved, that is, unnecessary and excessive washing was almost eliminated. Avoidance behaviour, on the other hand, increased at the beginning but then gradually diminished and eventually she was able to undertake a number of activities which previously she "would not dream of tackling". At first other aspects of her behaviour presented a bit of a problem. She fluctuated between resentful, aggressive behaviour, questioning the relevance of treatment and hospital standards of hygiene, and bouts of agitation and weeping in which the fear of "contamination" and "disease" was constantly expressed. She did, however, respond well to reassurance and encouragement and gradually became more co-operative and settled.

With the advent of freedom during the next phase of treatment, ritualistic washing re-emerged but only to the extent of seven per day on the average. The average number of avoidances was about five. Eventually these daily averages dropped to four and three respectively. Throughout this stage she appeared more co-operative, optimistic and

involved in treatment. Her fear of eventual consequences was expressed less frequently and with less conviction. Towards the end of this period her mood became depressed and she voiced strong doubts whether she would be able to maintain the improvement following discharge from the hospital. She also reproached herself for the illness and for being a "bad wife and mother".

Follow up. She and her husband have been seen six times over a period of 14 months since discharge. The main aspects of her progress are as follows: As regards her symptomatic behaviour, the frequency of washing and cleaning, as compared with pre-discharge level, remained virtually unchanged. The duration and thoroughness of these activities, however, increased considerably. Nevertheless she now spends only 15s. weekly on cleansing agents (pre-treatment amount was £3-10-0) and her hands are free of dermatitis. Her avoidance of "dirty objects" continues but if forced to tackle them she can refrain from washing. The strength of her belief in the consequences of contact with "dirt" remains considerably reduced. She goes out for walks, shopping and uses public transport; only occasionally feels apprehensive, particularly when dogs are around. More recently she started going to cinemas and joined a tennis club. For the last 6 months she has been working as a teacher in primary schools and enjoys it.

Her relationship with her daughter and husband improved greatly. She displays much less concern about their getting in touch with "dirt" and has become more tolerant and permissive towards them. She also has resumed marital sexual intercourse, but continues to be frigid. At the last interview her husband said: "We're more than pleased with the progress; now we are a united family, enjoying each other's company."

Case 2

The treatment procedures and management of this patient were essentially the same as those used for Case 1. The treatment sessions, carried out by the author, aimed at creating stress for the patient, e.g. she was required to "imagine having an intercourse with the Holy Ghost", to clean a smoking pipe, to swear, to eat sausages, or to walk straight without looking down and stopping. After each session special care was taken to prevent her from performing rituals; encouragement, reassurance, persuasion and occasional relaxation were used. She was also encouraged to discuss with a minister the validity of her belief in the "eternal damnation" for her thoughts.

Following 3 weeks of this regime, supervision and restrictions were gradually reduced. Her husband was required to sit in on a few treatment sessions in order to instruct him how to prevent the patient from engaging in ritualistic behaviour. After $2\frac{1}{2}$ weeks she was allowed to go home for a weekend and was discharged from the hospital a week later (total stay in the hospital—9 weeks; total time in treatment with the author—25 hr).

Response to treatment. The objective of the first stage was only partially achieved mainly because it was not possible to exert constant and strict supervision but also because of the nature of rituals, i.e. sudden onset and a great variety of quick actions. However, the average daily number was reduced initially from about eighty to twenty. As regards the frequency of "intruding thoughts", virtually no change was reported by her. In time, a gradual reduction of both phenomena took place and eventually she averaged 6·5 rituals and eight "thoughts" daily.

At first, treatment sessions with the author were very distressing for her and elicited a great deal of anxiety and weeping. These reactions rapidly subsided and eventually the

patient herself would request the author to deal with items which continued to present difficulties. Her co-operation was excellent and involvement in the treatment very high. She also expressed a strong faith in the therapist and displayed a strong attachment to him. Unlike in Case 1, the second phase did not produce an increase in symptomatic behaviour; in fact a further reduction occurred—two rituals and seven "thoughts" daily. Her co-operation, and involvement remained high. She also seemed to be less convinced about the validity of her belief in untoward consequences. Shortly before the discharge her optimism about the outcome of treatment abated somewhat and she became rather agitated.

Follow up. The patient has been followed up for 1 yr 10 months. During this period she and her husband were seen eighteen times. Originally the appointments were frequent and were then gradually extended. For 21 months she kept a thorough record of the daily number of rituals and intrusive thoughts. The chart shows mild fluctuations with the overall means of about four rituals and seven thoughts daily. Thus the improvement attained at the termination of treatment has been maintained.

Thoughts about the Holy Ghost, swear words and the performance of activities with "sexual connotations" only occasionally elicit rituals but these are not repeated any more. She does not seem to be fully aware of the onset of ritualistic behaviour—"I am taken by surprise"—but can stop herself immediately. Some "sexual acts" evoke apprehension and hesitation in undertaking them and some are frequently avoided, but on the whole she is capable of coping reasonably well with most. Travelling and walking present almost no difficulties. Soon after discharge she obtained a teaching post and was recently promoted to the unestablished grade.

All the symptoms are enhanced when she is alone, and when feeling angry or resentful. She also reports that the belief in, and fear of, the consequences of "sinful thoughts" and of non-performance of "acts of repentance" are present but their intensity remains reduced.

Both the patient and her husband are extremely pleased with the outcome.

DISCUSSION

In the present state of knowledge it would be unjustifiable to argue with any degree of assurance that the impressive improvement of these patients' chronic and severe illness was due to the treatment given. It cannot be strongly maintained, however, that a mere stay in the hospital and the relationship with the therapist *per se* could account for the improvement. Also, it seems unlikely that spontaneous recovery occurred during this period. Furthermore, the relevance of the treatment is strengthened in view of various previous unsuccessful therapeutic attempts which both patients received. Of particular importance here is the fact that Case 1 relapsed completely after systematic desensitization by reciprocal inhibition.

Even if there was sufficient evidence to demonstrate that the treatment method used here was responsible for the maintained improvement, one could not pin-point the relevant aspects of the treatment.

However, the favourable outcome in both patients is consistent with the formulation which provided the rationale for the therapeutic method adopted. Two aspects of the treatment are deemed as important: the realization by the patients that persistent non-performance of rituals did not lead to the immediate experience of unchecked arousal of anxiety; the patients' expectations of "disastrous consequences" were not fulfilled.

The main purpose of the treatment was the modification of the patients' expectations and some evidence, admittedly based only on the patients' verbal reports, indicates that this was achieved to some degree. One may assume that a completely successful modification of expectations would lead to a complete elimination of ritualistic behaviour. This may be extremely difficult to attain for cases whose expectations refer to a distant future, as in Case 2 who feared "eternal damnation", since reality testing could not be effected. Bridger and Mandel's findings (1964) suggest that verbal manipulations may not be effective for subjects who had "first signalling direct experience" and in order to change their expectancies and maladaptive patterns of behaviour undergoing of "new first signalling direct experiences" may be necessary.

The therapeutic approach adopted here requires that the treatment be intensive and a strict control over patients' behaviour exerted. This could not be achieved by one therapist. Nursing staff, given adequate instructions, are entirely capable of effecting the requirements. The treatment does not appear uneconomical in terms of time spent by the therapist in treatment and by nursing staff in supervision.

In view of the general lack of success with this type of disorder, it is hoped that research workers and other practitioners will consider and take up this method of treatment. The main effort should be concentrated on the efficacy of the method and the range of its application.

REFERENCES

BRIDGER W. H. and MANDEL I. J. (1964) A comparison of GSR fear responses produced by threat and electric shock. *J. psychiat. Res.* 2, 31–40.
COOPER J. E., GELDER M. G. and MARKS I. M. (1965) Results of behaviour therapy in 77 psychiatric patients. *Br. med. J.* 1, 1222–1225.
GRIMSHAW L. (1965) The outcome of obsessional disorders. *Br. J. Psychiat.* 111, 1051-1056.
KRINGLEN E. (1965) Onsessional neurotics. *Br. J. Psychiat.* 111, 709–722.
LOMONT J. F. (1965) Reciprocal inhibition or extinction? *Behav. Res. & Therapy* 3, 209–219.
METZNER R. (1963) Some experimental analogues of obsession. *Behav. Res. & Therapy* 1, 231–236.
MEYER V. and CRISP A. H. (1966) Some problems in behaviour therapy. *Br. J. Psychiat.* 112, 367–381.
WALTON D. and MATHER M. D. (1963) The application of learning principles to the treatment of obsessive —compulsive states in the acute and chronic phases of illness. *Behav. Res. & Therapy* 1, 163–174.
WOLPE J. (1958) *Psychotherapy by Reciprocal Inhibition.* Stanford University Press, Stanford.
WOLPE J. (1964) Behaviour therapy in complex neurotic states. *Br. J. Psychiat.* 110, 28–34.

Thoughts provoked by pain

H. C. PHILIPS

Department of Psychology, Shaughnessy Hospital, 4500 Oak Street, Vancouver, B.C., Canada

(Received 13 February 1989)

Summary—Despite the growing interest in the cognitive component of chronic pain, little information has been collected on the variety of thoughts provoked by pain experience. A new assessment instrument (the Cognitive Evaluative Questionnaire—CEQ) has been utilized with 127 chronic pain patients and their cognitions classified into seven discrete clusters. The results confirm the heterogeneity of pain cognitions, the majority of which are likely to play a role in enhancing or perpetuating chronic pain. The relationship of these cognitions to chronic avoidance behaviour is discussed.

INTRODUCTION

Chronic pain provokes diverse thoughts. Some are maladaptive (maintaining or exacerbating pain) and others help to minimize or curtail pain experience and behaviour.

The common attitude of patients to pain is firmly founded on the traditional medical model (Rachman and Philips, 1975; Philips, 1988). Pain is regarded as a sensory experience that reflects the type and extent of tissue damage or disturbance. It is therefore not surprising that many of the cognitions provoked by pain are negative and alarming. It is likely that many of these thoughts exacerbate pain and/or prevent active coping. Philips (1987) has hypothesized that this occurs because of the role that certain cognitions play in limiting and inhibiting behaviour.

Despite the growing interest in the cognitive component of chronic pain (Turk, Meichenbaum and Genest, 1983), little systematic information has been collected on the varied cognitive reactions of pain sufferers to pain increment. Bakal (1982) introduced a self-report instrument to help therapists identify these psychological antecedents and correlates of headache. This Headache Assessment Questionnaire (HAQ) consists of 48 statements describing the thoughts, feelings and/or attitudes provoked by the onset of headache. Penzien, Holroyd, Holm and Hursey (1985) provided information about the discriminant and construct validity of the scale. Their principal component analysis suggested that the scale has several dimensions: 'non-productive rumination', 'self-denigration', 'irritation over environmental difficulties', and 'tension or worry'. This study provides an important reminder that cognitive reactions to pain are unlikely to be homogeneous, and that it will be useful to consider the subclasses or types of thoughts provoked by continuing pain.

Progress in the management of the chronic pain problems will be aided by clarity about the nature and changes in chronic pain cognitions. For example, significant shifts in appraisal of both problem size and self-efficacy following successful behaviour treatment that emphasized self-management of pain (Philips, 1987a). She also suggested that cognitions associated with chronic pain (expectations and beliefs) play a prominent role in motivating the unadaptive avoidance behaviour that is so characteristic of chronic pain sufferers (Philips, 1987b). Certainly appraisals may act to maintain the pre-occupation with bodily symptoms often seen in these people. A more accurate method of assessing the thoughts of chronic pain patients, prior to treatment, would guide and focus cognitive approaches and allow for evaluation of cognitive changes as a result of treatment.

The major aim of the present study is to clarify the cognitive components of the chronic pain reaction in chronic pain sufferers.

METHOD

(1) Subjects

A group of 127 chronic pain patients (44 male, 83 female) were evaluated during a chronic pain assessment interview. The group contained 72 back pain sufferers, 26 headache cases (migraine, 'tension' or mixed headache types), and 26 with other pain loci (i.e. facial, knee, multiple loci, etc.). They reported histories of pain from 1 to 30 yr, the average being 5.5 yr.

(2) Measures

All Ss filled in the following inventories:

(i) the Cognitive Evaluation Questionnaire (CEQ).

This questionnaire was developed from the Bakal Headache Questionnaire (the HAQ, see Bakal, 1982) in order to make it appropriate for any type of chronic pain problem. (Copies are available from the author upon request). Ss are asked to indicate the extent to which a thought, feeling or attitude occurred to them at the onset of a severe pain attack, using a scale from 0 to 3, where 0 = indicated not at all, 1 = was equivalent to slightly, 2 = to fairly and 3 = to very much. This questionnaire produces 48 discreet ordinal responses.

(ii) Beck Depression Inventory (Beck, Ward, Mendelson, Mock and Erbough, 1961).

(iii) McGill Pain Questionnaire (Melzack, 1975).

(3) Procedure

Prior to participating in a chronic pain assessment interview, all Ss were asked to fill in the three measures.

(4) Statistical analysis

An exploratory cluster analysis was selected as the statistical method best suited to the classification of the 48 statements on the CEQ. This method allows the degree of 'similarity' of meaning (or sense) of the 48 questions to be established on the basis of Ss responses. It requires no assumptions with respect to data distribution and accepts ordinal measurement, allowing the data to give rise to groupings of statements.

Similarity between statements was determined by the Goodman–Kruskal γ Co-efficient (Roscoe, 1975) using the Complete Linkage Distance. This statistic was selected rather than the often-used Pearson Product Moment Correlation Co-efficient (Johnson and Wichern, 1982), because of the ordinal nature of the data.

RESULTS

(A) Using a cluster analysis, 48 statements of the CEQ were classified into 7 discreet groups or clusters, on the basis of the patients responses.

A pictorial representation of the cluster analysis is shown in Fig. 1. The distance measure used between statements is 1 less than the absolute magnitude of the Goodman–Kruskal Co-efficient. γ values fall between -1 and $+1$ with those close to $+1$ indicating positive agreement between the responses to any two statements. The dendogram shows the complete linkage distances.

Looking at this dendogram from the top (i.e. perfect agreement being $+1$), the splits were examined down to approx. 0.9 γ level. Eight splits were evident suggesting separate clusters. Being close to $+1$, they can be considered primary or fundamental groupings. The questionnaire items that fall into each of these eight groups are shown in Table 1.

Although there are some items that seem out of place, the majority in each cluster appear to make psychological sense as a subgroup of cognitions. A rough classification is offered for each of these eight in an attempt to simplify discussion of them.

(B) The correlation matrix show the degree of association between the seven clusters defined by the analysis above (Table 2). The co-efficients are lowest between Cluster 1 and the other clusters. None of the correlations are high enough to suggest redundant cognitions. The highest (cluster Nos. 5/7) have only 38% of variance in common. The clusters with the highest correlation make good psychological sense: helplessness and emotionality ($r = 0.62$); expectations of pain increase and emotionality ($r = 0.58$); a desire to withdraw/avoid and emotionality ($r = 0.57$).

(C) The correlations of each cluster with the Beck Depression Inventory and the McGill Pain Questionnaire are shown in Table 3. Cluster No. 1 ('positive coping') was virtually unassociated with the depression scores. The latter is most highly associated with Cluster Nos 3 and 7 (disappointment with self and emotionality). Helplessness (Cluster No. 5) although showing some link, does not stand out as being tighly associated with the Beck Depression Scores.

(D) The McGill Pain Questionnaire shows strong associations between the Affective (PRI) and all clusters (with the exception of Cluster No. 1). Not surprisingly, Cluster No. 7 (emotionality) has the highest correlation co-efficient ($r = 0.45$) with the Affective (PRI) component.

(E) Dividing the pain Ss into back pain ($N = 72$), headache ($N = 26$) and facial pain/other loci ($N = 29$), the extent to which they differed in the 7 clusters was assessed. The Kruskal–Wallis test showed significant differences on cluster Nos 5–7 ($P = 0.02$ for each cluster). This finding arises from the lower scores on these clusters for back pain sufferers only.

(F) No significant difference was found between sexes on cluster variables using the Kruskal–Wallis test.

(G) Dividing the Ss into three subdivisions based on the duration of the pain [0–11 months; 1–5 yr; and 5–30 yr (45, 42 and 40 Ds respectively)], no differences appeared in cluster scores—with one exception. Cluster No. 7 (emotionality) was significantly elevated ($P = 0.02$—Kruskal–Wallis) because of a drop in the scores on this cluster in the middle epoch (1–5 yr).

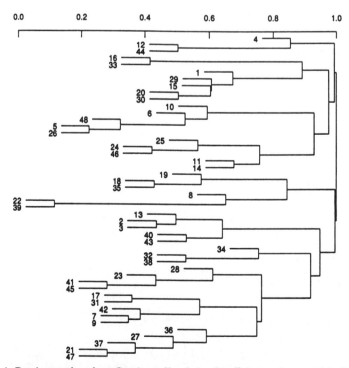

Fig. 1. Dendogram based on Goodman Kruskal γ Co-efficient, using complete linkage.

Table 1. The list of questionnaire items associated with each of the primary 'fundamental' groupings, or cluster variables

C No.	Cluster name	Question	Cognition
C1	Positive coping	4	I'm determined not to take any medications.
		12	I'm trying to relax to bring this pain under control.
		44	I'll just have to act as natural as I can.
C2	Desire to withdraw	16	I can tell this one won't be that bad.
		33	Oh well, now I have a good excuse not to do what I was supposed to do.
		1	I feel tired.
		29	When I stop and think about my pain, it seems to get worse.
		15	I wish little things wouldn't bother me as much as they do.
		20	I wish I could take the time to lie down.
		30	I wish I didn't have to do anything today.
C3	Disappointment with self	10	I don't want to upset anyone by telling them I am in pain.
		6	I am afraid of what people think about my pain.
		48	I feel guilty about having pain episodes.
		5	I am angry with myself for being in pain.
		26	I am disappointed with myself for having another bout of pain.
C4	Causal rumination	25	I wonder if they will ever find a cure for my pain.
		24	I wonder how long this will last.
		46	I am wondering why I am getting more pain.
		11	I wonder what it would be like to never be troubled by pain.
		14	I hate to take medicine, but it looks like I'll have to this time.
C5	Helplessness	19	I am thinking, "Why me. Why do I always feel pain?"
		18	I feel helpless.
		35	I can think of nothing other than my pain.
		8	I am concerned that there is something physically wrong with me.
		22/39	I guess all I can do is wait it out.
C6	Concern re: effects of pain	13	I am worrying about my future plans and commitments.
		2	I wonder if I'll have to cancel my plans.
		3	How am I going to concentrate with this awful pain?
		40	It's so hard to work with pain.
		43	I am afraid that my pain will get worse.
		34	I'm worried about my family obligations.
		32	I wish people would be more considerate.
		38	When I feel like this, I need comfort from friends and family.
C7	Emotional reactivity	28	I knew this was coming.
		23	Listening to this chatter makes me feel sick.
		41	I wish everyone would be quiet and leave me alone.
		17	I feel very worked up.
		31	I feel panic stricken.
		42	I feel totally frustrated because I have another period of pain.
		7	I am depressed because I am in pain.
		9	I feel frustrated because I let myself get overcome by pain.
		36	I have no patience with others.
		27	This pain is driving me crazy.
		37	I feel that I am being punished.
		21	I can't help feeling angry about what happened before.
		47	I get upset each time I think about what happened before.

Table 2. Intercorrelation matrix of cluster scores

	C1	C2	C3	C4	C5	C6	C7
C1		0.200	0.280	0.207	0.077	0.110	0.071
C2			0.487	0.375	0.392	0.442	0.574
C3				0.379	0.275	0.478	0.552
C4					0.447	0.402	0.442
C5						0.519	0.619
C6							0.576
C7							

Table 3. Spearman correlation between cluster variables and two psychological indices: Beck Depression Inventory, and McGill Pain Questionnaire (PRI score)

	C1	C2	C3	C4	C5	C6	C7
Beck depression scores	0.051	0.401	0.427	0.154	0.385	0.41	0.523
McGill Pain Questionnaire sensory (PRI)	0.212	0.286	0.220	0.133	0.116	0.174	0.220
Affective (PRI)	0.117	0.350	0.433	0.403	0.300	0.354	0.451
Evaluative (PRI)	−0.004	0.214	0.193	0.351	0.303	0.226	0.317

DISCUSSION

Using a data-driven statistical approach to the classification of the cognitions of chronic pain sufferers, seven separate clusters of reaction were delineated. One of these groups (C1) appears to contain thoughts that may well prove to be positive and therapeutic reactions to pain. The majority of self-management approaches to chronic pain teach relaxation response to pain, reduction or elimination of the use of medications to deal with pain, and the reduction and eliminations of demonstrations of pain (non-verbal pain behaviour). Thus, these statements are likely to be reported by patients after successful behavioural treatment. For this reason, as well as the fact that Cluster No. 1 correlates poorly with the other clusters, it has been felt wiser to consider this cluster differently from the other six. It is called 'positive coping' and it is not appropriate to sum it with the other cluster scores in deriving any single measure of maladaptive cognitive reaction.

The remaining six clusters emphasize the maladaptive nature of the majority of a cognitive reactions associated with continuing or incrementing pain experience. They are cognitions that support the passive, avoiding behaviour of people whose expectations of control over pain are low, and whose pain increments with activity. Categories have been suggested for each of these clusters on the basis of the questionnaire items which form the cluster. It was hoped to capture in these names the predominent characteristic of the cognitions of the cluster. The seventh cluster entails by far the largest number of items and had been called 'emotional reactivity'. It was felt necessary to retain this as one cluster because, in the Cluster Analysis, further splitting occurred at a greater distance than 0.9 γ co-efficient (see Fig. 1). However, the emotional reactions being summarized in this cluster include irritability, frustration, depression, anger and emotional upset.

Cognitive behavioural therapeutic methods focus on the modification of beliefs and attitudes such as those contained in the questionnaire. This is done in an attempt to lead the person to become an active manager of his own problem (Turk et al., 1983; Philips, 1988). Evidence of the changing attitudes of patients as a result of such interventions can be found in a recent study by Philips (1987). Significant shifts in appraisal of both problem size and self-efficacy followed the behavioural treatment.

This questionnaire is likely to be of value to cognitive—behaviour therapists working with pain patients. It will help to identify the prominent maladaptive cognitive reactions to be focused upon in treatment (i.e. causal ruminations and/or emotional reactivity). In addition, it will allow the evaluation of the treatment intervention in terms of changes in an individual's cognitions. The outcome of cognitive programs often are assessed by general behavioural indices of improvement, and have not included details of the cognitive changes that are assumed to be instrumental in leading to behavioural and subjective improvement.

It has been suggested that the cognitions of chronic pain patients—expectations, beliefs, predictions—may play a prominent role in motivating and/or maintaining the avoidance behaviour so characteristic of such patients (Philips, 1987b). A model has been proposed in which it was hypothesized that expectations about the effects of exposure as well as self-efficacy beliefs were linked to avoidance behaviour.

This investigation of the cognitions of chronic pain patients lends independent support to these predictions by validating at least two clusters of cognitions: concern with respect to pain increases (expectations of pain), and helplessness (low self-efficacy beliefs). Predictions from the Philips model of chronic pain can now be evaluated by investigation of the effect on these clusters of behavioural exposure and/or non-avoidance methods.

The Cluster Analysis results of this study are different from those found in the Discriminant Function Analysis of headache sufferers cognitions undertaken by Penzien et al. (1985). Despite the low proportion of headache sufferers in the current study (i.e. 20% only), differences in patient samples would not appear to explain the discrepancy between the studies. The current study found headache cases not to differ from back and other pain locii in cluster scores.

Unfortunately, Penzien et al. have published only a sample of the HAQ items with the largest loadings on each of the four major factors. However, from this information it seems probable that their results differ from those of the present study in more than factor or cluster names. The most likely explanation of this discrepancy is in the different methods of analysis used. Factor analytic methods assume continuous measurements and normal distributions while the data from the CEQ are non-continuous discreet ordinal judgements. As a consequence, distorted results may well have been forthcoming. The present study, however, does confirm the suggestion made by Penzien that the cognitions of chronic pain sufferers are heterogeneous, and would benefit from subdivision.

Development of this questionnaire is needed. An unequal number of statements fell in the seven clusters, making some more robust than others (i.e. Cluster No. 7 vs Cluster No. 1). Future studies need to be undertaken which amplify Cluster Nos 1, 3 and 4, following which a replication of this study would be useful. In the meantime, the questionnaire can be used by deriving percent cluster scores and/or summing clusters 2–7 into a cognitive score.

A check on consistency was built into the scale by Bakal by providing duplicate items embedded in the questionnaire (Nos 22 and 39). In this study, they form the bottom (i.e. first formed) cluster, having a γ co-efficient of $+0.89$. If one judges consistency of response on this basis, it appears that Ss answer the questionnaire with care. However, better evaluation of response consistency is needed. Further studies of the stability of cognitive reactions to chronic pain are necessary as current levels of pain may well affect the cognitive response reports. It will be necessary in such a study to attempt to collect reliability data with pain intensity levels controlled.

Cluster analysis is an exploratory technique designed to produce a hierarchical structure (without imposition of a model) from a list of input distances. Some experimenter choice must be made, with statistical guidance. The criteria for the choices rest on the psychological validity or potential usefulness of the final dendogram. The analysis depends in part on the prevailing understanding of chronic pain components and processes.

Acknowledgements—The author wishes to express gratitude to Peter Schumacher, Department of Statistics, UBC for his useful contribution to the statistical evaluation of the data. In addition, thanks are due to the Back Pain Clinic and Department of Psychology, Shaughnessy Hospital for making the data available.

REFERENCES

Bakal D. A. (1982) *The Psychobiology of Chronic Headache*. Springer, New York.
Beck A. T., Ward C. H., Mendelson M., Mock J. and Erbaugh J. (1961) An inventory for measuring depression. *Arch. gen. Psychiat.* **4**, 561–571.
Everitt B. (1980) *Cluster Analysis*, 2nd edn. Heineman, London.

Hunter M. (1983) The headache scale: a new approach to assessment of headache pain based on pain descriptions. *Pain* **16,** 361–373.

Johnson R. A. and Wichern D. W. (1982) *Applied Multivariate Statistical Analysis.* Prentice–Hall, Englewood Cliffs, N.J.

Melzack R. (1975) The McGill Pain Questionnaire: major properties and scoring methods. *Pain* **1,** 277–299.

Penzien M. S., Holroyd K. A., Holm J. E. and Hursey K. G. (1985) Psychometric characteristics of Babal Headache Assessment Questionnaire. *Headache* **25,** 55–58.

Philips H. C. (1987a) The effects of behavioural treatment for chronic pain. *Behav. Res. Ther.* **25,** 365–377.

Philips H. C. (1987b) Avoidance behaviour and its role in sustaining chronic pain. *Behav. Res. Ther.* **25,** 273–279.

Philips H. C. (1988) *The Psychological Management of Chronic Pain: A Manual.* Springer, New York.

Rachman J. and Philips H. C. (1975) *Psychology and Medicine.* Temple–Hall.

Roscoe J. T. (1975) *Fundamental Research Statistics for the Behavioural Sciences,* 2nd edn. Holt, Rinehart & Winston, New York.

Turk D. C., Meichenbaum D. and Genest M. (1983) *Pain and Behavioural Medicine. A Cognitive Behavioural Perspective.* Guilford Press, New York.

PSYCHOLOGICAL INTERVENTION FOR THE CONTROL OF PAIN

Matisyohu Weisenberg

Department of Psychology, Bar-Ilan University, Ramat-Gan 52100, Israel

Summary—The psychology of pain control has grown greatly in the past 25 years. Many psychololgical techniques have been applied successfully to the regulation of both acute and chronic pain. Many of these techniques rely upon anxiety reduction and/or the installation of perceived control. The connection between pain perception and anxiety and perceived control is, however, not yet fully understood.

The two major approaches to the treatment of chronic pain are the behavioral and cognitive–behavioral. Each approach has been shown to be effective in the treatment of chronic pain. However, which are the critical ingredients and what are the psychological limits of pain control via these and other approaches are still to be determined. What is lacking more than anything else is a comprehensive psychological theory of pain perception and control.

INTRODUCTION

During the past 25 years the field of pain control has grown at an ever-increasing rate. Before 1970, research centered mainly upon the sensory-physiology and psychophysics of pain (see Hardy, Wolff and Goodell, 1952). Within psychology *per se* there was minimal emphasis upon pain as a topic. In their classic text of experimental psychology, Woodworth and Schlosberg (1956) barely mention pain. Others used the phenomena of pain as a means of testing theoretical formulations such as cognitive dissonance (see Zimbardo, Cohen, Weisenberg, Dworkin and Firestone, 1966) and were less interested in studying pain itself.

Sternbach (1968) wrote one of the first books from a psychological perspective that went beyond the limited laboratory approach. The 1975 book by Weisenberg was a result of teaching and clinical experience in which it became readily apparent that clinicians were unaware of the findings of laboratory research, while researchers focused upon topics that were far less important to clinical practice.

Today, pain phenomena are considered an integral part of psychological theory, experimental research and clinical practice. New books, journals and chapters on pain abound. There has been considerable progress in understanding pain phenomena even if some of the old problems remain unresolved.

To understand pain phenomena from a psychological perspective it is important to deal with the definition of pain. It will then be possible to examine the two major factors implicated in the psychological regulation of pain: (1) anxiety and (2) perceived control. Theoretically, two approaches to the clinical treatment of pain have predominated: (1) behavioral and (2) cognitive approaches. The behavioral and cognitive views and techniques will be described. A brief assessment will be made of what we have achieved and what still appears to be missing.

DEFINING PAIN

The definition of pain is not merely an intellectual exercise, as it has had both conceptual and practical implications. Early laboratory work that mainly emphasized the sensory aspects of pain viewed pain in stimulus–response terms. Pain was defined as a reaction related to actual or impending tissue damage on the basis of the stimuli that arouse it, e.g. radiant heat, electric shock, bradykinin, etc., and on the basis of the responses measured to indicate evidence of its presence, e.g. expressions of hurt, withdrawal, blood pressure changes, etc. Following in this tradition Sternbach (1968) defined pain as an abstract concept that refers to "(1) a personal, private sensation of hurt; (2) a harmful stimulus which signals current or impending tissue damage; (3) a pattern of responses which operate to protect the organism from harm" (p. 12). As has been noted earlier (Melzack, 1973; Weisenberg, 1977) definitions of pain must adequately deal with identified pain phenomena. Especially not covered adequately by stimulus–response, tissue-damage definitions is the pain of clinical, pathological origin. It is not always possible to identify the stimuli leading to pain reports, especially in chronic pain (see Chapman and Bonica, 1985; Loeser, 1986; Weisenberg, 1980, 1983). A simple tissue-damage approach also must be examined with care. Pain such as causalgia can persist months after the original tissue damage has healed. The oft-repeated classical report of Beecher (1956) has shown that, despite exensive tissue damage, soldiers wounded in battle refused morphine in contrast to their civilian counterparts with similar amounts of tissue damage. The setting was shown to be more important than the tissue damage.

Conceptually, the Gate Control theory (Melack and Wall, 1965, 1982) is still the most relevant for an understanding of the various aspects of pain. Pain phenomena are viewed as consisting of several components, discriminable in time, space, and intensity However, pain also has an essential aversive–cognitive–motivational and emotional component that leads to behavior designed to escape or avoid the stimulus. Different neurophysiological mechanisms have been described for each system.

Great importance is attached to central nervous system processes. Higher cortical areas are involved in both discriminative and motivational systems influencing reactions on the basis of cognitive evaluation and past experience. More than any other theoretical approach, gate control emphasizes the tremendous role of psychological variables and how they affect the reaction to pain. Especially with chronic pain, successful pain control often involves changing the cognitive–motivational components while the sensory component remains intact. Hypnosis, anxiety reduction, desensitization, attention distraction as well as other behavioral approaches can be effective alternatives and supplements to pharmacology and surgery in the control of pain. Their effect is felt mostly on the cognitive-motivational components of pain.

Regardless of the correctness of the gate control wiring diagram or whether or not a gating mechanism actually exists, conceptualizing pain as having both sensory and cognitive–motivational components can lead to different views of pain control as compared with stimulus–response conceptions or other simple animal models. Bolles and Fanselow (1980), for example, presented a model in which fear and pain are viewed as conflicting processes. When the fear system is engaged it triggers the endorphin system to inhibit pain. The pain system, in turn, promotes rest and healing. Pain and fear are seen as competing. This view of pain phenomena runs counter to most clinical experience in which anxiety is seen as exacerbating pain rather than reducing it. The Bolles and Fanselow (1980) model, however, is based upon animal work that filters out the influence of such things as cognitions, social and cultural expectations, etc. It can thereby lead to different conceptualizations and likely treatment recommendations. For example, following through on Bolles and Fanselow model, to reduce pain of a pathological origin it might be desirable to frighten the patient.

There are other recent illustrations of a reconceptualization of pain phenomena in sensory terms. Algom, Raphaeli and Cohen-Raz (1986) and Algom (1986), for example, have proposed a functional theory of pain based upon laboratory psychophysical functions. The proposed model is presented as being more readily testable and quantifiable. Emotional components are viewed as important but secondary to the sensory. Clinically, however, and especially for chronic pain the functional approach does not appear as meaningful even if it has succeeded in demonstrating that certain aspects of gate control theory are not accurate.

The International Association of Pain (IASP) has tried to come to grips with the complexity of pain phenomena by categorizing and defining pain terms as well as the range of pain syndromes (1986). Each diagnostic entity has been given a number, a process reminiscent of DSM III (1980). IASP (1986) Repeated the definition of pain first published in 1979: "An unpleasant sensory and emotional experience associated with actual or potential tissue damage, or discribed in terms of such damage" (1986, p. S217). This definition attempts to overcome difficulties mentioned earlier. Pain is defined independent of the stimulus. Although pain is viewed in terms of tissue damage it is not dependent upon actual tissue damage. Conceptually, the definition accepts the notion that pain consists of both sensory and emotional components. Most relevant for the psychologist is the stress made by the notes on term usage. "Activity induced in the nociceptor and nociceptive pathways by a noxious stimulus is not pain, *which is always a psychological state* (italics added), even though we may well appreciate that pain most often has a proximate physical cause" (1986,

p. S217). Pain is viewed as a psychological experience and is not synonymous with the physiological activity occurring within the neuron.

The IASP definition was developed mainly for clinical use rather than for experimental activity. However, conceptually, it has great meaning as well. It also squarely lays down a challenge to psychologists who supposedly are the experts at dealing with psychological phenomena.

A further clinical refinement has been made by Loeser (1986) and Chapman and Bonica (1985). *Acute* pain is what occurs with tissue damage. With tissue healing most often the pain complaint disappears. *Chronic benign* pain is rarely associated with tissue damage. Whatever injury existed should have healed. *Chronic malignant* pain is similar to acute pain in that there is repeated and continued tissue damage. Both acute and chronic malignant pain require aggressive management using adequate levels of analgesia. Chronic benign pain, in turn, is made worse by aggressive treatment. Rest and inactivity, surgery and potent analgesic drugs contribute to the exacerbation of the problem. Psychological coping techniques, treating the depression as well as defining and working toward realistic life goals have helped patients to deal with the problems of chronic benign pain.

ANXIETY AND ITS EFFECT ON PAIN

Many of the psychological techniques for the reduction of pain involve anxiety reduction. Patients are taught to use a variety of anxiety- and stress-reducing procedures such as relaxation, hypnosis, modeling, biofeedback, as well as a variety of cognitive activities (see Weisenberg, 1977, 1980, 1983, 1984). Chapman and Bonica (1985) and Chapman (1986) have described a physiological substrate showing the interrelationship of pain and anxiety for both acute and chronic pain. Sternbach (1974) has tied anxiety most to acute pain. However, anxiety has been shown to be relevant to chronic situations as well. Spear (1967) reported that 45–50% of patients attending a hospital psychiatric clinic reported pain. Reports of both persistent and non-persistent pain most frequently occurred in patients suffering anxiety states. Similarly, Merskey (1968, 1980) reported that the most common psychiatric diagnoses found in psychiatric patients with persistent pain were anxiety neuroses, hysteria, and neurotic depression. Krishnan, France, Pelton, McCann, Davidson and Urban (1985) reported that anxiety was highly prevalent among chronic pain patients, especially among those with a major depression. Malow, West and Sutker (1986) performed a signal detection analysis of responses to pressure pain stimulation as a function of anxiety level among chronic drug abuse patients. Highly anxious compared with low and moderately anxious patients demonstrated lower pain thresholds, lower pain report criteria and decreased sensitivity.

The concept 'the fear of pain', especially when combined with an avoidance coping strategy, has recently been proposed as a key theoretical element of a model to explain the long-term exaggerated response to pain (Lethem, Slade, Troup and Bentley, 1983; Slade, Troup, Lethem and Bentley, 1983). Anxiety also has been reported to be an extremely likely outcome of treatment for cancer and is seen as one of the contributors to cancer pain and distress (see Bond, 1985). Bond (1985) consequently has recommended greater use of psychological treatment methods including psychotropic drugs for the treatment of cancer pain. In general, pain and anxiety have been associated with each other. The general conclusion has been that the greater the anxiety, the greater is the pain (Sternbach, 1968). To reduce pain, in turn, treatment involves reducing the anxiety.

However, even though control and reduction of anxiety are viewed as a means to reduce pain, the exact relationship of pain and anxiety is still not fully understood. Thus, prescribing diazepam or teaching muscular relaxation will not automatically by itself result in the absence of pain (see Lehrer, 1972). In preparing patients for surgery or for other procedures, Janis (1958, 1983), for example, has placed great emphasis upon an optimal level of anxiety as leading to more favorable post-surgical outcomes that include less use of narcotic analgesics as well as faster hospital discharge. However, other researchers have not been able to support the Janis contention (see Cohen and Lazarus, 1973; Taenzer, Melzack and Jeans, 1986).

In studies of hypnosis, Hilgard and Hilgard (1975) have reported that anxiety reduction does not imply reduction in pain perception. It is possible to have a reduction in anxiety occurring simultaneously with a reported increase in pain perception. Others, such as Wall (1979), have viewed pain as a need state to promote injury recovery rather than as a sensation. In the immediate state pain may not occur. Fight or flight activities may take precedence. Once relative safety and care can be obtained pain may be perceived. It is at this stage that anxiety becomes important and almost synonymous with pain. It is helpful in promoting recovery and preventing futher damage. Thus, it has been noted that men wounded in battle in which there is a high level of anxiety may not react at all to the pain of wounds during the battle or even for some time afterwards. Pain may be perceived only after the anxiety level of battle has been reduced. Thus, it would appear that knowledge of anxiety level *per se* is not adequate to predict reaction to pain.

The Bolles and Fanselow (1980) model mentioned earlier has taken a view almost opposite to those who treat pain patients. They postulate that fear *inhibits pain*. Bolles and Fanselow explain what appears, in their formulation, as the less common occurrence of increased reaction to pain as a consequence of fear as due either to prolonged muscle tension or to the confusion of fear and pain. That is, the person being provided with some amount of nociception is in reality reacting to fear while calling it pain. A person is really not feeling pain at the dentist's office after the injection of anesthesia into the tissue, only fear, which he has mislabeled as pain.

Yet, based upon clincial experience it is not possible to deny the centrality of anxiety. With all of the importance attributed to anxiety and its reduction in regard to pain control, it is surprising how little controlled research has been done to clarify its role. Of course, anxiety, too, is a complex concept. It has been used to refer to a state based upon the particular environment in which the person finds himself at the moment (state anxiety). It has also been used to refer to a trait (trait anxiety), that is, to a personality attribute reflecting the status of the person generally (Spielberger, Gorsuch and Lushene, 1970). Paul and Bernstein (1973) refer to anxiety as a complex response involving subjective feelings of apprehension and tension associated with sympathetic physiological arousal. Arousal can be due to an external stimulus source or to the memory of a past experience. In common with pain, anxiety is perceived as uncomfortable and leads to behaviors that will reduce it.

Weisenberg, Aviram, Wolf and Raphaeli (1984) were able to demonstrate differential effects of anxiety on pain perception and behavior. Under laboratory conditions of high anxiety, the same instructions could either lower or raise the pain reaction by being more or less consonant with the pain reaction. Ss who received electric shock as a pain stimulus were given a serial anticipation learning task under ego-arousal instructions whereby the anxiety was focused upon performing well (Task focus) or whereby the focus of the anxiety was placed upon the potential danger of the electric shock (Pain focus) or whereby the focus was placed both upon the learning and pain stimulus (Both focus). The Task focus condition yielded the lowest level of verbal pain ratings, lowest GSR to shock, but the largest number of learning errors compared with the Both focus group. The Pain focus condition was inbetween. The relationship between pain and rated anxiety accounted for some 34% of the variance. In a subsequent study of perceived control, the relationship of rated pain and anxiety accounted for only 10% of the variance (Weisenberg, Wolf, Mittwoch, Mikulincer and Aviram, 1985).

There seems to be little doubt that anxiety and pain are related. However, it is becoming clear that other factors must be added. Anxiety and pain are not synonymous. How anxiety affects the pain reaction must still be clarified.

One possibility is that anxiety could have an effect on the person's perception of the situation. Thus, Malow *et al.* (1986) found that their high anxious compared with moderate or low anxious Ss were not able to discriminate pain stimuli as well. Yang, Wagner and Clark (1983) found that chronic pain patients who were experiencing high levels of psychological distress were less able to discriminate harmful from innocuous situations on a paper and pencil rating task. Kent (1984) reported that high anxious compared with low anxious dental patients rated their expected dental treatment pain as higher, but reported actually experiencing less pain than the low anxious patients.

Anxiety may also function as a predisposing variable to create a mental set or schema (Beck, Rush, Shaw and Emery, 1979). Thus, in a study of cultural and racial differences in the reaction to pain, Weisenberg, Kreindler, Schachat and Werboff (1975) found that dental patients from Puerto Rico yielded the highest level of trait anxiety, whites the lowest, while blacks were in between. In a recent replication in Israel, Barak and Weisenberg (1986) found that dental patients who came from a mid-Eastern background displayed higher levels of trait anxiety than patients from a Western background. In both studies those patients who displayed a high level of trait anxiety also were more likely to display attitudes denying or avoiding dealing with pain. It is possible that anxiety, when tied together with other key variables such as instructional set or attitudes, could affect treatment outcome. This might be analogous to the results of Dworkin, Richlin, Handlin and Brand (1986) who demonstrated that successful treatment outcome for depressed or non-depressed chronic pain patients was based upon a different pattern of predictor variables. So, too, it is likely that a different set of variables could be important in determining treatment outcome depending upon the level of anxiety. It would also be necessary to separate state from trait anxiety as they may have different outcome implications (Taenzer et al., 1986).

PERCEIVED CONTROL AND ITS EFFECT ON PAIN

Perceived control has been shown and accepted to be a basic mediating variable for both acute and chronic pain (Chapman and Bonica, 1985; Chapman and Turner, 1986; Miller, 1980; Sternbach, 1974; Thompson, 1981). Clinically, treatment programs have placed great emphasis upon actively involving the patient so that he/she will achieve a degree of control over his/her pain. Sternbach (1974) and Gottlieb, Strite, Koller, Madorsky, Hockersmith, Kleeman and Wagner (1977) related perceived control as important ingredients in treatment to combat feelings of depression and learned helplessness (Seligman, 1975). Turk and Holzman (1986) have associated perceived control as affecting the patient's perceived self-efficacy (Bandura, 1977, 1982) of pain regulation.

Keeri-Szanto (1979) has described a technique whereby post-surgical patients are permitted to control the administration of their own narcotic medications. Patient-controlled, demand analgesia avoids many of the difficulties that occur in non-control situations. The required prescription has to be written once the patient indicates need for pain relief. To accomplish this the nurse must be summoned and convinced the patient 'really' is in pain and the drug must be signed out from the locked cabinet. The time it takes for the drug to be absorbed after injection also must be included. By the time all of the above has occurred, the drug level for which relief was originally requested is no longer the same and the pain has intensified. In contrast, with a patient-controlled, demand system patients do not abuse the amount of drug used. It was also possible to identify approximately 20% of the patients who were placebo responders and for whom lesser concentrations of narcotic were indicated. Drug administration can thus be accomplished in a way that leads to greater satisfaction of individual needs without necessarily using the most potent maximal dosages.

At this point in time numerous clinical studies have been performed on patient-controlled analgesia. The general conclusion is that for post-operative pain, the technique is safe, efficient, and often preferred by patients. It does not necessarily lead to greater pain relief (see Bollish, Collins, Kirking and Bartlett, 1985). Hill, Saeger and Chapman (1986) used patient-controlled analgesia for cancer patients undergoing bone marrow transplantation where there is severe pain for at least three weeks. They found that patients used approximately a third as much of morphine to achieve an equivalent level of pain control without the development of tolerance. However, patients did not always want to rely upon patient-controlled analgesia. At night, for example, they preferred continuous morphine infusion.

Numerous laboratory studies have indicated that providing subjects with some degree of control over the pain stimulation can reduce stress and increase pain tolerance. Bowers (1968), for example, has argued that lack of control increases anxiety and hence results in larger pain and stress reactions. Staub, Tursky and Schwartz (1971) related control to predictability. Uncertainty increases anxiety and results in less pain tolerance, while reduction of uncertainty increases tolerance. However, the issue of control and predictability, as with many other areas of pain perception, is not entirely clear. Corah (1973) tried to replicate a study showing that a control device introduced into the dental operatory would produce more cooperative behavior. Twenty-four children, ages 6-11, were provided with a two-button, green–red device to use during treatment. The control device group showed less response to high-arousal procedures as measured by GSR, but slightly more response during low-arousal procedures compared with a no-control group. Behavioral ratings of each group did not differ. Regarding the effectiveness of control these results are not entirely clear.

Both the studies of Geer, Davison and Gatchel (1970) and Glass, Singer, Leonard, Krantz, Cohen and Cummings (1973) demonstrated that providing the subject with the perception of behavioral control of shock resulted in less sympathetic arousal as measured by GSR. However, the change in ratings of painfulness as a function of perceived control was equivocal. Pain ratings were not obtained in the midst of the subject's performance, but rather at the end of the study. Once more the issue of control and pain reduction remains unclear.

In an analysis of control as a variable, Averill (1973) showed that it has been used to refer to behavioral control, cognitive control, or decisional control. He states that it is difficult to conclude that there is a direct relationship between stress and control. Reduction of uncertainty appears to be more important than maintaining behavioral control *per se*. Use of a warning signal to increase predictability does not always result in reduced stress and reactions to pain. The meaning of a warning signal must also be taken into account, e.g. does it mean continuous vigilance or does it imply that the person can relax during non-signalled tasks? Other factors that must be considered include the presence or absence of feedback that tells the subject how well he/she is controlling, the subject's ability to tolerate the information necessary for control, and what appears as larger short-term stress reactions but long-term adaptations. Abbott, Schoen and Badia (1984) concluded that unpredictable shocks are physiologically more stressful than predictable conditions when there are (1) either one or only a few sessions and (2) the stress is severe. However, when the experiment is conducted over several days and the stress is less severe, predictable conditions can be more stressful than unpredictable. Possibly this may be due to the greater habituation that occurs under unpredictable conditions because of the need to be on guard for a longer time—chronic physiological arousal. With the predictable conditions the subject can relax inbetween stressors and, as a consequence, adapt more slowly.

When predictability is kept constant, Miller (1980) has suggested the minimax hypothesis to account for the effects of perceived control. Control provides the person with a guaranteed upper limit on how bad the situation can become. A person with perceived control can insure having a lower maximum danger compared with the person without control. The minimax hypothesis views control as based upon an internal, stable attribution, e.g. the person's own response. When the situation is not controllable by the person himself/herself, external attributions must be considered, e.g. the experimenter, chance, etc. The external factor may or may not be able to guarantee the low maximum the person would like to have. Miller has suggested with some empirical support that an individual would be willing to turn over control to someone else when the person doubts his own self-efficacy in dealing with a threat, the action to reduce the threat is unclear or when the person perceived another to have more skill or expertise in dealing with the threat.

Who should control is a key issue in the health field. A patient who comes for treatment most often gives over control to his/her physician, nurse, physical therapist, etc. Not every person wants control even when he/she has the chance to exert such control. In breast cancer, for example, there are women who prefer to give the physician the right to decide what to do immediately following tissue examination. Other women prefer to have the right to decide upon surgery only after a full discussion of biopsy results (National Cancer institute, 1977). Post-mastectomy, Taylor, Lichtman and Wood (1984) found that belief that the patient could control her cancer *herself* or that *her physician* could control it was significantly associated with good adjustment.

To date there has been little systematic study of willingness to control on the part of the Ss. Yet, many of our psychological techniques for pain regulation depend upon the S's willingness to accept control, e.g. cognitive strategies, relaxation, etc.

Weisenberg *et al.* (1985) in a laboratory study compared five independent groups on perceived control. The groups were subject decision, subject behavior, subject decision plus behavior, experimenter control, and no control. For decisional control the S was told that at the end of each trial either he (subject control) or the experimenter (experimenter control) could decide to reduce the number of shocks he received on the next trial. For behavioral control the S was told that at the end of each trial he would connect the shocker to the shock source. In the combined condition the S could decide to reduce the number of shocks he received on the next trial and he would also connect the shocker to the shock source. Predictability was varied on a within-subject basis. In reality, all Ss received exactly the same number of shocks. Overall, the subject decision condition produced the strongest reaction to the pain stimulus, while the combined subject decision plus behavior condition yielded the lowest reactions to the pain. Unexpectedly, the experimenter control condition yielded the lowest pain reaction among Ss with high perceived self-efficacy for pain control, but one of the highest for Ss with low perceived self-efficacy for pain control. Predictability *per se* did not yield clear-cut results.

These results raise the question as to the degree of control to be given to a person in order to reduce the aversiveness of a situation. Is there a minimum amount needed? Is it better to avoid giving perceived control at all if the amount given is viewed as inadequate? It was expected that giving over control to the experimenter would lead to less distress among subjects with low perceived self-efficacy. Yet, the opposite results were obtained. In the clinic situation, the question is what happens? When a patient is in a situation that he/she feels he/she cannot control, when does giving over control to a competent other reduce distress and when does it increase distress? Does a person have to possess some degree of control before he can relinquish it to another? These are some of the questions that still must be answered.

BEHAVIORAL APPROACHES TO PAIN CONTROL

One of the most widely used treatment strategies for chronic benign pain is the behavioral approach to pain for which Fordyce (1976) has been its most well-known expositor. Fordyce has conceptualized pain behavior as the last step in the proces of nociception. Nociception, the first step, refers to stimuli that act on A-delta and C fibers. These can lead, but do not have to lead, to pain, a sensory experience based upon the perception of nociception. The third step, suffering, is a negative affective response generated in higher nervous centers by pain and by other situations as well, such as loss of loved objects, stress, anxiety, etc. Pain behaviors are the final step in the chain. They include speech, facial expressions, postural changes, seeking attention, refusing to work, etc. Pain behaviors are operants that are sensitive to the environmental contingencies and are not solely based upon nociception. In fact, pain behaviors are far from nociception in the conceptual chain and subject to many influences other than nociception.

Fordyce (1976) has placed great stress upon the distinction between acute and chronic pain when looking at pain behaviors. Acute, time-limited pain does lead to a variety of pain behaviors, e.g. grimacing, moaning, limping, etc. However, because of its short time duration it is more readily tied to its nociceptive stimulus and less subject to learning and conditioning. Acute pain may require some lifestyle changes temporarily. However, it ususally does not lead to a lasting change.

Chronic pain, however, persists for an extended period of time. Symptom behaviors continue to occur and are, therefore, more readily subject to learning and conditioning independent of the nociceptive stimuli that led to their original occurrence. In addition, the chronicity often leads to major, lasting changes in lifestyle, activities, and social relationships. Over time there is more and more rehearsal of sick behavior and less of well behavior. Once disability ceases, return to well behavior may become a formidable task.

In chronic pain, Fordyce distinguishes between respondent and operant pain behaviors. Respondent pain behaviors are those that are still tied to antecedent nociceptive stimuli and occur as a consequence of them. These behaviors can be dealt with by a variety of different strategies including medication, occasionally surgery, transcutaneous nerve stimulation, biofeedback, as well as a variety of cognitive coping strategies.

Operant pain behaviors are those which have existed for an extended period of time in an environment that has provided them with contingent reinforcement. Operant pain behaviors are usually not related to any given bodily site. They develop as a consequence of pain behavior becoming contingent upon reinforcement. Reinforcement can occur directly through such things as the positive consequences of pain medication or the attention of others. Reinforcement can occur indirectly through the effective avoidance of unpleasant circumstances, e.g. job, difficult social relationship, etc. Reinforcement can also occur as a consequence of the punishment of well behavior, especially by well-meaning family members who prevent the patient from doing such activity. Through reinforcement, pain behaviors may continue for reasons unrelated to the nociceptive tissue-damaging stimulation.

It should be pointed out that most cases of chronic pain involve a combination of respondent and operant pain behaviors. Fordyce's major treatment approach relates, however, mainly to operant pain behaviors. Treatment involves two major elements: (1) the reduction or elimination of pain behaviors, and (2) the restoration of well behaviors. This is done by changing the reinforcement patterns. Operant techniques are used to extinguish pain behaviors such as moans, requests for medication, or lack of physical activity because of pain. Attention is given for health-related activity; inattention for pain behavior. Well behaviors, including future activities, are planned out. Medication is managed to reduce or eliminate addiction. A time-contingent rather than complaint-contingent medication regimen is used in which the active ingredient is masked. The goal is to reduce the amount of active ingredients as treatment progresses. A carefully planned exercise program is initiated. Exercise is viewed as a well behavior in its own right as well as a building block to future behaviors. Rest and attention are used as reinforcers for meeting exercise quota and are with held for failure to meet the quota. A variety of graphs and records are kept to provide patients with feedback on progress. The spouse or family members are also trained. They are made aware of how they reinforce pain behaviors and are asked to become partners in reinforcing well behaviors.

There is great concern attached to generalization of well behaviors beyond the hospital environment. This is done by teaching the patient self-control and self-reinforcement. The patient's natural environment is also programmed. New behaviors and goals are also established. Patients are given passes to go home during treatment so that they can try out newly established behaviors in their natural environments. Following inpatient discharge, patients continue to come for treatment on a gradually reduced basis.

Most of the behavioral approaches are incorporated into multidisciplinary programs. Long-term follow-up studies indicate that these combined programs can be effective in dealing with chronic pain (Fordyce, Fowler, Lehmann, Delateur, Sand and Treischmann, 1973; Ignelzi, Sternbach and Timmermans, 1977; Keefe, Block, Williams and Surwit, 1981; Linton, 1986; Newman, Seres, Yospe and Garlington, 1978; Sternbach and Timmermans, 1977). What remains unclear in these programs is just what are the active ingredients. Must they be conducted only on an inpatient basis and how long must these programs be?

Some progress has been made to clarify the ingredients necessary for effective treatment. Sanders (1983) compared four behavioral treatment components in a multiple baseline additive design in the inpatient treatment of low back pain. Relaxation and social reinforcement of increased activity contributed to improvement, while functional pain behavior analysis and assertion training did not yield positive effects. A severe limitation of this study, however, is its being based only on four male patients. Four other patients were discarded.

White and Sanders (1985) divided eight chronic pain patients into two detoxification groups. Group one received an oral methadone cocktail on a time-contingent basis, while group two received it on a pain-contingent as needed basis. At detoxification the time-contingent group yielded lower pain and higher mood scores than the pain-contingent group. Theoretically, from a behavoral point of view the lower pain scores would be due to an extinction process, whereby the pain complaint–medication association was broken. However, it is also possible to explain these results in other ways. Time-contingent medication could have led to the reduction of anticipatory anxiety and pain and hence to a more relaxed person.

Kerns, Turk, Holzman and Rudy (1986) demonstrated the effectiveness of a behavioral pain treatment program on a ten-session outpatient basis. Treatment consisted of rationale, identification of pain and well behaviors, extinction of pain and reinforcement of well behaviors, training in altering environmental consequences through modeling, role-playing and behavior rehearsals, self-monitoring of medication, activity level and progress and progressive relaxation. There was also weekly contracting for increased well behaviors. At the end of the 10-week program and at a six-month follow-up, patients showed a significantly reduced use of the health-care system and progress on individually constructed behavioral goals. A component score related to pain severity and impact of the pain on the patient's life did not show change. It seems desirable to consider more than just the behavioral treatment.

COGNITIVE APPROACHES TO PAIN CONTROL

The cognitive approach to pain control is consistent with the *Zeitgeist* in psychology in which cognitive approaches have been increasingly applied both to theoretical and clinical issues. Most notable has been the application of cognitive theory to the problems of coping with stress (see Folkman, Lazarus, Dunkel-Schemer, DeLongis and Gruen, 1986; Roskies and Lazarus, 1980), depression (see Beck, 1976; Beck et al., 1979), as well as its broad clinical application to a variety of psychological problems (see Ellis, 1962; Meichenbaum, 1977).

According to Roskies and Lazarus (1980), how a person psychologically copes with stress depends upon his/her cognitive view of the situation. This cognitive evaluative view, referred to as appraisal, is a dynamic process that changes according to the person's perceived anticipated consequence of an event, its importance to his/her well-being, and the perceived resources he/she has available to cope with the threat. The appraisal process changes as events change.

Coping has been classified according to the mode of action used (direct action, action inhibition, information search, intrapsychic processes) and according to the function it serves (problem-oriented or palliative regulation of the emotional response). Changing how a person thinks and feels in a given situation is viewed as an effective means of problem-solving.

Along with other cognitive theorists (see Beck, 1976; Ellis, 1962), belief systems are seen as exerting influence upon the cognitive appraisal. Emotion is a consequence of the cognitive appraisal (Beck, 1976). To handle stress, the person must learn to modify his/her appraisal of the environment and to manage his/her stress more effectively. Eliminating stress per se is not as important as learning to cope with it and to master it. Coping involves both what a person does and what he/she thinks and says to himself/herself, rather than simply what he/she does. This is in contrast to the behavioral view of Fordyce (1976) who says that if there is no pain behavior, there is no problem of pain.

Effective coping depends upon a person's assessment of his/her competence. It is not enough to possess the relevant skills. The person must believe that he/she has them and believe he/she is capable of applying them as needed. Bandura (1977) has referred to this later notion as self-efficacy. A person's belief in his/her own effectiveness will determine whether he/she will try to cope or avoid a situation that he/she views as beyond his/her coping ability. Efficacy expectations can also determine how much effort a person will invest and how long he/she will persist in the face of aversive experiences.

The application of cognitive strategies to pain control has been most strongly espoused by Turk and his colleagues (see Turk, Meichenbaum and Genest, 1983; Holzman, Turk and Kerns, 1986). Several recent reviews of the cognitive approaches have also been published (Tan, 1982; Turner and Chapman, 1982; Weisenberg, 1984). Although there are still methodological and conceptual problems, it is generally agreed that the cognitive approach can help reduce the reactions to pain.

Three basic phases of treatment have been identified. Patients are taught to reconceptualize pain by emphasizing how pain can be controlled through thoughts, feelings, and beliefs. There is a skills acquisition phase during which patients are taught such things as relaxation, use of imagery and attention diversion. The third phase requires practice and consolidation of what is taught with special attention paid to situations that could lead to relapse (Marlatt and Gordon, 1980).

The varieties of cognitive strategies have recently been classified to promote greater clarity and uniformity of utilization of terminology (Fernandez, 1986). Three broad categories have been proposed: (1) imagery, e.g. incompatible imagery; (2) self-statement, e.g. stress innoculation; and (3) attention diversion, e.g. passive or active distraction. Each category has been further subdivided yielding a total of 10 strategies. How useful these classifications will be, however, is still something that must be demonstrated. As with the behavioral approach, there are several major questions to be addressed. There is still missing an overall theoretical approach to the cognitive control of pain that would permit the variety of techniques to be tied together (Weisenberg, 1984). Clinical evaluations are still being conducted. There is little doubt that a cognitive approach is effective. In fact, Kerns et al. (1986) reported the cognitive–behavioral approach to have a greater influence on ratings of pain severity than the behavioral approach alone.

However, the question of which strategy is appropriate under which conditions is still unclear. For example, both Keefe and Dolon (1986) and Turner and Clancy (1986) found that with chronic pain patients, attention diversion strategies were associated with poorer treatment outcomes. Perhaps this strategy is effective only with mild as opposed to severe pain (McCaul and Malott, 1984).

In a laboratory study, Peveler and Johnston (1986) reported that progressive relaxation affected overall arousal and also reduced the negative cognitions. The study was conducted to elaborate upon the mechanism whereby relaxation is effective. There is also evidence that in the treatment of migraine headache both relaxation alone or cognitive coping strategies were equally superior and effective compared with a placebo treatment group (Richter *et al.* 1986). Relaxation techniques are usually an integral part of a comprehensive cognitive treatment package. The question these data raise is how many of the cognitive ingredients are really necessary. These questions as well as others are still being researched.

WHAT HAVE WE ACHIEVED AND WHAT IS STILL MISSING?

There is little doubt that great progress has been made in the understanding and in the application of this knowledge to the treatment of pain. The laboratory currently is being used more and more in conjunction with clinical pain problems. Quite a number of treatment techniques have been developed and are being applied to both acute and chronic pain.

Turk and Holzman (1986) performed an analysis of the metaconstructs used in the treatment of chronic pain. The features found in common include providing the patient with a rationale for his/her pain and for the treatment approach. This helps the patient see his/her problem as more treatable and creates an expectancy for successful outcomes. Each treatment approach tries to instill hope in combating the pain. Treatment strategies are tailored to the individual patient. Patients are asked to be actively involved in the treatment and not simply passive recipients of care. New skills are taught. Outcome self-efficacy is emphasized. Patients are taught to attribute success to their own activity and control.

With all of the success in these procedures, however, there is still a great deal unknown. Theoretically, from a psychological perspective, Gate Control theory has been very important since 1965 by providing an entrée for the psychologist into the treatment of pain (Melzack and Wall, 1965). However, at this stage it would be appropriate to elaborate upon the psychological aspects of pain perception, filling in many of the gaps. Such a theory would go beyond the physiological connections and account for the influence of such things as anxiety and perceived control in the regulation of pain. It would also have to deal with the phenomena of chronic pain such as depression and learned helplessness.

Behavioral and cognitive–behavioral approaches have been accepted as effective means for controlling pain. Which of the major ingredients of each approach is most necessary for treatment success is still not clear. This, too, would be greatly helped by an overall theoretical update. As indicated previously (Weisenberg, 1984), factors such as belief and perceived self-efficacy may be more important than the specific approach adopted. There are still many limitations to the effective treatment of pain. Many patients are never treated successfully. It is now necessary to proceed to the next stage, whereby we extend these limits.

REFERENCES

Abbott B. B., Schoen L. S. and Badia P. (1984) Predictable and unpredictable shock: Behavioral measures of aversion and physiological measures of stress. *Psychol. Bull.* **96**, 45–71.
Algom D. (1986) A functional theory of pain. Unpublished manuscript, Bar-Ilan University, Ramat-Gan, Israel.
Algom D., Raphaeli N. and Cohen-Raz L. (1986) Integration of noxious stimulation across separate somatosensory communications systems: A functional theory of pain. *J. exp. Psychol. Human Perception and Performance* **12**, 92–102.
American Psychiatric Association (1980) *DSM III: Diagnostic and Statistical Manual of Mental Disorders.* American Psychiatric Association, Washington, D.C.
Averill J. R. (1973) Personal control over aversive stimuli and its relationship to stress. *Psychol. Bull.* **80**, 286–303.
Bandura A. (1977) Self-efficacy: Toward a unifying theory of behavioral change. *Psychol. Rev.* **84**, 191–215.
Bandura A. (1982) Self-efficacy mechanism in human agency. *Am. Psychol.* **37**, 122–147.
Barak E. and Weisenberg M. (1986) Anxiety and attitudes toward pain as a function of ethnic grouping and socioeconomic status. Unpublished manuscript, Bar-Ilan University, Ramat-Gan, Israel.
Beck A. T. (1976) *Cognitive Therapy and the Emotional Disorders.* International Universities Press, New York.
Beck A. T., Rush A. J., Shaw B. F. and Emory G. (1979) *Cognitive Therapy of Depression.* Guilford, New York.
Bolles R. C. and Fanselow M. S. (1980) A perceptual–defensive–recuperative model of fear and pain. *Behav. Brain Sci.* **3**, 291–301.
Bollish S. J., Collins C. L., Kirking D. M. and Bartlett R. H. (1985) Efficacy of patient-controlled versus conventional analgesia for postoperative pain. *Clin. Pharm.* **4**, 48–52.
Bond M. R. (1985) Cancer pain: Psychological substrates and therapy. *Clin. J. Pain* **1**, 99–104.

Bowers K. S. (1968) Pain, anxiety and perceived control. *J. consult. clin. Psychol.* **32**, 596–602.

Chapman C. R. (1986) Psychological control of acute pain in medical settings. *J. Pain Symptom Mmt* **1**, 9–20.

Chapman C. R. and Bonica J. J. (1985) *Chronic Pain (Current Concepts)*. The Upjohn Co., Kalamazoo, MI.

Chapman C. R. and Turner J. A. (1986) Psychological control of acute pain in medical settings. *J. Pain Symptom Mgt* **1**, 9–20.

Cohen F. and Lazarus R. S. (1973) Active coping processes, coping dispositions and recovery from surgery. *Psychosom. Med.* **35**, 375–389.

Corah N. L. (1973) Effect of perceived control on stress reduction in pedodontic patients. *J. dental Res.* **52**, 1261–1264.

Dworkin R. H., Richlin D. M., Handlin D. S. and Brand L. (1986) Predicting treatment response in depressed and non-depressed chronic pain patients. *Pain* **24**, 343–353.

Ellis A. (1962) *Reason and Emotion in Psychotherapy*. Lyle Stuart, New York.

Fernandez E. (1986) A classification system of cognitive coping strategies for pain. *Pain* **26**, 141–151.

Folkman S., Lazarus R. S., Dunkel-Schemer C., DeLongis A. and Gruen R. J. (1986) Dynamics of a stressful encounter: Cognitive appraisal, coping and encounter outcomes. *J. Person. soc. Psychol.* **50**, 992–1003.

Fordyce W. E. (1976) *Behavioral Methods for Chonic Pain and Illness*. C. .V. Mosby, St Louis.

Fordyce W. E., Fowler R. S., Lehmann J. F., Delateur B. J., Sand P. L. and Treischmann R. B. (1973) Operant conditioning in the treatment of chronic pain. *Archs Phys. Med. Rehab.* **54**, 399–408.

Geer J. H., Davison G. C. and Gatchel R. I. (1970) Reduction of stress in humans through nonveridical perceived control of aversive stimulation. *J. Person. soc. Psychol.* **16**, 734–738.

Glass D. C., Singer J. E., Leonard H. S., Krantz D., Cohen S. and Cummings H. (1973) Perceived control of aversive stimulation. *J. Person.* **41**, 577–595.

Gottlieb H., Strite L. C., Koller R., Madorsky A., Hockersmith U., Kleeman M. and Wagner J. (1977) Comprehensive rehabilitation of patients having chronic low back pain. *Archs Phys. Med. Rehab.* **58**, 101–108.

Hardy J. D., Wolff H. G. and Goodell H. (1952) *Pain Sensations and Reactions*. Hafner, New York.

Hilgard E. R. and Hilgard J. R. (1975) *Hypnosis in the Relief of pain*. William Kaufmann, Los Altos, CA.

Hill H. F., Saeger L. C. and Chapman C. R. (1986) Patient-controlled analgesia in cancer patients following bone marrow transplantation: A pilot study. Unpublished manuscript, Fred Hutchinson Cancer Research Center, Seattle, WA.

Holzman A. D., Turk D. C. and Kerns R. D. (1986) The cognitive–behavioral approach to the management of chronic pain. In *Pain Management: A Handbook of Psychological Treatment Approaches* (Edited by Holzman A. D. and Turk D. C.), pp. 31-50. Pergamon, New York.

Ignelzi R. J., Sternbach R. A. and Timmermans G. (1977) The pain ward follow-up analysis. *Pain* **3**, 277–280.

International Association for the Study of Pain (1979) Pain terms: A list with definitions and notes on usage. *Pain* **6**, 249–252.

International Association for the Study of Pain (1986) Classification of chronic pain: Descriptions of chronic pain syndromes and definitions of pain terms. *Pain (Suppl.)* **3**, S1–S226.

Janis I. L. (1958) *Psychological Stress*. John Wiley, New York.

Janis I. L. (1983) Stress innoculation in health care: Theory and Research. In *Stress Reduction and Prevention* (Edited by Meichenbaum D. and Jaremko M. E.), pp. 67–99. Plenum, New York.

Keefe F. J., Block A. R., Williams R. B., Jr. and Surwit R. S. (1981) Behavioral treatment of chronic low back pain: Clinical outcome and individual differences in pain relief. *Pain* **11**, 221–231.

Keefe F. J. and Dolan E. (1986) Pain behavior and pain coping strategies in low back pain and myofascial pain dysfunction syndrome patients. *Pain* **24**, 49–56.

Keeri-Szanto M. (1979) Drugs or drums: What relieves postoperative pain? *Pain* **6**, 217–230.

Kent G. (1984) Anxiety, pain and type of dental procedure. *Behav. Res. Ther.* **22**, 465–469.

Kerns R. D., Turk D. C., Holzman A. D. and Rudy T. E. (1986) Comparison of cognitive–behavioral and behavioral approaches to the outpatient treatment of chronic pain. *Clin. J. Pain* **1**, 199–203.

Krishnan K. R. R., France R. D., Pelton S., McCann U. D., Davidson J. and Urban B. J. (1985) Chronic pain and depression. II. Symptoms of anxiety in chronic low back pain patients and their relationship to subtypes of depression. *Pain* **22**, 289–294.

Lehrer P. M. (1972) Physiological effects of relaxation in a double-blind analog of desensitization. *Behav. Ther.* **3**, 193–208.

Lethem J., Slade P. D., Troup J. D. G. and Bentley G. (1983) Outline of a fear-avoidance model of exaggerated pain perception I. *Behav. Res. Ther.* **21**, 401–408.

Linton S. J. (1986) Behavioral remediation of chronic pain: A status report. *Pain* **24**, 125–141.

Loeser J. D. (1986) Pain and its management: An overview. In National Institutes of Health Consensus Development Conference, *Integrated Approach to Management of Pain*, pp. 17–19. Bethesda, MD.

Malow R. M., West J. A. and Sutker P. B. (1986) A signal detection analysis of anxiety and pain responses in chronic drug abuses. Paper presented at the *Annual Mtg American Psychological Association*, Washington, D.C.

Marlatt G. A. and Gordon J. R. (1980) Determinants of relapse: Implications for the maintenance of behavior change. In *Behavioral medicine: Changing health lifestyles* (Edited by Davidson P. O. and Davidson S. M.), pp. 410–452. Brunner/Mazel, New York.

McCaul K. D. and Malott J. M. (1984) Distraction and coping with pain. *Psychol. Bull.* **95**, 516–533.

Meichenbaum D. (1977) *Cognitive Behavior Modification*. Plenum, New York.

Melzack R. (1973) *The Puzzle of Pain*. Basic Books, New York.

Melzack R. and Wall P. D. (1965) Pain mechanisms: A new theory. *Science, N.Y.* **150**, 971–979.

Melzack R. and Wall P. D. (1982) *The Challenge of Pain*. Penguin Books, Harmondsworth.

Merskey H. (1968) Psychological aspects of pain. *Postgrad. med. J.* **44**, 297–306.

Merskey H. (1980) The role of the psychiatrist in the investigation and treatment of pain. In *Pain* (Edited by Bonica J. J.), pp. 249–260. Raven Press, New York.

Miller S. M. (1980) Why having control reduces stress: If I can stop the roller coaster, I don't want to get off. In *Human Helplessness: Theory and Applications* (Edited by Garber J. and Seligman M. E. P.), pp. 71–95. Academic Press, New York.

National Cancer Institute (1979) *Breast Cancer Digest*. National Institutes of Health, Bethesda, MD.

Newman R. I., Seres J. L., Yospe L. P. and Garlington B. (1978) Multidisciplinary treatment of chronic pain: Long-term follow-up of low-back pain patients. *Pain* **4**, 283–292.

Paul G. L. and Bernstein D. A. (1973) *Anxiety and Clinical Problems: Systematic Desensitization and Related Techniques.* General Learning Press, Morristown, NJ.

Peveler R. C. and Johnston D. W. (1986) Subjective and cognitive effects of relaxation. *Behav. Res. Ther.* **24**, 413–419.

Richter I. L., McGrath P. J., Humphreys P. J., Goodman J. T., Firestone P. and Keene D. (1986) Cognitive and relaxation treatment of paediatric migraine. *Pain* **25**, 195–203.

Roskies, E. and Lazarus R. S. (1980) Coping theory and the teaching of coping skills. In *Behavioral Medicine: Changing Health Lifestyles* (Edited by Davidson P. O. and Davidson S. M.), pp. 38–69. Brunner/Mazel, New York.

Sanders S. H. (1983) Component analysis of a behavioral treatment program for chronic low-back pain. *Behav. Ther.* **14**, 697-705.

Seligman M. F. P. (1975) *Helplessness: On Depression, Development and Death.* W. H. Freeman, San Francisco.

Slade P. D., Troup J. D. G., Lethem J. and Bentley G. (1983) The fear-avoidance model of exaggerated pain perception II. *Behav. Res. Ther.* **21**, 409–416.

Spear F. G. (1967) Pain in psychiatric patients. *J. Psychosom. Res.* **11**, 187–193.

Spielberger C. D., Gorsuch R. L. and Lushene R. E. (1970) *Manual for the State–Trait Anxiety Inventory.* Consulting Psychologists Press, Palo Alto, CA.

Staub E., Tursky B. and Schwartz G. S. (1971) Self-control and predictability: Their effects on reactions to aversive stimulation. *J. Person. soc. Psychol.* **18**, 157–162.

Sternbach R. A. (1968) *Pain: A Psychophysiological Analysis.* Academic Press, New York.

Sternbach R. A. (1974) *Pain patients: Traits and Treatment.* Academic Press, New York.

Taenzer P., Melzack R. and Jeans M. E. (1986) Influence of psychological factors on postoperative pain, mood and analgesic requirements. *Pain* **24**, 331–342.

Tan S. Y. (1982) Cognitive and cognitive–behavioral methods for pain control: A selective review. *Pain* **12**, 201–228.

Taylor S. E., Lichtman R. R. and Wood J. V. (1984) Attributions, belief about control and adjustment to breast cancer. *J. Person. soc. Psychol.* **46** 48–502.

Thompson S. C. (1981) Will it hurt less if I can control it? A complex answer to a simple question. *Psychol. Bull.* **90**, 89–101.

Turk D. C. and Holzman A. D. (1986) Commonalities among psychological approaches in the treatment of chronic pain: Specifying the meta-constructs. In *Pain Management: A handbook of Psychological Treatment Approaches* (Edited by Holzman A. D. and Turk D. C.), pp. 257–267. Pergamon, New York.

Turk D. C., Meichenbaum D. and Genest M. (1983) *Pain and Behavioral medicine: A Cognitive–Behavioral Perspective.* Guilford Press, New York.

Turner J. A. and Chapman C. R. (1982) Psychological interventions for chronic pain: A critical review. *Pain* **12**, 23–46.

Turner J. A. and Clancy S. (1986) Strategies for coping with chronic low back pain: Relationship to pain and disability. *Pain* **24**, 355–364.

Wall P. D. (1979) On the relation of injury to pain: The John J. Bonica Lecture. *Pain* **6**, 253–264.

Weisenberg M. (1975) *Pain: Clinical and Experimental Perspectives.* C. V. Mosby, St Louis, MO.

Weisenberg M. (1977) Pain and pain control. *Psychol. Bull.* **84**, 1008–1044.

Weisenberg M. (1980) Understanding pain phenomena. In *Contributions to medical psychology*, Vol. 2 (Edited by Rachman S.), pp. 79–111. Pergamon, Oxford.

Weisenberg M. (1983) Pain and pain control. In *Diagnosis and Intervention in Behavior Therapy and Behavioral Medicine* (Edited by Daitzman B. R.), pp. 90–149. Springer, New York.

Weisenberg M. (1984) Cognitive aspects of pain. In *Textgbook of Pain* (Edited by Wall P. D. and Melzack R.), pp. 162–172. Churchill Livingstone, Edinburgh.

Weisenberg M., Aviram O., Wolf Y. and Raphaeli N. (1984) Relevant and irrelevant anxiety in the reaction to pain. *Pain* **20**, 371–383.

Weisenberg M., Kreindler M. L., Schachat R. and Werboff J. (1975) Pain: Anxiety and attitudes in black, white and Puerto Rican patients. *Psychosom. Med.* **37**, 123–135.

Weisenberg M., Wolf Y., Mittwoch T., Mikulincer M. and Aviram O. (1985) Subject versus experimenter control in the reaction to pain. *Pain* **23**, 187–200.

White B. and Sanders S. H. (1985) Differential effects on pain and mood in chronic pain patients with time- versus pain-contingent medication delivery *Behav. Ther.* **16**, 28–38.

Woodworth R. S. and Schlosberg H. (1956) *Experimental Psychology.* Henry Holt & Co, New York.

Yang J. C., Wagner J. M. and Clark W. C. (1983) Psychological distress and mood in chronic pain and surgical patients: A sensory decision analysis. In *Advances in Pain Research and Therapy*, (Edited by Bonica J. J., Lindblom U. and Iggo A.), pp. 901–906. Raven Press, New York.

Zimbardo P. G., Cohen A. R., Weisenberg M., Dworkin L. and Firestone I. (1966) Control of pain motivation by cognitive dissonance. *Science N.Y.* **151**, 217–219.

THE BEHAVIOURAL TREATMENT OF OBSESSIONAL-COMPULSIVE DISORDERS, WITH AND WITHOUT CLOMIPRAMINE

*S. Rachman, J. Cobb, S. Grey, B. McDonald, D. Mawson, G. Sartory and R. Stern

Institute of Psychiatry, De Crespigny Park, London, SE5 8AF

(Received 21 March 1979)

Summary—The effects of behavioural treatment alone, and in combination with clomipramine, were assessed on 40 patients with chronic obsessional-compulsive disorders, using a 2 × 2 factorial design. These effects were assessed by behavioural measures and mood measures.

The behavioural treatment was followed by significant improvements on most behavioural measures. Clomipramine administration was followed by significant improvements on mood scales and some behavioural measures. There were no significant interactions between these two experimental conditions.

INTRODUCTION

The major aims of this study were to examine the immediate and long-term therapeutic effects of behavioural treatment alone, and combined with clomipramine, an anti-depressant drug. The behavioural treatment consisted of exposure *in vivo*, participant modelling and self-imposed response prevention (see Rachman, Hodgson and Marks, 1971). The present report deals mainly with the effects of the behavioural treatment, and the drug effects are described in detail elsewhere (Marks *et al.*, 1979).

This behavioural method of treatment was selected because three sources of evidence (case studies, clinical series and small controlled studies) had indicated its value in the management of chronic and severe obsessive-compulsive rituals (for reviews see Beech, 1974; Boulougouris and Rabavilas, 1977; Marks, 1978; Rachman and Hodgson, 1979). The present study was planned as a more rigorous and extensive evaluation of the method, while at the same time investigating the value of clomipramine. Earlier research had shown that exposure both with and without modelling was capable of producing significantly greater improvements than a relaxation training control comparison (Rachman *et al.*, 1971; Hodgson *et al.*, 1972). The effectiveness of exposure with modelling received support from a study by Roper *et al.* (1976), and a 2-yr follow up of the first twenty patients treated by these methods showed that the improvements were stable (Marks *et al.*, 1975).

Nevertheless some patients made little or unstable progress, and clinical observations suggested that the presence of significant depression retarded progress. In view of the acknowledged association between depression and obsessional disorders (Beech, 1974; Lewis, 1936; Rachman and Hodgson, 1979), and the therapeutic claims made on behalf of clomipramine (e.g. Capstick, 1975; Fernandez and Lopez-Ibor, 1967), it was decided to investigate the value of supplementing the behavioural treatment with this drug. The effects of exposure plus clomipramine were compared with those of exposure plus placebo.

The present study also differs from its predecessors in comprising a larger sample of patients, with ten in each of four treatment conditions, and in incorporating a random allocation to the first period of psychological treatment.

* Address reprint requests to: S. Rachman, Psychology Department, Institute of Psychiatry, De Crespigny Park, London, SE5 8AF, England.

METHOD

Design

A 2 × 2 factorial design was used to investigate the effects of behavioural treatment vs relaxation and clomipramine vs placebo (see Fig. 1). 40 patients were randomly assigned to either clomipramine or placebo, and these groups were subdivided into either exposure or relaxation groups, thus giving four groups of 10 patients each.

Patients

Eleven male and 29 female obsessional-compulsive patients with a mean age of 35 yr, were selected for the trial. The mean duration of the problem was 12 yr.

Patients were considered suitable for the trial if they had handicapping obsessional-compulsive rituals of at least 1 yr duration, were aged between 18 and 59 yr, had no history of psychosis, and had not had previous adequate behavioural treatment.

Of the 69 patients who met the selection criteria, two had problems which were so severe that immediate treatment was required and one was too depressed to be put into a drug trial involving placebo treatment. Seventeen patients refused the offer of treatment within the trial and one improved immediately after screening. Thus 48 patients entered the trial. Five patients dropped out at the end of the four week out-patient phase (2 of these were on clomipramine and had already improved sufficiently). Of the 43 patients who started the inpatient phase one patient receiving clomipramine became manic at the beginning of relaxation training, one patient on placebo developed a paranoid psychosis during the active behavioural treatment, and one clomipramine patient became suicidally depressed during active behavioural treatment. These three patients were withdrawn from the trial in order that alternative treatment could be given.

Procedure

All the patients attended hospital weekly as outpatients for a 4-week period during which they received drugs. Clomipramine or placebo was given, starting at 10 mg nocte and rising to 225 mg nocte unless excessive side effects prevented this. At the end of the four week period patients receiving clomipramine were on a mean dose of 164 mg, with mean blood plasma levels of the drug reaching 157 ng/100 ml. The patients receiving placebo were on a mean dose of 134 mg. There were no traces of either clomipramine or its metabolite in the blood plasma of any of the patients in the placebo condition. For a full discussion of the significance of blood levels of clomipramine and its metabolite see Stern et al. (1979). Patients were admitted to hospital at this point, and were allocated to one of three trained therapists (see Table 1).

Psychological treatment, either relaxation or exposure plus response prevention, began on the day after admission, following a detailed interview. The sessions lasted 45 min and took place each week-day morning. After 15 sessions of treatment, relaxation patients were switched to exposure treatment, and all patients continued with exposure for 15 more sessions.

After the 6-week inpatient phase the patients were discharged from hospital unless their clinical condition made further treatment desirable. Domiciliary sessions were carried out when necessary, and in cases where the patient lived a long way from hospital a local therapist was enlisted to provide treatment cover after discharge. During the follow-up period, only essential psychological treatment was given, and in some cases the patients brought their families to a six-weekly therapeutic group. From week 36 medication was tailed off over 4 weeks so that patients were off all capsules by week 40.

Psychological treatment

(1) *Relaxation.* The patients were told that relaxation training would help them to deal with tension more effectively. They were asked to alternately tense and relax differ-

Table 1. Procedure: administration of clomipramine/placebo and behavioural treatment/relaxation in the four groups over time. Assessments were made in all patients at the indicated times. All patients stayed in hospital between weeks 4 to 10. (C refers to the clomipramine condition and P to placebo; E and R stand for behavioural treatment and relaxation, respectively)

			Weeks		
	0 Assessment (M1)	4 Assessment (M2)	7 Assessment (M3)	10 Assessment (M4)	18 Assessment (M5)
Group 1 (CE)		Clomipramine	Behavioural treatment and clomipramine		Clomipramine
Group 2 (CR)		Clomipramine	Relaxation and clomipramine		Clomipramine
Group 3 (PE)		Placebo	Behavioural treatment and placebo	Placebo	
Group 4 (PR)		Placebo	Relaxation and placebo	Placebo	

ent parts of the body in turn. A standard half-hour tape recording of instructions was used to ensure some uniformity in treatment, but the therapist was present at all times to model how to relax, provide encouragement and deal with queries. The therapist praised any improvement reported by the patient but avoided specific discussion of rituals. Part of each session was spent relaxing without the aid of the tape, and patients were instructed to practise regularly between sessions.

(2) *Exposure.* The patients were told that by repeatedly facing the situation which gave rise to discomfort and resisting carrying out rituals they would gradually learn that the discomfort dissipates. The dominant theme of the obsessions was usually tackled first; and the therapist began by modelling activities which the patient usually avoided, then refraining from ritualising, and demonstrating his lack of serious concern about the consequences. Patients were then encouraged to carry out similar tasks themselves at as fast a pace as they could tolerate. For example, a compulsive handwasher was taken to the hospital dustbin and, after watching the therapist touch the dustbins and then rub his hands over his face and hair, was asked to do the same himself. Some patients were willing to expose themselves to feared situations immediately while others needed one or two sessions of modelling before they were prepared to participate. When a patient could not be persuaded to tackle a task the therapist would present a less difficult one. After exposure, patients were asked not to carry out rituals for the rest of the session and to resist ritualising for a specified time thereafter.

In addition to exposure the treatment involved modelling and retraining of day-to-day habits which the patient had been carrying out in a ritualistic way. Many patients were unsure of the 'normal' way to do things and found that non-ritualistic behaviour itself could evoke discomfort. Thus a compulsive handwasher might find it difficult to wash his hands quickly, whether he had been near a source of contamination or not; in this case the therapist would model brief handwashing and give some guidance as to the occasions on which it was reasonable to wash. All patients were instructed to carry out exposure tasks between sessions, with comfort and encouragement from the nursing staff where needed, and patients kept records of their performance on these tasks. These records enabled patients and therapists to monitor progress more accurately. At weekends the patients usually went home and were asked to carry out tasks similar to the ones completed in hospital. Before and after discharge some patients had treatment at home for problems involving rituals. Where relatives were involved in the rituals, they were seen with the patient for advice about helping the patient to continue self-exposure treatment to refrain from carrying out rituals. Relatives were asked to refrain from helping the patient to complete rituals.

Assessments

Assessments took place at weeks 0, 4, 7, 10, 18, 36, 44, 62 and 114. The follow-up assessments after week 18 are discussed by Marks *et al.* (1979). Patients, therapists and the independent assessors were all blind with regard to the drug conditions, and the assessor was blind to the psychological treatment conditions.

(1) *Four target problems.* Patients worked out with the assessor their four main compulsive rituals to be treated (e.g. 'touching everything 10 times'). The patient and assessor separately rated these 4 target problems on a 0–8 scale for 'discomfort' and for 'time taken by ritual per day' (see Marks *et al.*, 1977). A disadvantage of these scales is that not all patients' rituals can readily be rated on both discomfort and time. Nevertheless, the scales are usually sensitive to clinical improvement (Marks *et al.*, 1977, 1978).

(2) *Compulsive activity checklist.* As a measure of the extensiveness of rituals, patient and assessor separately completed a compulsive activity check-list modified from that devised by Hallam (see Philpott, 1975) which appears in Marks *et al.*, (1977, pp. 78–79). It lists 39 everyday activities (e.g. 'brushing teeth', 'washing clothes'), each to be rated on a 0–3 scale, and has a total score range of 0–117. It is sensitive to clinical improvement (Marks *et al.*, 1977, 1978).

The inter-rater reliability of target problems and checklist measures was $r = 0.86$ for target problems and $r = 0.95$ for the checklist ($n = 28$). Checklist scores of assessor and patients correlated, $r = 0.83$ ($n = 40$).

(3) *Behavioural avoidance test*. The patient was asked to carry out 5 tasks which usually gave rise to rituals. The assessor rated (a) Performance, (1 = task executed, 0 = task avoided, giving a maximum score of 5) and (b) discomfort in carrying out the task on a 0–8 scale. Scores for the 5 items were pooled, yielding a maximum of 40 for discomfort.

(4) *Wakefield depression scale*. This self-rating scale (Snaith et al., 1971) is a modified and shortened version of Zung's self-rated Depressive Scale (Zung, 1965). It consists of twelve 0–3 items, with a range of 0–36. It has a test-retest reliability of $r = 0.68$, and correlates $r = 0.87$ with the widely used Hamilton Depression Scale.

(5) *Hamilton depression scale*. Items 1–17 were used on this assessor-rated scale of depression. The score range is 0–48 (Hamilton, 1967).

(6) *Free floating anxiety* was rated by the assessor on a 0–8 scale used by Gelder and Marks (1966).

(7) *Social adjustment rating scales* were completed by the blind assessor, and include items on family and other social life, leisure and work activities (Marks et al., 1974).

RESULTS

The design affords comparison between behavioural treatment and relaxation at week 7 only. The means and SDs of variables are shown in Table 2. Two-way analyses of variance, testing the effects of behavioural treatment, clomipramine and their interaction, were carried out on measures at that occasion (see Table 3). Pre-treatment scores (week 0) were co-varied out.

Behavioural treatment had a significant effect on performance and discomfort ratings of the behavioural avoidance test, (see Figs. 1 and 2), as well as the assessor-rated compulsive activity check-list (see Fig. 3) and combined time of targets (Fig. 4). Clomipramine had a significant effect on the two depression measures (see Fig. 5 and 6), namely the Wakefield and Hamilton questionnaire as well as anxiety ratings, assessor-rated combined discomfort scores of targets and both self and assessor-rated activity check-lists. The interaction term of the two experimental conditions was not significant on any of the measures. The results suggest that although both treatment modes are followed by significant improvement, their combined effect is additive rather than one potentiating or facilitating the effect of the other mode, as had been predicted.

The means of the behaviourally treated groups suggest that further improvement took place during the second half of treatment, i.e. between weeks 7 and 10. This assumption was borne out by comparisons of scores at week 7 with those at week 10 within the groups initially treated with behavioural therapy. The two groups improved further on all measures except for discomfort ratings of the behavioural avoidance test. Although in the absence of a control group, this further improvement cannot be unambiguously attributed to the action of behavioural treatment, the results suggest that the full effect of behavioural treatment was not attained at week 7, the time at which it was compared to the control treatment.

The evaluation of the drug effect was based on all measurement occasions, at which clomipramine was contrasted with a placebo control, whilst all other conditions (i.e. hospital stay, behavioural treatment) were kept the same. Thus, measures at weeks 4, 10 and 18 were transformed into orthogonal polynomial indices resulting in a mean level score and the linear and quadratic trend over these occasions. The presence of trends as well as their interaction with the drug condition were tested (see Table 4). Scores at week 0 were co-varied out in the interaction analysis.

The significant linear trend which is present in all measures confirms that the patient sample improved over time. The significant quadratic trend of all measures indicates that the improvement was greater between weeks 4 and 10, that is, during the hospital stay, than between weeks 10 and 18. The interaction of mean level of repeated measures

Table 2. Means and SDs (in brackets) of measures

Measures			0	4	Weeks 7	10	18
Combined		CE	4.6 (2.7)	4.1 (2.7)	1.5 (1.3)	1.1 (1.3)	0.9 (1.1)
targets:		CR	3.9 (2.3)	1.9 (1.5)	1.8 (1.3)	1.0 (1.0)	
	Time	PE	4.1 (2.9)	4.2 (2.3)	2.5 (2.5)	1.7 (2.0)	1.9 (1.9)
		PR	2.7 (1.2)	3.0 (1.5)	3.0 (1.2)	2.1 (1.2)	
Self		CE	6.1 (1.4)	5.6 (1.8)	2.6 (1.7)	1.7 (1.7)	1.4 (1.5)
		CR	6.1 (1.2)	5.5 (1.1)	4.1 (1.0)	1.4 (1.7)	
	Discomfort	PE	6.7 (1.1)	6.5 (1.0)	4.6 (2.1)	2.9 (2.2)	3.3 (2.3)
		PR	5.6 (1.8)	5.3 (1.8)	5.0 (2.1)	2.8 (2.0)	
		CE	6.5 (2.8)	5.8 (2.8)	2.1 (2.1)	1.3 (1.6)	1.3 (1.7)
	Time	CR	7.4 (0.7)	6.3 (1.5)	3.6 (2.1)	1.7 (1.5)	
		PE	7.3 (1.0)	7.1 (1.0)	3.9 (2.4)	2.2 (2.1)	3.1 (2.3)
		PR	7.1 (1.3)	6.8 (1.7)	5.9 (1.9)	3.8 (1.9)	
Assessor		CE	7.1 (1.4)	6.1 (2.0)	2.9 (2.0)	1.7 (1.6)	1.4 (1.5)
		CR	7.2 (1.1)	6.9 (1.0)	4.3 (1.4)	1.2 (1.5)	
	Discomfort	PE	7.5 (0.7)	7.0 (1.2)	4.9 (1.8)	3.0 (1.8)	3.2 (2.6)
		PR	7.1 (1.2)	6.7 (1.6)	5.8 (1.6)	3.1 (2.1)	
Activity		CE	43.8 (21.6)	41.7 (23.5)	20.8 (20.0)	11.3 (14.1)	10.4 (15.5)
checklist	Self	CR	48.0 (21.2)	37.3 (19.0)	30.5 (15.4)	14.4 (20.2)	
		PE	41.1 (22.8)	47.8 (22.6)	31.1 (23.3)	12.2 (8.0)	21.2 (19.7)
		PR	31.1 (19.0)	32.8 (20.1)	28.5 (16.6)	19.1 (12.1)	
		CE	47.1 (15.4)	40.6 (18.6)	20.1 (15.6)	12.5 (13.7)	10.5 (14.3)
		CR	48.2 (19.4)	41.1 (16.1)	28.0 (18.1)	12.1 (15.0)	
	Assessor	PE	51.6 (26.7)	53.1 (22.4)	31.3 (20.5)	16.8 (13.1)	24.1 (21.1)
		PR	40.3 (16.9)	39.4 (17.3)	35.5 (18.1)	20.8 (23.2)	
Behavioural		CE	0.6 (0.7)	1.2 (0.9)	4.1 (1.3)	4.7 (0.6)	4.6 (0.6)
avoidance test		CR	0.9 (1.0)	1.6 (1.3)	3.3 (1.3)	4.6 (0.5)	
		PE	0.9 (1.2)	1.8 (1.5)	4.1 (1.1)	4.6 (0.5)	3.9 (1.7)
	Performance	PR	0.7 (1.1)	1.3 (0.8)	2.0 (1.1)	3.2 (1.6)	
Behavioural		CE C	37.7 (2.8)	34.1 (5.8)	15.4 (11.9)	7.0 (10.0)	7.6 (8.2)
avoidance test	Discomfort	CR	37.4 (3.8)	32.6 (5.8)	20.4 (10.6)	8.1 (9.1)	
		PE P	38.5 (1.7)	35.2 (3.9)	16.9 (10.0)	12.7 (8.3)	15.8 (12.7)
		PR	37.0 (4.4)	33.0 (3.9)	30.3 (6.0)	21.3 (12.0)	
Anxiety		CE C	3.0 (1.9)	3.1 (1.5)	2.2 (1.8)	2.1 (1.6)	1.4 (1.5)
		CR	4.1 (2.2)	3.6 (1.8)	1.5 (1.8)	0.9 (1.4)	
		PE P	4.1 (2.8)	3.7 (1.8)	3.7 (2.0)	3.1 (2.2)	2.9 (2.3)
		PR	3.5 (2.3)	3.4 (2.7)	2.7 (2.1)	2.8 (1.9)	
Wakefield		CE C	21.1 (5.8)	18.3 (5.2)	15.4 (8.6)	11.1 (7.5)	10.1 (7.0)
		CR	26.7 (6.1)	21.6 (6.7)	14.9 (5.6)	11.8 (8.5)	
		PE P	25.5 (7.9)	25.3 (9.4)	21.2 (11.1)	18.0 (12.9)	19.1 (11.1)
		PR	18.9 (6.7)	19.1 (6.8)	18.4 (6.4)	13.3 (7.1)	
Hamilton		CE C	13.9 (7.8)	11.3 (7.4)	8.1 (8.3)	5.1 (3.3)	4.3 (4.3)
		CR	18.3 (9.9)	10.3 (6.3)	6.5 (5.0)	3.8 (3.9)	
		PE P	15.7 (10.6)	16.5 (10.2)	16.5 (11.1)	12.1 (8.4)	10.2 (9.9)
		PR	13.1 (8.6)	11.0 (8.4)	13.7 (6.3)	8.5 (6.6)	

Table 3. Analysis of variance of behavioural treatment and clomipramine at week 7 significance level of F-ratios

Variables		Behavioural Treatment	Clomipramine	B × C
Self combined targets	Time	N.S.	N.S.	N.S.
Self combined targets	Discomfort	N.S.	N.S.	N.S.
Assessor combined targets	Time	0.05	N.S.	N.S.
Assessor combined targets	Discomfort	N.S.	0.04	N.S.
Self activity checklist		N.S.	0.02	N.S.
Assessor activity checklist		0.01	0.006	N.S.
Behavioural avoidance test	Performance	0.02	N.S.	N.S.
Behavioural avoidance test	Discomfort	0.007	N.S.	N.S.
Anxiety ratings		N.S.	0.03	N.S.
Wakefield		N.S.	0.005	N.S.
Hamilton		N.S.	0.0002	N.S.

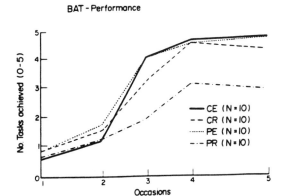

Fig. 1. Mean performance measures of the behavioural avoidance test in the four treatment groups. The five measurement occasions refer to assessments at weeks 0, 4, 7, 10 and 18, respectively (C = clomipramine, P = placebo, E = behavioural treatment, R = relaxation.)

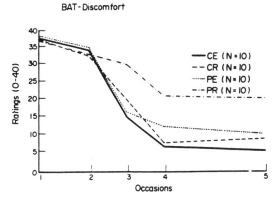

Fig. 2. Mean discomfort ratings of the behavioural avoidance test in the four treatment groups.

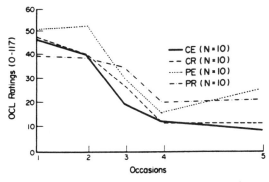

Fig. 3. Mean assessor rated compulsive activity-checklist in the four treatment groups.

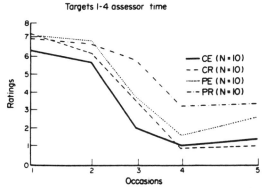

Fig. 4. Mean assessor rated scores for combined time of targets in the four treatment groups.

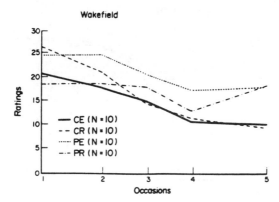

Fig. 5. Mean scores of the Wakefield questionnaires in the four groups.

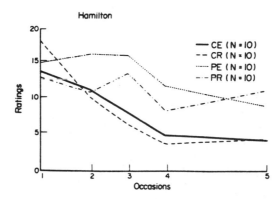

Fig. 6. Mean scores of the Hamilton scale in the four groups.

by drug condition revealed that clomipramine had a significant effect on all measures except performance scores of the behavioural avoidance test. On a number of measures, (i.e. the combined target discomfort ratings, both self and assessor-rated, as well as Wakefield scores), the drug effect increased over time as indicated by the linear trend by drug condition interaction. None of the drug by quadratic trend interactions were significant.

Relations of measures

A principal component analysis of measures at week 0 yielded 4 components with an Eigenvalue greater than 1 (Table 5). The first component represents a general factor

Table 4. Results of the analysis of variance comparing drug and placebo groups. Repeated measures (weeks 4, 10, 18) were transformed into orthogonal polynomials

Variables		Repeated measures Linear trend	Quadratic trend	Repeated measures by drug condition Mean level	Linear trend
Self combined targets	Time	0.0001	0.0001	0.003	N.S.
	Discomfort	0.0001	0.0001	0.002	0.02
Assessor combined targets	Time	0.0001	0.0001	0.003	N.S.
	Discomfort	0.0001	0.0001	0.004	0.05
Self activity		0.0001	0.0001	0.004	N.S.
Assessor activity checklist		0.0001	0.0001	0.003	N.S.
Behavioural avoidance test	Performance	0.0001	0.0001	'N.S.	N.S.
Behavioural avoidance test	Discomfort	0.0001	0.0001	0.006	N.S.
Anxiety ratings		0.0007	0.03	0.02	N.S.
Wakefield		0.0001	0.0001	0.002	0.005
Hamilton		0.002	0.006	0.001	N.S.

Table 5. Principal components of measurments at week 0

		Principal components			
		1	2	3	4
Eigen value		5.70	2.40	1.25	1.13
% of variation		38.03	15.98	8.34	7.51
Correlation with measures:					
Self combined targets	Time	−0.54			
Self combined targets	Discomfort	−0.64			
Assessor combined targets	Time	−0.53			
	Discomfort			0.61	
Self activity		−0.84			
Assessor activity checklist		−0.85			
Behavioural avoidance test	Performance		−0.70		
Behavioural avoidance test	Discomfort		0.71		
Anxiety ratings		−0.57			−0.57
Wakefield		−0.84			
Hamilton		−0.75			

which correlates with the depression measures as well as most self-report measures of compulsive activities, but not with the behavioural avoidance test and assessor-rated discomfort ratings of targets. The second component was correlated with both the performance and discomfort score of the behavioural avoidance test and can be described as a behavioural factor of compulsive ritualising. The remaining two factors are correlated with discomfort ratings of targets on the one hand and anxiety ratings on the other.

Effects of clomipramine in a mildly depressed group

A sub-sample of 10 non-depressed patients, half of whom were on the drug and the other half on placebo, were extracted from the total sample of patients. According to the clinical cut-off point on the Wakefield Scale, only two out of the 40 patients were classified as not depressed: the sample must therefore be regarded as mildly depressed. Selection of the samples was carried out on the basis of the patient's scores on both the Hamilton and Wakefield tests of depression. Thus, patients were selected if their score was within the lower quartile in both tests or else, in the lower quartile of at least one test and below the median on the other test. The analysis applied to the data was identical to the one carried out on the total sample of patients i.e. an analysis of variance which tested the drug condition by repeated measures interaction, including weeks 4, 10 and 18, whilst co-varying week 0. None of the measures yielded a significant drug effect except for the patients' self-assessed time on the target problems (p 0.05) i.e. there was little sign of a direct effect of clomipramine on obsessional behaviour. The notion of the drug's direct anti-obsessional effect was not supported by the present data.

DISCUSSION

The behavioural treatment was followed by significant changes on the performance and discomfort ratings of the avoidance test, the obsessional-compulsive checklist, and the assessor-rated targets (time), but relative to the relaxation control condition had no significant effects on the measures of mood. These results are almost certainly an underestimate of the extent of the improvements achieved by behavioural treatment because the major comparisons were made at week 7 i.e. before 20 of the 40 patients had completed the second of their three-week periods of behavioural treatment. As reported above, this group of patients continued to show significant improvement during the period of treatment that took place from weeks 7 to 10. Comparisons carried out at week 10 would have shown more extensive changes attributable to the behavioural treatment. Unfortunately a weakness in the experimental design did not make allowance for the evaluation of the continuing changes that occurred during weeks 7–10.

Leaving aside this difficulty, the significant effects of treatment are consistent with earlier research on the subject (see reviews by Beech and Vaughan, 1979; Rachman, Hodgson and Marks, 1971, 1973; Marks, 1978; Rachman and Hodgson, 1979). As in the earlier studies in this series, the behavioural treatment was not followed by significant reductions in adverse mood, relative to the control condition. This finding is inconsistent with the reports given by Meyer and Levy (1974, p. 250) and Boersma *et al.* (1976). Short of a direct comparison between methods employed by these different research teams, it is difficult to resolve the apparent inconsistency. However it seems likely that the difference can be traced to the broader and more intensive treatment programme employed by Meyer and his colleagues. More important, our results emphasise the need to incorporate a control condition, because its absence might have led to the misleading conclusion that improvements in mood were attributable to behaviour therapy.

The results of the behavioural treatment were *behavioural* and *specific*. The compulsive behaviour changed as predicted, and was not accompanied by alterations in other aspects of the person's problems. The absence of concomitant mood or other changes emphasises the specificity of the therapeutic changes observed to follow this form of treatment. Such specificity, although it is moderately disappointing for clinicians, is of theoretical significance. It encourages the view that there is a direct connection between the treatment provided and the effects observed; the specificity discourages explanations which rest on the operation of non-specific factors such as, for example, the influence of the therapist–patient relationship.

The clomipramine was followed by several broad improvements, reflected in measures of mood and of rituals. These encouraging changes are consistent with the persuasive but as yet unconfirmed claims made by Capstick (1975) and several others. The stability of these improvements needs to be determined. The interesting question of distinguishing between the primary and secondary effects of this anti-depressant drug cannot be adequately resolved by our findings, but it would appear that the mood-relieving effects of the drug were primary and the improvements observed in obsessional-compulsive problems were secondary. If the drug had produced a direct effect on obsessional-compulsive problems, then non-depressed obsessional patients would have improved on measures of obsessionality more on receiving clomipramine than comparable patients improve with placebo.

We obtained clear evidence of the anti-depressant effect of clomipramine, but little sign that it had a direct anti-obsessive effect. Surprisingly, we obtained no evidence of an interaction between behavioural treatment and clomipramine. Although our original prediction, based largely on clinical experience, was not borne out, further investigations are worth undertaking if only because the separate effects of the two forms of treatment are so clear. It is of course possible that our failure to obtain evidence of an interaction between the two methods of treatment arose from weaknesses in the experimental design. As mentioned earlier, the major comparison took place at week 7, and there are reasons for concluding that neither the behavioural treatment nor the clomipramine had at this stage achieved their full effects. It is possible that with better timing, an interaction between the two techniques might become evident.

It should be said that when a patient has both sets of problems, depressed mood and obsessional difficulties (see principal components analysis), the combined application of behavioural treatment and clomipramine is justified. The behavioural treatment can be expected to have a specific behavioural effect while the drug can be expected to improve the patient's mood state.

The results obtained in the clomipramine treated groups suggest, on the other hand, that significant depression probably helps to maintain compulsive behaviour; the application of the anti-depressant medication was followed by reductions in depression and in compulsions. Further clarification of the close and interesting connection between depression and compulsions can be achieved in future research by instituting tighter controls on the timing of the interventions and the assessments. For example, it would be helpful to know whether the improvements in compulsive problems occur *after* a significant decline in depression, and if so, the duration of the lag. Further consideration of these problems is given in Rachman and Hodgson (1979). However, a decline in depression is not always accompanied by a decline in compulsions (e.g. the relaxation control condition in Rachman *et al.*, 1973). Hence, influences other than depression must also be implicated in maintaining compulsive behaviour.

The principal components analysis yielded a major general component which might reflect the wide ramifications of this disorder and/or failure to include an adequate number of independent assessment instruments. Our confirmation of the close association between obsessional-compulsive problems and depression is worth pursuing, providing one can exclude the possibility that the high scores obtained by the depressed patients on all tests of obsessionality (excluding the behavioural tests) are not unduly influenced by an elevation of complaint behaviour reported in depressed populations. The specificity of the effects of the behavioural treatment is confirmed by this analysis; the behavioural tests, which constituted a separate component, were observed to pick up the effect of the behavioural treatment. Further research into the primary and secondary effects of both forms of treatment and a renewed search for evidence of an interaction between the two techniques, are justified. The design and execution of controlled investigations into the critical question of the stability of therapeutic changes remains a major problem beset with practical and ethical obstacles. Finally, the results of the behavioural treatment were behavioural and specific, rather than non-specific. It is of course fitting that a form of treatment which focuses on the direct modification of behaviour should produce alterations in behaviour. This finding shows that the term *behaviour therapy* is appropriately used here, and it helps to validate one of the critical claims made on behalf of this particular form of behaviour therapy. It modifies the problem behaviour, and in the correct direction.

Acknowledgements—This research was supported by a grant from the Medical Research Council. We wish to thank Prof I. Marks for his valuable assistance.

REFERENCES

BEECH H. R. (Editor) (1974) *Obsessional States.* Methuen, London.

BEECH H. R. and VAUGHAN M. (1978) *Behavioural Treatment of Obsessional States.* John Wiley, Chichester.

BOERSMA K., DEN HENGST S., DEKKER J. and EMMELKAMP P. M. G. (1976) Exposure and response prevention in the natural environment: a comparison with obsessive-compulsive patients. *Beh. Res. Ther.* **14,** 19–24.

BOULOUGOURIS J. C. and RABAVILAS A. (Editors). (1977) *The Treatment of Phobic and Obsessive-Compulsive Disorders.* Pergamon Press, Oxford.

CAPSTICK N. (1975) Clomipramine in the treatment of the true obsessional state: a report on four patients. *Psychosomatics* **16,** (1), 21–25.

FERNANDEZ J. and LOPEZ-IBOR J. J. (1967) Monochlorimipramine in the treatment of psychiatric patients resistant to other therapies. *Act. Luso. Es. Neurol.* **26,** 119–147.

GELDER M. G. and MARKS I. M. (1966) Severe agoraphobia: a controlled prospective trial of behaviour therapy. *Br. J. Psychiat.* **112,** 309–319.

HODGSON R., RACHMAN S. and MARKS I. M. (1972) The treatment of obsessive-compulsive neurosis: followup and further findings. *Behav. Res. Ther.* **10,** 181–189.

HAMILTON M. (1969) Standardised assessment and recording of depressive symptoms. *Psychiat. Neurol. Neurochir.* **72,** 201–205.

LEWIS A. J. (1934) Melancholia: A clinical survey of depressive states. *J. ment. Sci.* **80,** 277–378.

MARKS I. M. (1978) Exposure treatments (Chapter 7): Conceptual Issues (pp. 163–203, Chapter 8): Clinical Applications (pp. 204–242). In *Behavior Modification* (Edited by W. S. AGRAS) Little Brown.

MARKS I. M., HODGSON R. and RACHMAN S. (1975) Treatment of chronic obsessive-compulsive neurosis by in vivo exposure. *Br. J. Psychiat.* **127,** 349–365.

MARKS I. M., HALLAM R. S., PHILPOTT R. and CONNOLLY J. (1977) *Nursing in Behavioural Psychotherapy.* Research Series of Royal College of Nursing, London.

MARKS I. M., BIRD J. and LINDLEY P. (1978) Behavioural nurse therapists. *Behav. Psychother.* **6,** 25–35.

MARKS et al. (1979) Clomipramine and exposure for compulsive rituals (In preparation).

MEYER V., LEVY R. and SCHNURER A. (1974) The behavioural treatment of obsessive-compulsive disorders. In *Obsessional States* (Edited by H. R. BEECH). Methuen, London.

PHILPOTT R. (1975) Recent advances in the behavioural measurements of obsessional illness. *Scot. med. J.* **20,** 33–40.

RACHMAN S., HODGSON R. and MARKS I. M. (1971) Treatment of chronic obsessive-compulsive neurosis. *Behav. Res Ther.* **9,** 237–247.

RACHMAN S., MARKS I. M. and HODGSON R. (1973) The treatment of obsessive-compulsive neurotics by modelling and flooding *in vivo*. *Behav. Res. Ther.* **11**, 463–471.

RACHMAN S. and HODGSON R. (1979) *Obsessions and Compulsions*. Prentice-Hall, Englewood Cliffs, NJ.

ROPER G., RACHMAN S. and MARKS I. M. (1976) Passive and participant modelling in exposure treatment of obsessive-compulsive neurotics. *Behav. Res Ther.* **13**, 271–279.

SNAITH *et al.* (1971) Assessment of the severity of primary depressive illness. *Psychol. Med.* **1**, 143–149.

STERN *et al.* (1979) Clomipramine: plasma Levels, side effects and outcome in obsessive-compulsive neurosis (In preparation).

COGNITIVE-BEHAVIORAL TREATMENT WITH AND WITHOUT RESPONSE PREVENTION FOR BULIMIA

G. Terence Wilson,[1]* Kathleen L. Eldredge,[2] Delia Smith[3] and Barbara Niles[4]

[1]GSAPP, Rutgers University, Box 819, Piscataway, NJ 08854, [2]V.A. Medical Center, Palo Alto. Calif., [3]Western Psychiatric Institute Pittsburgh, Palo Alto and [4]V.A. Medical Center, Boston, Mass., U.S.A.

(Received 26 March 1991)

Summary—We compared cognitive-behavior therapy (CBT) with and without exposure and response prevention (ERP) in the treatment of eating disorder patients who both binged and purged, and reported abnormal attitudes concerning body weight and shape. Both treatments produced significant and comparable reductions in binge-eating and purging, eating patterns, and attitudes about weight and shape at posttreatment. Treatment effects were generalized to improvements in different measures of general psychopathology, and were maintained over follow-ups of 3 and 12 months. The findings are consistent with prior research showing that CBT is an effective treatment for patients with the core features of bulimia nervosa. Furthermore, the data suggest that the addition of in-session exposure and response prevention does not enhance the effectiveness of the basic CBT program.

INTRODUCTION

Rosen and Leitenberg (1982) developed exposure and response prevention (ERP) as a behavioral technique for the treatment of bulimia nervosa based on their anxiety model of the disorder. As these authors put it, "... binge eating and vomiting seem linked in a vicious circle by anxiety. ... Eating elicits this anxiety (binging dramatically so); vomiting reduces it. Once an indivdiual has learned that vomiting following food intake leads to anxiety reduction, rational fears no longer inhibit overeating. Thus the driving force of this disorder may be vomiting, not binging ..." (p. 118). The analogy is to the behavioral treatment of obsessive-compulsive disorders. Treatment is aimed primarily at preventing vomiting in response to exposure to the binge-eating that typically elicits it. Although the specific technique has been implemented in different ways (Wilson, 1988), the common denominator is that the patient is requested to bring to each therapy session her characteristic binge foods and then consume them to the point at which she would typically induce vomiting. Under the guidance of the therapist the patient is encouraged not to vomit but to cope with the anxiety and learn that it will gradually extinguish over the remainder of the therapeutic session. The procedure is hypothesized to uncouple the learned association between eating-induced anxiety and vomiting.

Initial findings from an uncontrolled clinical series (Giles, Young & Young, 1985) and single-case experimental design studies (Leitenberg, Rosen, Gross, Nudelman & Vara, 1984; Rossiter & Wilson, 1985) suggested that ERP was a broadly effective form of treatment. The effectiveness of ERP was subsequently evaluated in three controlled outcome studies. Wilson, Rossiter, Kleifield and Lindholm (1986) compared ERP in combination with a verbal cognitive restructuring (CR) method with CR alone. The former was superior to the latter, the posttreatment abstinence rates for binge-eating and vomiting being 71 and 33% respectively. The small sample size militated against a statistically significant difference between the two treatments in terms of mean percent reduction in binge-eating and vomiting. Moreover, as Wilson (1988) pointed out, interpretation of this study must take into account the fact that the CR treatment omitted important behavioral components of a comprehensive and now relatively standard cognitive-behavioral treatment (CBT) program for bulimia nervosa (Fairburn, 1985). Hence the short-term superiority of combining ERP with CR does not show that ERP enhances the effectiveness of CBT.

---

*Author for correspondence.

Leitenberg *et al.* (1988) compared a combination of a more representative CBT treatment with two different forms of ERP (one conducted in multiple settings, the other in a single setting), with CBT only, and a wait-list control. As in the Wilson *et al.* (1986) study, treatment was conducted in small groups. All three treatments were significantly more effective than the wait-list control at posttreatment and a 6 month follow-up. CBT plus either form of ERP did not differ significantly from CBT only across a variety of behavioral and attitudinal measures of outcome, with the exception of mean vomiting frequency and one part of a test meal at the follow-up. Only 36% of the CBT patients and 33.3% of the patients in the combined treatment were abstinent at follow-up (Agras, Schneider, Arnow, Raeburn & Telch, 1989b). In all, this pattern of results provides little evidence of the value of adding the ERP technique to CBT treatment.

A third study compared individual CBT with a combination of CBT and ERP, as well as a form of supportive treatment (including self-monitoring of binge/purge behavior), and a wait-list control (Agras, Schneider, Arnow, Raeburn & Telch, 1989a). At posttreatment the three treatments showed significant improvement whereas the wait-list controls did not. Only CBT differed significantly from the wait list controls on frequency of purging, and at the 6 month follow-up CBT (80% mean reduction) was significantly superior to CBT plus ERP (50% mean reduction). Abstinence rates at follow-up were 59 and 20% respectively. In this study ERP seems to have had a negative effect, detracting from the effectiveness of CBT. This effect could be attributable to the demands of ERP procedure making it impossible to implement fully the CBT treatment within what was a relatively brief treatment (14 sessions of 1 h duration). That a combination of two specific treatments produces a less effective outcome than that of either of the treatments separately administered is not unprecedented in the behavior therapy literature (Franks & Wilson, 1977).

The purpose of the present study was to evaluate the utility of adding ERP to CBT treatment in a way that overcame some of the limitations of the previous three studies. The goal was to compare individual, comprehensive CBT treatment with and without a limited number of intensive ERP sessions. By including a 1 yr follow-up we could assess the longer-term effects of both treatments, and compare their relative effects, a comparison that the reversal design of the Wilson *et al.* (1986) study precluded. We planned the study to ensure that the addition of ERP would not undermine the implementation of the full CBT treatment, as might have been the case in the Agras *et al.* (1989a) investigation.

METHOD

Subjects

All patients were recruited through announcements of the treatment program in campus and community newspapers, and from referrals from local health professionals. Respondents were contacted by phone and provided they reported binge-eating and self-induced vomiting at least once a week, were invited to a diagnostic and assessment interview. Interviewees were included in the study if: (a) they met modified DSM-III-R criteria for bulimia nervosa (the two modifications were that *S*s binged and vomited at least once a week rather than twice weekly; and perceived excessive consumption of food was counted as a binge provided loss of control was present); (b) weighed within 15% of the range for medium frame for their height on the 1983 Metropolitan Life Insurance Norms; (c) suffered from the eating disorder for a minimum of 12 months; (d) were not currently in any form of treatment for eating disorders; and (e) consented to a medical examination and blood tests conducted by their personal physician or the student health service. The mean age of *S*s in the CBT treatment was 19.8 yr, and 21.6 yr for those in the CBT/ERP treatment. Fourteen were college students. The physical examinations revealed no instance of medical problems or abnormal blood chemistry. Eligible *S*s were randomly assigned to a 20 session treatment program of either CBT or CBT plus ERP.

Procedure

The Eating Disorder Examination (EDE) (Cooper & Fairburn, 1987), a semi-structured clinical interview, was administered to all *S*s. The EDE provides the most comprehensive and discriminating assessment of the specific psychopathology of bulimia nervosa (Rosen & Srebnik, 1990), and has been validated in several studies (Rosen, Vara, Wendt & Leitenberg, 1990; Wilson & Smith, 1989). All Ss were weighed using a physician's balance beam scale, and completed the following questionnaires: the Beck Depression Inventory (BDI; Beck, Ward, Mendelson, Mock & Erbaugh, 1961); the Symptom Checklist 90 (SCL-90; Derogatis, 1977); the Eating Self-efficacy Questionnaire (ESQ; Glynn & Ruderman, 1982); the Rosenberg (1979) Self-esteem Scale (RSE); and the Social Adjustment Scale (SAS) (Weissman & Bothwell, 1976).

Treatments. Twenty sessions of individual treatment were administered over a 20 week period on the same schedule recommended by Fairburn (1985), namely twice a week for the first 4 weeks, weekly for the next 2 months, and once a fortnight for the remaining 8 weeks. The CBT treatment was administered according to a written manual.* The initial treatment sessions were devoted to developing an effective therapeutic relationship, assessing high risk situations for binge-eating/ purging, clarifying treatment goals and enhancing patients' commitment to eliminating binge-eating and purging, and introducing cognitive restructuring (CR) adapted from Beck's (1976) cognitive therapy. In this CR dysfunctional thoughts were identified and challenged according to the following three-step format: (1) the situation in which the thought arose was noted; (2) the dysfunctional thought was identified; and (3) the thought was challenged. Ss were given a list of typical cognitive distortions (Burns, 1980) to help them identify dysfunctional thoughts. Weekly homework assignments on identifying and altering dysfunctional thoughts were a key aspect of the treatment. The primary content of CR was constant concern about body weight and fear of gaining weight. Food and eating patterns were analysed in this context. Rigid rules about 'good' vs 'bad' foods and unrealistic, perfectionistic standards of eating and personal conduct were challenged with a view to adopting a more flexible realistic approach. Therapy emphasized helping Ss to define their self-worth in terms other than physical appearance and moving them towards an acceptance of their body shape and weight. In addition, CR, especially in the later sessions, addressed emotional and interpersonal antecedents of binge-eating. Specific behavioral assignments were designed to modify dysfunctional thoughts. Ss were weighed by the therapist at each session.

The middle range of treatment sessions focused on changing eating behavior directly. The goals were to develop regular eating patterns comprising three meals a day with provision for healthy snacks, and to incorporate, in a graduated manner, previously avoided foods into their meals. Self-control strategies and problem-solving skills (viz., finding alternative ways of responding to particular situations) were used to assist patients in coping with high-risk situations for binge-eating. CR and a delay technique were used to help patients learn to cope with the negative affect and specific urges that frequently triggered a binge. The remaining treatment sessions continued to address the importance of a regular pattern of healthy and flexible eating, and explicitly addressed relapse prevention (Marlatt & Gordon, 1985).

ERP sessions were introduced between session 10 and 13, using the procedure described by Wilson *et al.* (1986). Ss were asked to bring their typical binge food to treatment sessions. They were then asked to eat to the point where they would feel compelled to vomit. It is not the quantity of food that is decisive here, but Ss' feeling that they had transgressed some subjective standard or rule that would normally trigger vomiting. When this point was reached, they were asked to focus attention on physical discomfort and fears of weight gain and to write these down. Subjective Units of Distress (SUDS) ratings were taken after 1 min and then after every 2 min for a period of 15 min. Thereafter, SUDS were taken after 5 min and then every 10 min for the remainder of the session. During this part of the session Ss were encouraged to discuss their thoughts and feelings with the therapists about having eaten and not vomited. Using the CR strategies described above, the therapist tried to develop Ss' sense of personal efficacy about coping with negative emotions and resisting the urge to vomit. ERP sessions were framed as behavioral experiments that allow Ss to disconfirm, on the basis of their own experience, their fears about losing control, being swept away by irresistible urges to vomit and uncontrollably gaining weight. In explaining the nature and purpose of ERP, the therapists addressed the possibility that Ss might gain some weight. It was pointed out, however, that the majority of clients who had received this treatment had not gained weight. Ss were informed that self-induced vomiting does not ensure elimination of all calories ingested in a binge. In the event that weight gain occurred, Ss were told that they would be taught

---

*A copy of this manual may be obtained by writing to the first author.

healthier, more effective methods of weight control. *S*s were instructed to try to refrain from vomiting, even if they binged, between sessions. ERP sessions required roughly 90 min to conduct.

Therapists. Four advanced level graduate students (all women), with specific experience in CBT in general and the treatment of bulimia nervosa in particular, served as therapists. Each therapist administered both treatment methods. All four therapists met weekly as a group with the first author to discuss treatment and resolve problems. The first author systematically monitored the implementation of both treatments by all therapists by listening to tape-recordings of randomly selected sessions.

Assessment of treatment effects

Changes in the specific psychopathology of bulimia were assessed by readministering the EDE and EDI. An independent assessor, unfamiliar with the treatment conditions, conducted the EDE interviews. Changes in general psychopathology were assessed by readministering the BDI, SAS, ESQ, SCL-90, and RSE.

Follow-up

*S*s were contacted by phone for each of the first 2 months at which time they answered a brief, standardized set of questions assessing episodes of binge-eating and purging, weight, and eating habits.* At the third month *S*s visited the clinic where they again answered these questions and completed the following self-report measures—EDI, BDI, SCL-90, SAS, ESQ, and RSE. Phone contacts were repeated monthly until the eleventh month. At 12 months *S*s were readministered the EDE by the same independent assessor as at posttreatment and completed the same set of questionnaires administered at the pre- and posttreatment, and 3 month follow-up assessments.

At both the 3 and 12 month follow-ups *S*s were questioned about any additional treatment they may have sought. At 3 months, one *S* in CBT reported having had two sessions at a university counselling center. In CBT/ERP, one *S* had joined Weight Watchers for 3 weeks before withdrawing, and one had received inpatient treatment (medication—desipramine) for 43 days at a local psychiatric hospital. At 12 months, in the CBT/ERP condition, one *S* reported outpatient treatment (medication—month 12). Another CBT/ERP *S* reported receiving treatment (medication—fluoxetine) for depression.

RESULTS

Drop-outs

Five *S*s (22.7%) dropped out of treatment, three from CBT, and two from CBT/ERP. The drop-outs did not differ from *S*s who completed treatment on measures of specific eating disorder psychopathology (binge/purge frequencies, EDE subscales) or more general psychopathology (SCL-90, BDI, EDI subscales, SAS, and RSE) at pretreatment. At the 12 month follow-up evaluation we were unable to contact an additional *S* in CBT, and two *S*s in CBT/ERP.

Credibility

Five 4-point scales were used to assess the credibility of treatment for *S*s. In response to the question "How would you rate the quality of the service you received?" mean scores for the CBT and CBT/ERP conditions were 3.9 and 3.5. For the question "Did you get the kind of service you wanted?" the means were 3.9 and 3.6; for the question "If a friend were in need of similar help, would you recommend our program to her?" the means were 3.9 and 3.8; for the question "Have the services you received helped you to deal more effectively with your problems?" the means were 3.9 and 3.8, and for the question "If you were to seek help again would you come back to our program?" the means were 3.9 and 3.4. These scores indicate that *S*s viewed both treatments as highly and equally credible.

---

*Telephone contacts were initiated by one of the therapists from the study, although not necessarily the therapist a particular *S* had seen.

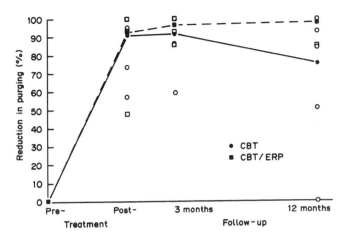

Fig. 1. Mean and individual S percentage reductions in binge-eating and purging at posttreatment and
3 and 12 month follow-ups. Only Ss who completed treatment were included.

Treatment effects

Binge/purge frequencies. The two treatment groups did not differ at pretreatment on frequency of binge-eating, defined as either subjectively or objectively large episodes of overeating (Cooper & Fairburn, 1987), or the combined total. The monthly means for combined subjective and objective binges were 17.4 for CBT, and 21.2 for CBT/ERP. Nor did the two groups differ on purge frequency at pretreatment (CBT = 23.1; CBT/ERP = 21.4).

All statistical analyses were conducted on a log transformation of the data. A repeated measures ANOVA of all Ss, including dropouts whose last recorded binge/purge frequencies were used in the analysis, showed a significant decrease in both total binge, $F(1,20) = 60.80$, $P < 0.0001$, and purge, $F(1,20) = 82.65$, $P < 0.0001$, frequencies from pre- to posttreatment. An ANOVA of only Ss who completed treatment shows the same finding for total binge, $F(1,15) = 137.4$, $P < 0.0001$, and purge, $F(1,15) = 122.3$, $P < 0.0001$, frequencies from pre- to posttreatment. The mean percentage reductions for completers for binge-eating were 94.53 for CBT, and 91.36 for CBT/ERP. The results for purging were almost identical, the comparable figures being 90.65 and 92.48%. There were no pre-post × treatment condition interactions. Figure 1 summarizes the mean and individual S reductions in total binge and purge frequencies from pre- to posttreatment.

The mean abstinence rates at posttreatment for all Ss for binge-eating, including drop-outs as failures, were 63.6% for CBT and 54.6% for CBT/ERP. The comparable rates for purging were 45.5 and 54.6%. If only completers are included, the rates for binge-eating were 87.5% for CBT, and 66.7% for CBT/ERP. The comparable rates for purging were 62.5 and 66.7%.

Weights and eating patterns

Ss in the two treatment conditions did not differ on body mass index (BMI) at either pre- or posttreatment. The respective means for CBT were 22.02 and 22.62, and 22.3 and 22.44 for CBT/ERP. Clearly there was no overall change in BMI from pre- to posttreatment.

The Restraint and Eating Concern subscales of the EDE provide detailed assessment of patients' eating. The Restraint subscale measures avoidance of any eating at all, of particular foods, reactions to breaking dietary rules, and desire for an empty stomach. The Eating Concern subscale measures preoccupation with food or calories, fear of losing control over eating, social eating, eating in secret, and guilt about eating. There were no differences between the two treatment groups at pretreatment. Repeated measures ANOVAs showed a significant change on the Eating Concern subscale, $F(1,15) = 70.84$, $P < 0.0001$, and on the Restraint subscale, $F(1,15) = 28.16$, $P < 0.0001^*$ (see Fig. 2). The absence of any significant Time × Treatment Condition effect indicates that the two treatments had equivalent effects.

---

*The overall ANOVA for restraint was marginally significant, $F(18,15) = 2.24$, $P = 0.06$. The subsequent F-test for a Time (Pre–Post) effect should be interpreted cautiously.

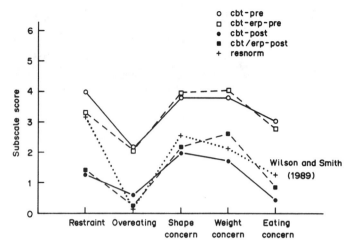

Fig. 2. Mean EDE subscale scores for CBT and CBT/ERP at pre- and posttreatment.

Attitudes to body weight and shape. There were significant pre- to posttreatment changes on both the EDE subscales of attitudes toward body weight, $F(1,15) = 23.08$, $P < 0.0002$, and shape, $F(1,15) = 36.18$, $P < 0.0001$, but no Time × Treatment Condition interaction. Figure 2 summarizes these treatment effects.

General psychopathology. Table 1 summarizes the mean pre- and posttreatment scores of both treatment groups on the BDI, SCL-90, SAS, RSE, and the EDI subscales of Perfectionism, Interoceptive Awareness, Ineffectiveness, Interpersonal Distrust, and Maturity Fears. At pretreatment the two treatment groups did not differ on any of these measures. Repeated measures ANOVAs showed an overall significant pre- to posttreatment effect on the BDI, SAS, RSE, and all scales of the EDI (see Table 1). The sole Time × Treatment Condition effect was on the SCL-90, $F(1,14) = 5.82$, $P < 0.05$, indicating that CBT produced a greater reduction on this measure than CBT/ERP.

Follow-up

Binge/purge frequencies. Figure 1 summarizes the individual and mean binge/purge frequencies for *S*s in both treatments at 3 and 12 month follow-ups. Repeated measures ANOVAs showed no significant effect of Time for either treatment, indicating overall maintenance of treatment-produced improvement. There was, however, a significant effect of Treatment Condition for purge (but not binge) frequency, $F(1,13) = 21.71$, $P < 0.0001$. The abstinence rates at three months for binge-eating were 75% for CBT and 33.3% for CBT/ERP. The comparable figures for purging were 62.5% and 55.6%. At 12 months the abstinence rates for binge-eating were 62.5% for CBT and 66.7% for CBT/ERP. For purging the figures were 42.12 and 85.7%. Fisher Exact Tests (2 Tail) showed no differences between the two treatments at either follow-up period.

Table 1. Pre- and posttreatment scores of CBT and CBT/ERP on measures of general psychopathology

| | Pretreatment | | | | Posttreatment | | | | | |
| | CBT | | CBT/ERP | | CBT | | CBT/ERP | | | |
	M	(SD)	M	(SD)	M	(SD)	M	(SD)	F	P
BDI	16.5	(8.5)	19.3	(10.5)	4.24	(3.5)	8.0	(6.9)	34.97	<0.0001
SAS	2.4	(0.49)	2.4	(0.64)	1.8	(0.41)	2.0	(0.46)	18.25	<0.001
RSE	23.3	(2.3)	23.3	(5.0)	32.2	(5.1)	28.0	(5.3)	18.38	<0.001
SCL-90 (GSI)	1.85	(0.57)	1.28	(0.56)	0.44	(0.08)	0.97	(0.54)	5.82*	<0.03
EDI										
IA	12.0	(8.0)	13.4	(4.1)	2.3	(2.8)	2.9	(2.8)	58.17	<0.0001
IN	11.1	(5.4)	11.6	(6.7)	3.0	(2.5)	4.6	(5.1)	30.59	<0.0001
MF	5.6	(5.7)	4.1	(7.5)	2.9	(2.7)	3.6	(5.4)	4.77	<0.01
P	10.0	(4.0)	9.1	(4.4)	5.9	(5.3)	6.9	(4.9)	9.12	<0.01
ID	7.9	(5.5)	7.3	(4.0)	4.3	(5.7)	5.0	(5.0)	8.04	<0.02

*A Treatment × Time interaction.

Bodyweight. At 12 months, the mean BMI for CBT *S*s ($n = 7$) was 21.88 (SD = 2.57). For CBT/ERP *S*s ($n = 6$) the mean BMI was 22.21 (SD = 1.25).

Attitudes to weight and shape. Repeated measures ANOVAs showed no significant changes from posttreatment to the 12 month follow-up for any EDE subscale. Nor were there differences between the two treatments at 12 months. The means for CBT and CBT/ERP respectively were 1.45 and 0.99 (Restraint); 1.0 and 0.42 (Overeating); 1.82 and 1.91 (Shape Concern); 2.25 and 2.03 (Weight Concern); and 1.13 and 0.66 (Eating Concern).

Similarly, there were no significant differences from posttreatment to either follow-up on the Drive for Thinness (DT) or Body Dissatisfaction (BD) subscales of the EDI. Nor did the two treatments differ from each other. At 12 months, the means for DT and BD for CBT were 5.3 (SD = 6.8) and 10.7 (SD = 10.3), and for CBT/ERP 10.8 (SD = 7.1) and 16.2 (SD = 9.1).

DISCUSSION

A limitation of this study was the small number of *S*s, and the findings must be interpreted cautiously with this in mind. The results indicate that adding ERP to a comprehensive CBT treatment neither enhances nor undermines the effectiveness of CBT. The data are consistent across a variety of different measures in indicating no difference between CBT plus ERP, and CBT alone. This finding, given Agras *et al.*'s (1989a) negative results and Leitenberg *et al.*'s (1988) at best equivalent results, leads us to echo Agras *et al.*'s (1989a) recommendation that ERP should not be routinely added to a comprehensive CBT treatment. The most conservative analysis of treatment outcome, counting drop-outs as treatment failures, yielded mean percentage reductions of 74.89 and 77.99% in binge-eating in CBT and CBT/ERP respectively. The comparable figures for purging were 85.38 and 79.28%. This measure of improvement compares favorably with previous studies. Leitenberg *et al.* (1988) reported mean reductions in purging frequency of 67 and 40% respectively in their CBT plus ERP and CBT alone treatments. Agras *et al.* (1989a) reported a 77% mean reduction in purging in their most effective treatment condition (CBT) after excluding drop-outs. When we exclude drop-outs our mean percentage reductions improve to 94.5 and 90.7% for binge-eating and purging in the CBT treatment and 91.4 and 92.5% in the CBT/ERP treatment. The drop-out rate in the present study (22.7%) was the same as that reported by Agras *et al.* (1989a), and consistent with other studies of CBT.

Abstinence or remission rates show a similar pattern of findings. Including all 22 *S*s in the analysis, 63.64% of CBT and 54.55% of CBT/ERP were abstinent from binge-eating at posttreatment, while the rates for purging were 45.45 and 54.55% respectively. If we exclude drop-outs, the percentages of patients who reported the absence of binge-eating at the end of treatment were 87.5 and 66.7%. The comparable figures for purging were 62.5 and 66.67%. Agras *et al.* (1989a) obtained a 56% abstinence rate at the end of their most effective treatment (CBT alone). Consistent with previous studies (Fairburn, Jones, Peveler, Carr, Solomon, O'Connor, Burton & Hope, 1991; Leitenberg *et al.*, 1988), CBT had broad therapeutic effects. Improvements in specific eating disorder psychopathology were not restricted to frequency of binge-eating and purging, but also included dietary restraint, concern about eating, and specific eating patterns. Figure 2 shows that posttreatment EDE subscale means were similar to scores obtained from normal, non-bulimic restrained eaters (Wilson & Smith, 1989). Indeed, the levels of dietary restraint at posttreatment were lower than that of the normal restrained eaters in the Wilson and Smith (1989) study.

Generalized improvement extended to associated psychopathology, such as depression, social adjustment, self-esteem, and overall psychological distress. We can conclude that CBT for bulimia produces wide-ranging therapeutic improvement without any sign of symptom substitution. The single difference between the two treatments was the superiority of CBT on the GSI of the SCL-90. There is no *a priori* reason to expect an advantage for CBT alone, and in the absence of any other difference it does not allow us to infer that CBT alone would be more effective than CBT plus ERP.

Treatment effects were maintained over time. As in other studies that included a 1 yr follow-up (Fairburn *et al.*, 1986; Wilson *et al.*, 1986), the present study showed that treatment effects were maintained at both 3 and 12 month follow-ups. The follow-up data must be viewed cautiously because a total of 5 of the 17 *S*s who completed treatment subsequently received some form of treatment. Of these, three received antidepressant medication that precludes unambiguous ascription of long-term improvement to the psychological treatments described here. In addition, all *S*s were contacted by phone for follow-up assessments during the first 2 months, and the fourth through eleventh months, and visited the clinic at 3 months. This degree of contact can plausibly be seen as a form of maintenance. The apparent superiority of CBT/ERP over CBT alone at the 12 month follow-up on mean percentage reduction in purging is difficult to interpret because of the small number of *S*s. It may simply reflect the impact of the two *S*s who dropped out at this point.

A theoretical analysis of the mechanisms responsible for behavior change in CBT and ERP explains the absence of significant differences between the two treatments. In-session, structured ERP is simply one of several ways of systematically exposing patients to feared cues (in the case of bulimic patients, the consumption of 'forbidden foods') with a view to extinguishing unrealistic anxiety or enhancing self-efficacy for coping with anxiety without resorting to purging (Wilson, 1988). The same learning principle is inherent in the routine instructions in CBT to eat three meals a day, including 'bad' foods that have been avoided for fear of losing control and binge-eating, without subsequent purging. The latter is functional exposure (Fairburn, 1985). It is self-administered exposure, whereas in-session ERP is therapist-assisted exposure. It is, therefore, not surprising that to the extent that there is sufficient exposure to relevant food cues without compensatory purging in CBT treatment, the addition of ERP should not significantly increase effectiveness.

It could be argued that the number of ERP sessions in the present study was insufficient to demonstrate a differential effect. Although we cannot rule out the possibility that a greater number of ERP sessions might have produced an effect, several points must be considered in evaluating this possibility. First, we included fewer ERP sessions than Agras *et al.* (1989a), but our sessions were 90 min in duration compared with their 60 min sessions. Second, the data show that the two *S*s who received the fewest (two) ERP sessions did not differ at posttreatment from those who received either three or five ERP sessions. Were the number of ERP sessions critical, we might expect differences among these *S*s. Third, it is not as if the CBT/ERP treatment was ineffective. It produced greater reductions in binge-eating and purging than Leitenberg *et al.* (1988) treatments.

From a practical and methodological perspective, adding ERP to CBT without curtailing the time necessary for implementing CBT resulted in more time being devoted to the combined treatment. The plan was to keep this imbalance in treatment duration as small as possible. In several cases patients received only three sessions of ERP because they had already begun to change their behavior—eating more flexibly, refraining from purging, and showing only mild discomfort during in-session ERP. Clinically there seemed to be little point in requiring continued ERP sessions especially since some patients resisted this prospect. [Problems posed by resistance to in-session ERP have been noted before (Wilson, 1988).]

The absence of any difference between the two treatments in the present study, given the absence of either a wait-list control or alternative comparison condition, makes unequivocal interpretation of the results difficult. Nonetheless, the results show that CBT is an effective treatment for normal weight bulimic patients who both binge and purge. Of the several studies that have included a wait-list control group, none has shown any real improvement (Fairburn, 1988; Fairburn, Agras & Wilson, 1991), let alone the statistically and clinically significant change we obtained. CBT is clearly superior to repeated assessment and the passage of time. What we cannot infer from this study is how our CBT would have compared with an alternative form of treatment.

Comparing results across different treatment settings is complicated by several procedural differences among the studies. One issue is how, and for how long, binge/purge frequencies are measured, Agras *et al.* (1989a), Leitenberg *et al.* (1988), and Wilson *et al.* (1986) all based their results on patients' self-monitoring of frequencies of binge-eating and purging over the last week of treatment. In contrast, in the present study, following Fairburn *et al.* (1991), we derived our posttreatment results from patients' self-reported frequencies gathered during the EDE for the previous 28 days. On the one hand, it can be argued that taking into account a full month as opposed to a single week for assessing the presence and frequency of binge-eating and purging provides a more searching and hence stringent evaluation of outcome. In this sense our results could be interpreted as a more conservative index of the effectiveness of cognitive-behavioral treatment.

On the other hand, critics may argue that self-monitoring provides a more rigorous measure of binge-purge frequencies than retrospective recall, even during the structured format of the EDE. Yet Rosen *et al.* (1990) found a very high correlation ($r = 0.81$) between the EDE assessment of vomiting and *S*s' own self-monitoring of this behavior, indicating that the EDE measure is valid.

Acknowledgements—We are grateful to Elaine Wilson, Ph.D., for conducting the independent, posttreatment and follow-up EDE evaluations, and Lynn Gale, Ph.D., for help with the statistical analyses. This paper was completed while the first author was a Fellow at the Center for Advanced Study in the Behavioral Sciences on financial support provided by the John D. and Catherine T. MacArthur Foundation.

REFERENCES

Agras, W. S., Schneider, J. A., Arnow, B., Raeburn, S. D. & Telch, C. F. (1989a). Cognitive-behavioral and response prevention treatments for bulimia nervosa. *Journal of Consulting Clinical Psychology, 57*, 215–221.

Agras, W. S., Schneider, J. A., Arnow, B., Raeburn, S. D. & Telch, C. F. (1989b). Cognitive-behavioral treatment with and without exposure plus response prevention: A reply to Leitenberg and Rosen. *Journal of Consulting Clinical Psychology, 57*, 778–779.

Beck, A. T. (1976). *Cognitive therapy and the emotional disorders.* New York: International Universities Press.

Beck, A. T., Ward, C. H., Mendelson, M., Mock, J. E. & Erbaugh, J. K. (1961). An inventory for measuring depression. *Archives of General Psychiatry, 4*, 561–571.

Burns, D. (1980). *Feeling good.* New York: Morrow.

Cooper, Z. & Fairburn, C. G. (1987). The Eating Disorder Examination: A semi-structured interview for the assessment of the specific psychopathology of eating disorders. *International Journal of Eating Disorders, 6*, 1–8.

Derogatis, L. R. (1977). *The SCL-90 manual I: Scoring, administration and procedures for the SCL-90.* Baltimore: Clinical Psychometric Research.

Fairburn, C. G. (1985). In Garner, D. M. & Garfinkel, P. E. (Eds), *Handbook of psychotherapy for anorexia nervosa and bulimia* (pp. 160–192). New York: Guilford Press.

Fairburn, C. G., Agras, W. S. & Wilson, G. T. (1991). The research on the treatment of bulimia nervosa: Practical and theoretical implications. In Anderson, G. H. & Kennedy, S. H. (Eds), *The biology of feast and famine: Relevance to eating disorders.* New York: Academic Press. In press.

Fairburn, C. G., Jones, R., Peveler, R. C., Carr, S. J., Solomon, R. A., O'Connor, M. E., Burton, J. & Hope, R. A. (1991). Three psychological treatments for bulimia nervosa: A comparative trial. *Archives of General Psychiatry, 48*, 463–469.

Franks, C. M. & Wilson, G. T. (Eds) (1977). *Annual review of behavior therapy: Theory and practice.* New York: Brunner/Mazel.

Garner, D. M., Olmsted, M. P. & Polivy, J. (1983). Development and validation of a multidimensional eating disorder inventory. *International Journal of Eating Disorders, 2*, 15–34.

Giles, T. R., Young, R. R. & Young, D. E. (1985). Behavioral treatment of severe bulimia. *Behavior Therapy, 16*, 393–405.

Glynn, S. M. & Ruderman, A. J. (1986). The development and validation of an Eating Self-Efficacy Scale. *Cognitive Therapy and Research, 10*, 403–420.

Leitenberg, H., Rosen, J., Gross, J., Nudelman, S. & Vara, L. (1988). Exposure plus response-prevention treatment of bulimia nervosa. *Journal of Consulting Clinical Psychology, 56*, 535–541.

Marlatt, G. A. & Gordon, J. (Eds) (1985). *Relapse prevention.* New York: Guilford Press.

Rosen, J. C. & Leitenberg, H. (1982). Bulimia nervosa: Treatment with exposure and response prevention. *Behavior Therapy, 13*, 117–124.

Rosen, J. C. & Srebnik, D. (1990). Assessment of eating disorders. In McReynolds, P., Rosen, J. C. & Chelune, G. (Eds), *Advances in psychological assessment* (Vol. 7). New York: Plenum Press.

Rosen, J. C., Vara, L., Wendt, S. & Leitenberg, H. (1990). Validity studies of the Eating Disorder Examination. *International Journal of Eating Disorders, 9*, 519–528.

Rosenberg, M. (1979). *Conceiving the self.* New York: Basic Books.

Rossiter, E. M. & Wilson, G. T. (1985). Cognitive restructuring and response prevention in the treatment of bulimia nervosa. *Behaviour Research and Therapy, 23*, 349–359.

Weissman, M. M. & Bothwell, S. (1976). Assessment of social adjustment by patient self-report. *Archives of General Psychiatry, 33*, 1111–1115.

Wilson, G. T. (1988). Cognitive-behavioral treatments of bulimia nervosa: The role of exposure. In Pirke, K. M., Vandereycken, W. & Ploog, D. (Eds), *The psychobiology of bulimia nervosa* (pp. 137–145). Springer, Berlin.

Wilson, G. T., Rossiter, E., Kleifield, E. I. & Lindholm, L. (1986). Cognitive-behavioral treatment of bulimia nervosa: A controlled evaluation. *Behaviour Research and Therapy, 24*, 277–288.

HABIT-REVERSAL: A METHOD OF ELIMINATING NERVOUS HABITS AND TICS*

N. H. Azrin and R. G. Nunn

Anna State Hospital, Anna, Illinois, U.S.A. and Rehabilitation Institute, Southern Illinois University
Carbondale, Illinois, U.S.A.

(Received 12 July 1973)

Summary—No clinical treatment for nervous habits has been generally effective. The present rationale is that nervous habits persist because of response chaining, limited awareness, excessive practice and social tolerance. A new procedure was devised for counteracting these influences: the client practiced movements which were the reverse of the nervous habit, he learned to be aware of each instance of the habit and to differentiate it from its usual response chain and he was given social approval for his efforts to inhibit the habit. The treatment was given during a single session to 12 clients who had diverse nervous habits such as nail-biting, thumb-sucking, eyelash-picking, head-jerking, shoulder-jerking, tongue-pushing and lisping. The habits were virtually eliminated on the very first day for all 12 clients and did not return during the extended follow-up for the 11 clients who followed the instructions.

Nervous habits and tics are psychological disorders which are highly resistant to general types of treatment. As concluded by Eriksson and Persson (1969) "some patients become permanently disabled and resistant to every form of treatment. Judging from the literature, no single form of treatment is universally effective" (p. 351). Similarly, Yates (1970) described tics as "notoriously resistant to almost any form of treatment" (p. 201).

Different theoretical explanations of nervous habits have been proposed, each of which has served as the basis for different types of treatment. The psychoanalytic view as expressed by Mahler and Luke (1946) considers tics as "erotic and aggressive instinctual impulses ... which are continually escaping through pathological discharge" (p. 441). The treatment derived from this view is to provide counseling that persuades the client that these impulses are the cause of his problem ('giving him insight') and to teach him to channel these impulses elsewhere. A second theoretical view is that nervous habits are caused by tension. Two types of treatment are based on this rationale; one is negative practice (Yates, 1958; Jones, 1960; Rafi, 1962) in which the client is required to perform the tic rapidly thereby preventing the tension reduction that otherwise would result. The second method of treatment that follows this tension reduction rationale is treatment by tranquilizing relaxant drugs (Connell et al., 1967; Challas and Brauer, 1963). A third theoretical account is that nervous habits are learned responses that are maintained by operant reinforcement. The treatment derived from this theory has been to arrange for aversive stimuli for the response in order to counteract the effect of these reinforcers (Brierly, 1967; Bucher, 1968).

* This research was supported by the State of Illinois Department of Mental Health and by Grant No. 21662 from the National Institute of Mental Health. Gratitude is expressed to Joanna Flores who drew the artwork for the figures, and to Dr. Renzaglia for providing facilities and assistance. Reprints may be obtained from either author, Behavior Research Laboratory, Anna State Hospital, Anna, Illinois 62906 U.S.A.

Present rationale

The present rationale is that a nervous habit originally starts as a normal reaction. The reaction may be to an extreme event such as a physical injury or psychological trauma (see also Yates, 1970), or the symptom may have started as an infrequent, but normal, behavior that has increased in frequency and been altered in its form. The behavior becomes classified as a nervous habit when it persists after the original injury or trauma has passed and when it assumes an unusual form and unusually high frequency. Under normal circumstances the nervous habit would be inhibited by personal or social awareness of its peculiarity or by its inherent inconvenience. The movement may, however, have blended into normal movements so gradually as to escape personal and social awareness. Once having achieved this transformation, the movement is performed so often as to become a strongly established habit that further escapes personal awareness because of its automatic nature. For some tics, the continuing execution of the movement may even strengthen the specific muscles required for that movement and the opposing muscles become relatively unused, thereby causing difficulty for conscious inhibition of the tic and further contributing to the low level of awareness of the tic movement. Also, social reinforcement in the form of sympathy may result, especially for those movements that have had a medical origin.

This analysis of nervous habits suggests several methods of treatment. The client should learn to be aware of every occurrence of the habit. Each habit movement should be interrupted so that it no longer is part of a chain of normal movements. A physically competing response should be established to interfere with the habit. When atrophy has resulted from the disuse of the antagonistic muscles, those antagonistic muscles should be strengthened. Social reinforcement should be reversed or eliminated.

METHOD

The procedure was evaluated by a within-subjects comparison. A measure was obtained of the extent of the problem prior to counseling and was considered to be the baseline level. This baseline level was compared with the measures taken after counseling.

Clients

Twelve clients were treated. Five clients contacted the counselor in response to a newspaper advertisement, three were children who were referred by their parents at the suggestion of their teacher, one was referred by a psychologist who had unsuccessfully treated the client for $2\frac{1}{2}$ yr, and the other three by various types of word of mouth knowledge of the service. No client was excluded. Their clients ages varied from 5 to 64 yrs; eight were female and four were male. Educational level varied from a pre-school child to a client who had an M.A. degree. All clients had been previously treated for their habits by various professionals such as a psychiatrist, psychologist, physician, dentist, speech therapist, or for the children, by their parents and teachers. All of the adult clients reported that their nervous habit seriously interfered with their functioning. Some of the habits caused medical problems; in the case of gum-sucking, by causing softness of the gum and mouth surfaces. Dental problems were caused by the thumb-sucking. The student teacher who lisped was told her teaching duties were unsatisfactory because of the lisping. Interference with all normal physical activities was caused by the head and shoulder tics. Problems of social appearance were caused by the eyelash picking and by the nail-biting. For all clients, the habits had been a long-standing problem of at least 3 yrs duration; for five clients the problem had existed continuously for at least 7 yrs.

Types of nervous habits

Eleven of the clients had one habit; one client had two. Figure 1 (left-hand column)

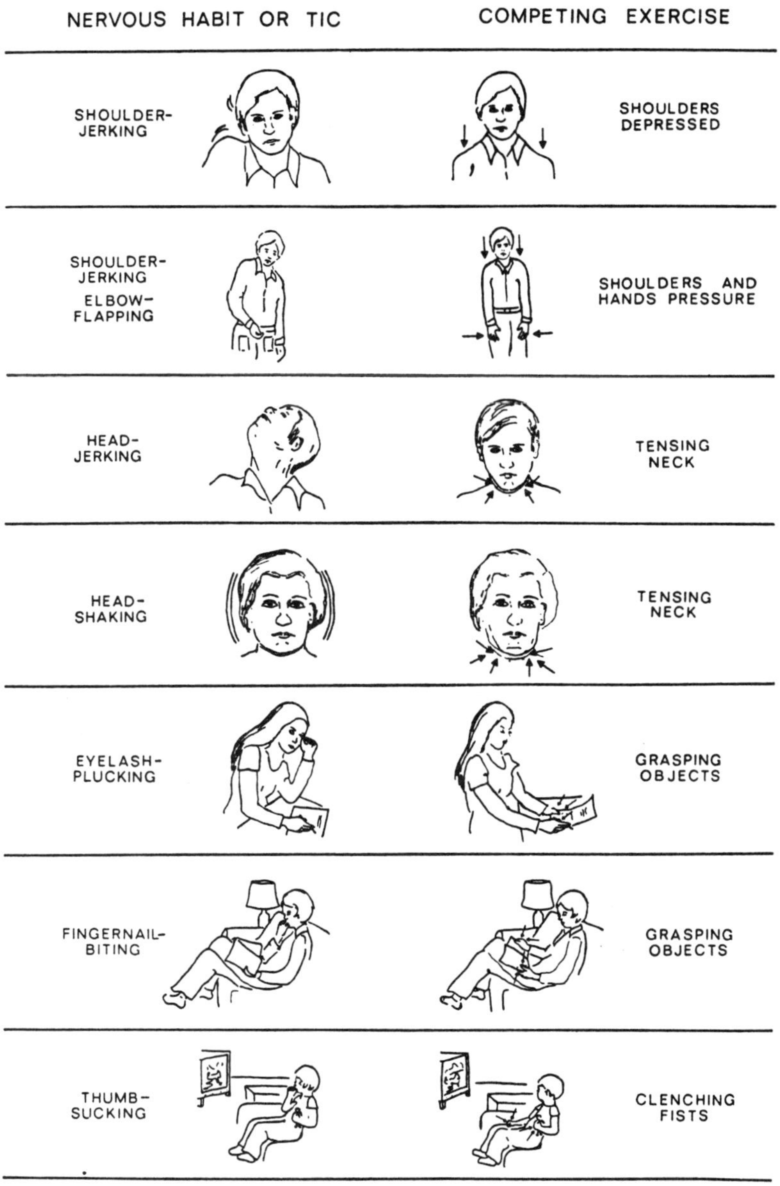

NERVOUS HABIT OR TIC	COMPETING EXERCISE
SHOULDER-JERKING	SHOULDERS DEPRESSED
SHOULDER-JERKING ELBOW-FLAPPING	SHOULDERS AND HANDS PRESSURE
HEAD-JERKING	TENSING NECK
HEAD-SHAKING	TENSING NECK
EYELASH-PLUCKING	GRASPING OBJECTS
FINGERNAIL-BITING	GRASPING OBJECTS
THUMB-SUCKING	CLENCHING FISTS

FIG. 1. A pictorial representation of the various types of nervous tics or habits. The left hand column illustrates the different tics or habits. The adjacent illustration in the right hand column illustrates the type of competing exercise used for that nervous tic or habit. The arrows in each of the Competing Exercise illustrations show the direction of isometric muscle contraction being exerted by the client.

illustrates the appearance of the different types of habits. Two clients experienced a shoulder-jerking tic; for one of them the right shoulder jerked upward suddenly about 5 in. and then immediately fell. For the other client the right shoulder jerked upward and forward while his elbow simultaneously jerked against his rib cage. Two or three of the shoulder jerks usually occurred in rapid succession followed by an interlude preceding the next series of spasm-like movements. For one client, his head jerked violently upward such that he was facing almost directly upward and slightly turned to one side at the end of the movement. One client's head moved rapidly up and down and side to side in short rapid movements with the neck stationary, resembling the tremor-like movements seen in Parkinson's disease. One client pressed her tongue firmly against the gum-line of her upper front teeth while she sucked against the roof of her mouth. Also, she found herself pressing her tongue firmly into the spaces between her lower back molars in the manner one uses the tongue to dislodge particles of food. Another client stroked her eyelashes repeatedly, such that the upper and lower eyelashes of both eyes were entirely plucked out. Another client lisped on all 's' and 'z' sounds. Although this problem is not ordinarily considered a nervous habit, but rather a speech problem, it was included here because of its apparent amenability to the present type of treatment. Four clients bit their fingernails resulting in the absence of all projecting portions of all 10 fingernails. Two clients (both children) sucked continually, one on her thumb, the other on her index and middle fingers.

Recording

The incidence of the nervous habit was recorded by the client. Each client stated about how often the habit was occurring during the previous week either in terms of the number of incidents per minute or day or in terms of the percentage of their time each day that they experienced the habits. Each client selected the measure that was more meaningful to him in view of the nature of the habit. For the first 2 weeks after treatment, the client reported each day the incidence of the habit. After about 2 weeks, these measures were obtained at less frequent intervals of about twice per week. After several weeks elapsed, the measure was taken only about twice per month. For every client, a validating report was also obtained from individuals who were in a position to observe the client frequently, such as a spouse, parent, teacher, roommate, co-worker or boyfriend. The counselor had face-to-face contact after counseling with all but two of the clients. Since the other two clients were at a great distance, the counselor relied heavily on detailed validating reports from their family members. For the young clients below 14 yrs of age, the primary measures were obtained from the parents and secondarily from the client or his teachers. The reports of the validating observer were generally in agreement with the primary observer. When the primary observer reported a large number of incidents on a given day, then the validating observer in virtually every case reported that the habit was a problem that day. Similarly, in virtually every instance in which the client reported zero incidents on a given day, the validating observer reported having seen no instances on that day.

Awareness training

The client was made very much aware of the nervous habit by means of several procedures. In one procedure, the Response Description Procedure, the client was required to describe the details of the movement to the counselor, using a mirror if necessary, while he re-enacted several instances of the typical movement. In the second procedure, the Response Detection Procedure, the counselor taught him to detect each instance of the movement by alerting the client when an instance of the tic occurred. A third procedure was the Early Warning Procedure wherein the client was given practice in detecting the earliest sign of the habit movement, such as when the hand of the nail-biters first approached the face. The fourth procedure was the Competing Response Practice (described below) in which the client maintained heightened awareness of the nervous habit by tensing for a few minutes the muscles that were incompatible with the movement. The fifth procedure, Situation Awareness Training created awareness of the situations in which the habit occurred by having the client recall all situations, persons, and places where the habit was likely to occur and having him describe how the habit was performed in each of those situations.

Competing response practice

This part of the procedure was derived in part from the over-correction rationale described elsewhere (Foxx and Azrin, 1972; Foxx and Azrin, 1973a; Foxx and Azrin 1973b; Azrin *et al.*, 1973) for treating other types of psychological disorders by having the client practice a behavioral pattern opposite to that of the problem behavior. A major departure from the overcorrection approach is the attempt to minimize any aversiveness of the required practice since the objective was to have the client maximally motivated to carry out the practice.

Each client was taught a specific response pattern that would be incompatible with the nervous habits and would, therefore, prevent the habit from being continually intertwined in normal activities. In addition, the incompatible movement was designed to have the characteristics of (1) being opposite to the nervous movement, (2) capable of being maintained for several minutes, (3) producing heightened awareness by an isometric tensing of the muscles involved in the movement, (4) being socially inconspicuous and easily compatible with normal ongoing activities but, still incompatible with the habit and (5) strengthening the muscles antagonistic to the tic movement for the muscle tics.

The clients were instructed to engage in the competing responses for about 3 min following either the temptation to perform a tic or the actual occurrence of a tic.

A different type of exercise was used for the different types of nervous habits. Figure 1 pictorially illustrates the exercise in the right-hand column; the left-hand column depicts the nervous habit. The exercises were as follows:

Head jerking. The competing response for the backward head-jerking tic consisted of isometric contraction of the neck flexors (sternocleidomastoid group) by pulling the chin in and down. For the first day, the client pushed his chin onto his sternum, but once having the necessary strength to control the jerking movement, isometric tension in the stationary eyes-forward position was substituted for the more conspicuous chin-on-sternum exercise.

Shoulder jerking. The same client also displayed an upward jerking of the right shoulder; the competing response of isometrically contracting the shoulder depressors was used to strengthen the muscles which work in opposition to this upward jerking movement.

Head-shaking. The client who displayed the head-shaking tic was instructed to slowly contract isometrically her neck muscles until the head was perfectly still.

Forward shoulder-jerking. The competing response for the client who displayed an upward and forward jerking of his right shoulder consisted of the client pushing his hands down and backward against some objects, such as the chair arms while sitting, or against his leg while standing.

Tongue-pushing. For the client who constantly sucked against the roof of her mouth while poking against the gum line of her upper teeth, the competing response required that she press her tongue against the roof of her mouth (in a position different than that while performing the habit) and against the bottom of her mouth for each incident of the habit.

Lisping. For lisping, the client was instructed to jut her jaw slightly forward, placing her tongue against the gumline of her lower teeth and to press her tongue against the gum line for each incident of lisping. Whenever possible, she was also instructed to repeat the word she had lisped 50 times correctly (the lisper and gum-sucker are not depicted in the Figure).

Eyelash picking, thumbsucking and fingernail biting. For the nervous habits of eyelash picking, fingernail biting and thumb-sucking, each client was instructed to place his hands down by his sides, and to clench his fists until they could feel tension in their arms and hands. In the case of the small thumb-sucking children, the parents were asked to manually guide their child's hands through an open-close exercise 20 times, while gradually fading out their manual assistance for each uncorrected incident performed by the child. Whenever the clenching exercises for nail-biting and eyelash picking interfered with the client's ongoing activities, they were instructed merely to grasp an object or objects appropriate to that situation and squeeze until they could feel a slight amount of tension.

Habit control motivation

Preliminary efforts with other clients had indicated that little success would result if the client was only casually interested in eliminating his habit. Sufficiently strong motivation was indicated if the adult client sought out the treatment himself, rather than being urged to do so by others. Several procedures were used to increase further the client's motivation to be rid of the nervous habit. The first procedure was the Habit Inconvenience Review in which the counselor and client reviewed, in detail, the inconveniences, embarrassment and suffering that resulted from the habit. This existing motivation for controlling the habit was supplemented by Social Support Procedures introduced once the client had demonstrated he could control his habits during the counseling session. His family and close friends were instructed to strengthen his motivation by (1) commenting favorably on his efforts and improved appearance when they noted a habit-free period, (2) reminding him of the need to 'practice your exercises', when they noted an instance of the habit overlooked by the client and (3) the counselor telephoned the clients regularly after treatment praising the client for his efforts in inhibiting the habit. These calls also were used to obtain the data regarding the frequency of the habit. The frequency of the calls has been noted above under 'Recording'.

A special motivational problem existed with children since the parents and not the child desired to be rid of the habit, the parents having presented the child for treatment. For these very young, often uncooperative children, the parents and teachers increased their child's motivation to control his habit by manually guiding the child's hands through the required exercises whenever the child failed to initiate the exercises himself. Similarly, the uncooperative older children were further motivated to control their habit by requiring them to perform their exercises in the bedroom whenever they failed to initiate the exercises themselves. In all other instances, the exercises were designed to be non-aversive and non-interfering with normal activities.

Another special motivational problem existed for those tics such as the head and shoulder jerks that seemed neurologically caused and therefore not subject to voluntary control. In such instances, the family and friends believed effort at self-control futile. For these clients a Public Display Procedure was used. The family was required to observe the demonstration of self-control during the counseling sessions, and the friends and teachers or fellow employees were notified of this ability by the client and counselor immediately after the counseling session.

Generalization training

During the counseling sessions, the client was given practice and instructions as to how he should control his nervous habit in his everyday situations. First, the counselor had him practice his exercise until he was performing it correctly, this period usually requiring less than 5 min. To teach the client to be aware of the habit movement in many situations, the counselor used a Symbolic Rehearsal Procedure in which the client was to imagine common and habit-eliciting situations and to imagine that he detected a habit movement and was performing the required exercise. This symbolic rehearsal utilized the list of situations obtained previously from the client in the Situation Awareness Procedure described previously and required about 15 min. To provide actual practice in detecting the habit movement and exercising for 3 min thereafter, the counselor engaged the client in casual conversation on a variety of habit-irrelevant topics for about $\frac{1}{2}$ hr. During that time, the client was to detect the movement himself, but if he failed to do so, the counselor reminded him using as minimal a suggestion as possible such as staring at the moving limb, or saying 'hmm' or raising his eyebrows, at which time the client would assume the competing exercise for three minutes while the conversation continued uninterrupted.

RESULTS

Table 1 shows the pre- and post-treatment (3rd week) frequency of the nervous habit for each of the clients individually. For every client the habit was reduced by at least 90 per cent; for 10 of the 12 clients, the habit was absent during the 3rd week after treatment.

TABLE 1. DESCRIPTION AND FREQUENCY OF OCCURRENCE OF THE NERVOUS TICS AND HABITS FOR EACH OF 12 CLIENTS PRE-TREATMENT AND 3 WEEKS POST-TREATMENT BY THE HABIT-REVERSAL METHOD

Client	Nature of tic or habit	Pre-treatment occurrence of tic or habit	Post-treatment (3rd week) occurrence of tic or habit
14-yr-old male	Head and shoulder jerking	8000/day	12/day
14-yr-old male	Elbow-flopping, shoulder jerking	250/day	0
64-yr-old female	Head shaking	75% of day	0
59-yr-old female	Gum-sucking, tongue pressing	100% of day	8% of day
21-yr-old female	Lisping on 's' or 'z' sounds	100% of time	0
31-yr-old female	Eyelash picking	50% of day	0
6-yr-old female	Thumb-sucking	100% of day	0
5-yr-old female	Finger-sucking	85% of day	0
28-yr-old female	Fingernail-biting	50% of day	0
28-yr-old female	Fingernail-biting	300/day	0
21-yr-old female	Fingernail-biting	20/day	0
8-yr-old male	Fingernail-biting	50% of day	0

Figure 2 shows the day-by-day changes for all clients averaged together. Each data point of Fig. 2 is the percentage reduction in the rate of occurrence of the habit from the pre-treatment level (see Table 1 for the pre-treatment level). The data points are for each day for the 1st month and for monthly periods thereafter. All 12 clients are represented for the first 3 weeks; one client having terminated her treatment efforts after 3 weeks. At the time of this writing, sufficient time had elapsed that data for seven clients were available for 5 months. The data shows that the habit reversal training reduced the nervous habits by an average of about 95 per cent on the 1st day after training, about 97 per cent after the 1st week, and about 99 per cent after the 3rd week. This average reduction of about 99 per cent was evident for as long as data was available, which was a period of 7 months for the earliest clients (not shown in Figure). The habit reversal method was rapid, requiring only one counseling session for all the clients. Two clients were given a second session 2 months and 5 months respectively after the first one. One client, a 21-yr-old female nail-biter, decided to abandon her successful efforts after 3 weeks; no further data could be obtained thereafter.

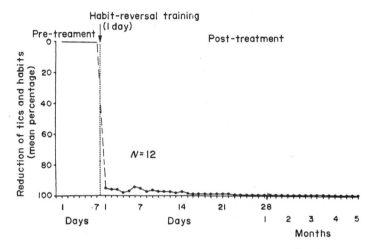

FIG. 2. The mean percentage reduction of nervous habits following treatment by the Habit-Reversal method. The pre-treatment level is designated as 0 per cent reduction and was obtained for the 7-day period immediately preceding treatment. The Habit-Reversal Training required about 2 hr on the day designated by the arrow and dotted line. The Post-Treatment data points are given daily for the first 28 days and monthly thereafter. Each data point is the average reduction relative to the pre-treatment level. The data points are for all 12 clients up to Day 21, for 11 clients for 7 weeks, for nine clients for 2 months and for seven clients for 5 months.

The 11 continuing clients were able to perform their exercises and continued to do so. When asked whether the exercises caused difficulties, all of the adult clients stated that the exercises seemed meaningful, were easy to perform and did not interfere with their ongoing · activities. In response to direct questioning, the clients and their validating observers stated that no new habit appeared when the treated habit was eliminated.

DISCUSSION

The habit reversal procedure appears to be an extremely effective method of eliminating nervous habits. The new method had a substantial effect, having eliminated, or virtually eliminated, the habits. The method was rapid, requiring only one or two counseling sessions. The treatment was durable in that the nervous habits remained absent after treatment and only one or two special telephone calls were usually needed to overcome the occasional relapses of some of the clients. (Preliminary results of a study in progress by Nunn and Azrin indicate that relapses can be eliminated almost entirely for the nail-biting habit by a modified procedure.) The method was a general treatment for many types of nervous habits as seen by its effectiveness on such diverse habits as head-jerking, lisping, nail-biting and thumb-sucking. Given that the client was movitated, the method seemed to be effective for all types of individuals: very young children as well as adults, males as well as females, those with high frequency or severe habits as well as those with lower frequency or milder habits. A possible side-effect of the treatment was that the competing response might itself become a nervous habit. As noted, however, no such 'symptom substitution' occurred, possibly because the treated habit was eliminated so rapidly thereby requiring only infrequent practice of the competing response. The habit reversal methods appear to be a general as well as an effective treatment for nervous habits.

Evaluation of the clinical value of the present method requires comparison with the clinical results obtained with other methods of treating nervous habits. Many procedures have produced some benefit in restricted office, laboratory or hospital situations, such as self-monitoring of the tic (Thomas et al., 1971); TV feedback and light aversion (Bernhardt et al., 1972); and noise termination (Barrett, 1962). We are concerned here only with methods that have produced clinical benefits that have occurred in the clients' everyday life. Four such methods are psychotherapy, drugs, shock-aversion and negative practice. In the major clinical evaluation of psychotherapy (Paterson, 1945; Mahler and Luke, 1946) about one-quarter of the clients were cured with treatment lasting several months. Combining the findings of the two major studies of aversion therapy (Brierly, 1967; Bucher, 1968), about three-quarters of the clients were cured. Haloperidol, the most effective of the drug treatments have been evaluated in a number of studies (Challas and Brauer, 1963; Stevens and Blachly, 1966; Connell et al., 1967; Shapiro and Shapiro, 1968). A complicating factor of this drug is its serious side effects at high doses. At safe dosages that could be used continuously, the haloperidol eliminated the tics for about one-half of the clients (Connell et al., 1967; Ford and Gottlieb, 1969). Negative practice has been evaluated in a large number of case studies (Yates, 1958; Jones, 1960; Rafi, 1962; Walton, 1961, 1964; Clark, 1966 and in one large sample study, Smith, 1957). Overall, negative practice has eliminated the tics for about one-third of the clients. The present method appears to be clinically more useful than any of the alternative treatments since it was effective for virtually all clients and required only one or two sessions.

REFERENCES

AZRIN N. H. and FOXX R. M. (1974) *Toilet Training in Less than a Day: How to do it.* Simon & Schuster, New York (in press).

AZRIN N. H., KAPLAN S. J. and FOXX R. M. (1973) Autism reversal: A procedure for eliminating the self-stimulatory behaviors of the institutionalized retarded. *Am. J. of ment. Defic.* (in press).

BARRETT B. H. (1962) Reduction in rate of multiple tics by free operant conditioning methods. *J. nerv. ment. Dis.* **135,** 187–195.

BERNHARDT A. J., HERSEN M. and BARLOW D. H. (1972) Measurement and modification of spasmodic torticollis: an experimental analysis. *Behav. Therapy* **3,** 294–297.

BRIERLY H. (1967) The treatment of hysterical spasmodic torticollis by behavior therapy. *Behav. Res. & Therapy* **5,** 139–142.

BUCHER B. D. (1968) A pocket-portable shock device with application to nailbiting. *Behav. Res. & Therapy* **6,** 389–392.

CHALLAS G. and BRAUER W. (1963) Tourette's disease: relief of symptoms with R1625. *Am. J. Psychiat.* **120,** 283–284.

CLARK D. F. (1966) Behavior therapy of Gilles De La Tourette's syndrome. *Br. J. Psychiat.* **112,** 771–778.

CONNELL P. H., CORBETT J. A., HORNE D. J. and MATTHEWS A. M. (1967) Drug treatment of adolescent tiqueurs: a double blind trial of diazepam and haloperidol. *Br. J. Psychiat.* **113,** 375–381.

ERIKSSON B. and PERSSON T. (1969) Gilles De La Tourette's Syndrome: two cases with an organic brain injury. *Br. J. Psychiat.* **115,** 351–353.

FORD C. V. and GOTTLIEB F. (1969) An objective evaluation of haloperidol in Gilles De La Tourette's syndrome. *Dis nerv. System* **30**, 328–332.

FOXX R. M. and AZRIN N. H. (1972) Restitution: A method of eliminating aggressive–disruptive behavior of retarded and brain damaged patients. *Behav. Res. & Therapy* **10**, 15–27.

FOXX R. M. and AZRIN N. H. (1973a) The elimination of autistic self-stimulatory behavior by overcorrection. *J. appl. Behav. Anal.* **11**, 35–48.

FOXX R. M. and AZRIN N. H. (1973b) *Toilet Training the Retarded: A Rapid Program for Day and Nighttime Independent Toileting.* Research Press, Champaign, Illinois.

JONES H. G. (1960) Continuation of Yates' treatment of a tiqueur. In *Behavior therapy and the neuroses.* (Ed. EYSENCK, H. J.), pp. 25–258. Pergamon Press, Oxford.

MAHLER M. S. and LUKE J. A. (1946) Outcome of the tic syndrome. *J. nerv. ment. Dis.* **103**, 433–445.

PATERSON M. T. (1945) Spasmodic Torticollis: Results of psychotherapy in 21 cases. *Lancet* **2**, 556–559.

RAFI A. A. (1962) Learning theory and the treatment of tics. *J. psychosom. Res.* **6**, 71–76.

SHAPIRO A. K. and SHAPIRO E. (1968) Treatment of Gilles De La Tourette's syndrome with haloperidol. *Br. J. Psychiat.* **114**, 345–350.

SMITH M. (1957) Effectiveness of symptomatic treatment of nail biting in college students. *Psychol. Newsletter* **8**, 219–231.

STEVENS J. R. and BLACHLY P. H. (1966) Successful treatment of the maladie des tics. *Am. J. Dis. Child* **112**, 541–545.

THOMAS E. J., ABRAMS K. S. and JOHNSON J. B. (1971) Self-monitoring and reciprocal inhibition in the modification of multiple tics of Gilles De La Tourette's syndrome. *J. Behav. Therapy and Psychiat.* **2**, 159–171.

WALTON D. (1961) Experimental psychology and the treatment of a tiqueur. *J. Child Psychol. Psychiat.* **2**, 148–155.

WALTON D. (1964) Massed practice and simultaneous reduction in drive level—further evidence of the efficacy of this approach to the treatment of tics. In *Experiments in behavior therapy* (Ed. EYSENCK, H. J.), pp. 398–400. Pergamon Press, Oxford.

YATES A. J. (1958) The application of learning theory to the treatment of tics. *J. abnorm. soc. Psychol.* **56**, 175–182.

YATES A. J. (1970) *Behavior therapy.* Wiley, New York.

BEHAVIOURAL APPROACHES TO BEREAVEMENT

R. W. RAMSAY

Department of Psychology, University of Amsterdam, 8 Weesperplein, Amsterdam, Holland

(*Received* 30 *July* 1976)

Summary—Persons who get "hung up" in an unresolved grief reaction appear to be similar in many ways to those who develop phobias. As behaviour therapy approaches to phobias have been highly successful, similar tactics have been tried out with persons involved in pathological grief, with gratifying success. The characteristics of grief reactions are briefly described, as is Eysenck's theory on the development and maintenance of phobias. This theory is applied to explain how and why some people develop pathological grief reactions. A modified flooding technique of confrontation with pain-evoking stimuli is described and some results are presented. The psychoanalytic literature gives indications as to what kinds of emotional reactions the therapist can expect.

In this paper I would like to point out some links between depression and phobias, and then go on to describe a behaviour therapy approach, which has been shown to be highly effective in the treatment of phobias, applied to one type of depression: pathological grief reactions.

The symptoms of depression can be described in terms of subjective feelings and of the observable behaviour of the depressed person. There are feelings of hopelessness, helplessness, failure, sadness, unworthiness, guilt, anxiety, loneliness, and sometimes feeling of persecution. The behaviour that accompanies these feelings may be isolation, withdrawal, apathy, slowness in thought and speech, agitation, poor sleep, loss of appetite, cringing, crying and an inability to tackle even simple tasks. Beck (1967) summarizes the most common symptoms:

a. Sad, apathetic mood;
b. Negative self-concept (self-reproach, self-blame);
c. Desire to hide, to stay away from others;
d. Loss of sleep, appetite, and sexual desire;
e. Change in activity level; becoming either lethargic or agitated.

The analytic theories of the causation of depressions tend to emphasize emotional reactions that occur to real or symbolic bereavements. The behavioural formulations tend to derive more from social reinforcement theory. For example, Seitz (1971) states that depression may be regarded as a function of inadequate or insufficient reinforcers. A depressed person can be viewed as on an extinction trial: some significant reinforcer has been withdrawn, weakening the person's behavioural repertoire.

A second mainstream of behavioural theorizing is the model of depression as "learned helplessness" (Seligman, 1975). This holds that anxiety is the initial response to stress, but if there is no way to control the situation or decrease the stress, anxiety is replaced by depression.

Grief reactions

One form of depression is a grief reaction as a result of the loss of a significant object, be it a loved one, wealth, position, or self-esteem. Averill (1968) uses the term bereavement behaviour to denote the total response pattern, psychological and physiological, displayed by an individual following the loss of a significant object, with two components: mourning and grief. Mourning refers to the conventional behaviour as determined by the mores and customs of the society; grief is the stereotyped set of psychological and physiological reactions of biological origin.

Mourning as a ritual may contain little or no affect, and grief may occur outside of the mourning procedure—the two response patterns may occur independently of each other but they are generally closely related and implement each other. The grief reactions, however, are the therapist's only concern. Averill summarizes the major features of grief as follows:

a. "Grief is a complex but stereotyped response pattern which includes such psychological and physiological symptoms as withdrawal, fatigue, sleep disturbances, and loss of appetite;

b. it is elicited by a rather well-defined stimulus situation, namely, the real or imagined loss of a significant object (or role), and it is resolved when new object relations are established;

c. it is a ubiquitous phenomenon among human beings and appears in other social species as well, especially in higher primates;

d. it is an extremely stressful emotion, both psychologically and physiologically, and yet behavior during grief is often antithetical to the establishment of new relations, and hence the alleviation of the stress."

Components of grief reactions

Some authors (e.g. Bowlby, 1960; Hodge, 1972) refer to *stages* of grief which imply a progression; others (Siggings, 1967) refer to *components*. In my experience there is a sequential character to the process, but with so much "regression" to earlier stages that it may be better to use the term components and qualify it by saying that some components predominate early in the process, and others at a later stage. For example, denial and despair are common in the early period of loss, aggression is rare; later, aggression may be prominent but lapses into denial and depression are frequent. The main components of grief are described in detail in various works (e.g. Bowlby, 1960; Siggins, 1967; Parkes, 1972); here it is sufficient to say that the most common ones are shock and numbness, denial that the loss has occurred, depression, anxiety, guilt, aggression, and at last, as the loved object is relinquished, a re-integration into a new way of life.*

Pathological grief reactions

The grief responses to a significant loss are not always present—the "normal" reactions of shock, despair, and recovery are often distorted, exaggerated, prolonged, inhibited, or delayed. These terms are, of course, for easy reference, and no hard dividing line can be drawn between normal and pathological. However, there is reasonable agreement in the literature that grief *has* to be worked through; if it is not, the person will continue to have troubles of some sort. Lindemann (1944) states with regard to the grief work that "one of the big obstacles to this work seems to be the fact that many patients try to avoid the intense distress connected with the grief experience and to avoid the expression of emotion necessary for it." Hodge (1972) puts it more strongly: "The problems must be brought into the open and confronted, no matter how unpleasant it may be for the patient. *The grief work must be done.* There is no healthy escape from this. We might even add that the grief work *will* be done. Sooner or later, correctly or incorrectly, completely or incompletely, in a clear or a distorted manner, *it will be done.* People have a natural protective tendency to avoid the unpleasantness of the grief work, but it is necessary and the more actively it is done the shorter will be the period of grief. If the grief work is not actively pursued, the process may be fixated or aborted or delayed, with the patient feeling that he may have escaped it. However, almost certainly a distorted form of the grief work will appear at some time in the future." (italics in the original).

Phobias

In Eysenck and Beech (1971) a theoretical course of development of phobic behaviour is traced. In the first place there is a single traumatic event, or else a series of sub-trauma-

* Note. For a more detailed explanation of these components, see Ramsay and Happée (1976).

tic events producing unconditioned but strong emotional reactions. At the second stage conditioning takes place, in the sense that previously neutral stimuli become connected with the unconditioned stimulus or stimuli. From now on, the conditioned as well as the unconditioned stimuli produce strong emotional behaviour. Stimulus and response generalization take place, and the complex of maladaptive reactions becomes persistent. The third stage, in order to account for lack of extinction in certain cases, is as follows: approaching the conditioned stimulus gives rise to conditioned fear and anxiety reactions; withdrawing from the conditioned stimulus would reduce the emotional response, thus being positively reinforcing; hence the subject would become conditioned to avoid the conditioned stimulus, thus making extinction impossible. It is not always possible to avoid all the conditioned stimuli completely, so an additional factor is postulated to account for the lack of extinction in these cases. This is incubation, or the "Napalkov phenomenon" (Eysenck, 1967). Under certain conditions, not yet clearly understood, it has been found that the response strength increases over time with or without further presentation of unreinforced conditioned stimuli. Thus, an originally fairly weak unconditioned stimulus–unconditioned response bond can result in time in a conditioned response that is of such strength as to seem out of proportion to the situation. In clinical practice, when using systematic desensitization and flooding, it has been observed that when strong conditioned responses are aroused for short periods of time, they tend to increase in strength instead of to extinguish.

Phobias and grief

Here I would like to propose a link between grief and phobias. Phobic reactions are characterized by anxiety in, and avoidance of, an objectively harmless situation (Marks, 1969; Barendregt, 1973). A person whose prepotent response pattern is to avoid confrontations and to escape from difficult situations is a potential phobic. The loss of a significant object entails as a consequence that numerous stimuli and situations will evoke the pain and anguish that the loss causes. A person whose prepotent response pattern is to avoid confrontations and to escape from difficult situations will not tackle the "grief work" and will tend to get "stuck" in the grief reactions. If these two suppositions are correct, then we should expect to find a number of reactive depressives with phobic patterns of life, and a number of phobics suffering pathological grief. The latter statement gains some support from Chabot (1975) who in a review of 105 intake interviews of phobic patients in Prof. Barendregt's Phobia Project (see Barendregt, 1973) found that no less than 41 of the 105 reported depressive feelings. This is not to say that they were all reactive depressives, but in clinical practice it is not rare to hear statements such as: "The problems started just after the death of my mother" or "After we moved from X to Y I started having trouble going out and meeting people". The main point to be made here is that there are some superficial similarities between phobias and pathological grief reactions, and if we take it further and look at the behaviour of people suffering from unresolved grief, we see avoidance behaviour similar to that of phobics. Many of the former will not enter situations which will evoke the sense of loss; certain streets are avoided, personal belongings are not touched, "linking objects" (Volkan et al., 1976) are locked away, certain tunes are never played. The stimuli and situations which could get the grief work going, which could elicit the undesired responses so that extinction could take place, are avoided. From Eysenck's theoretical explanation of how phobic reactions develop and are maintained, we would expect some grieving people to get "hung up" or even to become more depressed and miserable over time as they avoid and escape.

This explanation can, of course, be supplemented by the social reinforcement theory (Seitz, 1971) that depression is a function of inadequate or insufficient reinforcers. A widow whose reinforcers consisted of doing everything with and for her husband suddenly finds herself left with no positive reinforcers when he dies. Everything now is meaningless to her. A further supplement to the theorizing about depressions is Seligman's (1975) concept of "learned helplessness". We are powerless in the face of death or an important loss, all action is futile, and so the person stops responding in ways that would eventually alleviate the stress. No "working through" the bereavement takes place.

To summarize so far, a person suffering from pathological grief has lost a major portion of the positive reinforcers in life, has learned that nothing helps to relieve the stress, and so either does nothing in the way of confronting himself with the situations which could lead to an extinction of the negative conditioned emotional responses, or, like the phobic, actively avoids those situations.

Treatment of phobics by means of flooding and prolonged exposure to the conditioned stimuli which arouse the conditioned emotional responses has been shown to be highly effective (Marks, 1972). In a limited number of single case studies carried out by myself and colleagues, flooding and prolonged exposure has been found to be highly effective in the treatment of pathological grief reactions. This is not to say that the technique is simple. Systematic desensitization has been shown to be effective with phobics, but for grief we have found no gentle equivalent; the therapist can grade the confrontation in a roughly hierarchical fashion, but the emotional reactions, when they occur, are usually intense. In the selection of stimuli which elicit phobic reactions, the procedure is usually fairly straightforward: most phobics can produce lists of situations which frighten them and which are regularly avoided. With grief, it takes much searching to find the stimuli which will elicit the conditioned emotional responses. From the psychoanalytic literature we have descriptions of grief processes and the emotions involved, so that the therapist knows in advance what to expect in the way of nature and content of the emotional responses. Most people are emotionally inhibited, they have learned to suppress feelings; part of the therapist's task is to help the client give structure to the process of feeling and expression, to relearn how to feel, to code it correctly, and to express it in an appropriate way.

From the Rogerian school we have learned a lot about how to listen to the client, to know "where the client is" (Gendlin, 1974) and then to help him further in his emotional work. From the psychoanalysts we have learned about the structure of bereavement processes. From the Gestalt therapists we have learned much, but the treatment remains basically a behaviour therapy approach of flooding, repeated confrontation, with prolonged exposure and response prevention where the client tries to escape or avoid.

Although others have described brief therapy programmes for these problems, I do not altogether agree with their theoretical views. Volkan *et al.* (1976) say that "Although necessary in treatment, the emotional storm is not curative without the interpretation that brings it under close scrutiny of the patient's observing ego". We use no interpretations and our clients recover; where Volkan and his colleagues take an average of three months, we achieve the same in that number of weeks. We further disagree that "It is his [the therapist's] training in understanding the psychodynamic processes we have been describing, his ability to interpret and intervene, that enables him to unfreeze the previously frozen processes of grieving by the use of the linking object". Our behaviour therapists are not dynamically trained, yet still achieve remarkable success. We cannot feel for Volkan's reticence in the use of linking objects: "We should certainly object strongly to any view of the linking object as a mechanical aid in the treatment of established pathological mourning" whereas he himself warns that "although the linking object has magical powers for the patient, it should provide no magical short cut for the therapist, who must employ in his introduction of this symbol the highest awareness of the unconscious psychological processes." That just appropriates the magic while consciously refusing to name it as such. We regard linking objects simply as stimuli which will elicit the undesirable emotional responses that need to be extinguished. I would go so far as to suggest that psychoanalytic interpretation and the gaining of insight into the various defence mechanisms used by the patient is really dealing only with *symptoms* of an underlying problem; the behaviour therapy techniques here described deal with the core of the problem: pathological grief as emotional responses that have gone wrong. That is as basic as you can get.

REFERENCES

AVERILL J. R. (1968) Grief: its nature and significance. *Psychol. Bull.* **70,** 721–748.

BARENDREGT J. T. (1973) Onderzoek van fobieën. In *Klinische Psychologie in Nederland* (Eds A. P. CASSEE, P. E. BOEKE, and J. T. BARENDREGT). Van Loghum Slaterus, Deventer.

BECK A. T. (1967) *Depression: Clinical, Experimental and Theoretical Aspects.* Harper and Row, New York.

BELLAK L. and BERNEMAN N. (1971) A systematic view of depression. *Am. J. Psychother.* **25,** 385–393.

BOWLBY J. (1960) Grief and mourning in infancy and early childhood. *Psychoanal. Study Child* **15,** 9–52.

CHABOT B. E. (1975) 105 intake-gesprekken voor gesprekstherapie: een samenvattend overzicht met beknopt kommentaar. *Bulletin, Afd. Persoonlijkheidsleer, Univ. of Amsterdam,* **4,** 26–46.

EYSENCK H. J. (1967) Single-trial conditioning, neurosis and the Napalkov phenomenon. *Behav. Res. and Therapy,* **5,** 63–65.

EYSENCK H. J. and BEECH H. R. (1971) Counterconditioning and related methods. In *Handbook of Psychotherapy and Behavior Change: an empirical analysis* (Eds A. E. BERGIN and S. L. GARFIELD). Wiley, New York.

FREUD S. (1917) Mourning and Melancholia. S.E. vol. 14.

GENDLIN E. T. (1974) Client-centered and experiential psychotherapy. In *Innovations in Client-Centered Therapy* (Eds D. A. WEXLER and L. N. RICE). Wiley, New York.

HODGE J. R. (1972) They that mourn. *J. Religion & Health* **11,** 229–240.

LINDEMANN E. (1944) Symptomatology and management of acute grief. *Am. J. Psychiat.* **101,** 141–148.

MARKS I. M. (1969) *Fears and Phobias.* Academic Press, New York.

MARKS I. M. (1972) Perspective on flooding. *Seminars in Psychiatry* **4,** 129–138.

PARKES C. M. (1972) *Bereavement: Studies of grief in adult life.* International Universities Press, New York.

RAMSAY R. W. (1976) A case study in bereavement therapy. In *Case studies in Behaviour Therapy* (Ed. H. J. EYSENCK). Routledge & Kegan Paul, London.

RAMSAY R. W. and HAPPÉE J. A. (1976) The stress of bereavement and its treatment. In *Anxiety and Stress* (Eds C. D. SPIELBERGER and I. G. SARASON) in press.

SEITZ F. C. (1971) Behaviour modification techniques for treating depression. *Psychotherapy; Theory, Research & Practice* **8,** 181–184.

SELIGMAN M. E. P. (1975) Helplessness. Freeman, San Francisco.

SIGGINS L. D. (1967) Mourning: a critical survey of the literature. *Int. J. Psychiat.* **3,** 418–432.

VOLKAN V. D., CILLUFFO A. F. and SARVAY T. L. (1976) Re-grief therapy and the function of the linking object as a key to stimulate emotionality. In *Emotional Flooding* (Ed. P. OLSEN). *Vol.* 1 in New Directions in Psychotherapy. Human Sciences Press, New York.

INVITED ESSAY

ON THE PUTATIVE UNIQUENESS OF CANCER PAIN: DO PSYCHOLOGICAL PRINCIPLES APPLY?*

DENNIS C. TURK[1]† and EPHREM FERNANDEZ[2]

[1]Departments of Psychiatry and Anesthesiology, Pain Evaluation and Treatment Institute, University of Pittsburgh School of Medicine, Pittsburgh, PA 15213 and [2]Western Psychiatric Institute and Clinic, University of Pittsburgh, Pittsburgh, PA 15260, U.S.A.

(Received 26 July 1989)

Summary—A large volume of evidence has supported the important role of psychological principles and variables related to the perception of, and response to, nociceptive stimulation. On the basis of this research, a number of psychological interventions have been developed and used successfully with pain patients. Despite the evidence, there has been a tendency for practitioners to neglect the contributing role of cognitive, affective, and behavioral factors in reports of pain by cancer patients. Cancer seems to hold a unique status in medicine and society at large. In this paper, the cancer pain literature is briefly reviewed and evidence is presented for various psychological determinants of the pain report and response that may be extended to pain associated with cancer. The implications of these data for understanding and treatment of cancer patients are described.

Every year, more than 15 million people receive a diagnosis of cancer accounting for over 5 million deaths worldwide (Bonica, 1979). In the U.S.A. and other Western countries, 10% of the annual deaths are attributed to cancer. Advances in early detection, chemotherapy, radiotherapy, immunotherapy, and surgery have resulted in increased life expectancy among patients who formerly would have died within a few months of diagnosis. These individuals experience pain to varying degrees. After reviewing several epidemiologic studies, Bonica (1984) concluded that moderate to severe pain is present in 40–45% of patients initially following the cancer diagnosis, in 35–40% of patients at intermediate stages of the disease, and in 60–85% of those with advanced cancer. Extrapolating from these data, over $\frac{1}{2}$ million Americans with intermediate to advanced cancer will report moderate to severe pain annually.

Despite the magnitude of the problem, pain *per se* has received disproportionately little attention in oncology. Cancer is viewed primarily as a potentially lethal disease. Eradication of the disease is the central concern while the problem of cancer pain is relegated to a distant secondary concern. When cancer pain has received attention, it has typically been regarded as exclusively a biomedical problem requiring physical interventions such as potent analgesic medication and surgery.

Psychological research on cancer has also ignored issues related to pain and pain control. The tendency has been to focus on dispositional factors, individual differences among survivors (cf. Fox, 1978), and response to relatively discrete events (e.g. diagnosis, depression associated with impending death) (Massie & Holland, 1987). Thus, although cancer is a chronic disease, often extending over years, most psychological research has focused on the extreme phases of the disease—the beginning and the end of its natural history (Turk & Salovey, 1985).

When psychological modalities are mentioned they are viewed as directly tied to physiological factors. Thus, biofeedback and relaxation are recommended to reduce muscle tension that might exacerbate pain associated with tumors impinging on physical structures (e.g. distension of internal organs, impingement on nerves). Hypnosis and other cognitive coping strategies are suggested as being useful in helping to distract patients away from the nociceptive stimulation. Note, however,

---

*Completion of this paper was supported in part by grants DE 07514 from the National Institute of Dental Research and ARNS 38698 from the National Institute of Arthritis, Musculoskeletal and Skin Diseases awarded to the first author.
†To whom all correspondence should be addressed.

that the psychological strategies are all tied to an assumption that the report of pain is directly linked to nociception and tissue pathology.

Psychological factors such as anxiety, expectancy, cognitive appraisal, self-efficacy, perceived control, along with principles of respondent conditioning, operant conditioning, and observational learning have been shown to influence reports and experience of acute pain, chronic non-malignant pain, and acute recurrent pain, but have been ignored in the cancer pain literature. The gate control model of pain (Melzack & Casey, 1968; Melzack & Wall, 1965) postulating motivational–affective, cognitive–evaluative, as well as sensory–discriminative contributions to the perception of pain that has played such a central role in pain research and treatment appears to have had little impact in cancer pain. In short, the fund of knowledge about pain in general seems to be underutilized in the cancer pain area.

Examination of the literature confirms that cancer pain is placed in a category of its own, drawing little generalizability from other types of pain. It is viewed primarily as a symptom of disease bearing an isomorphic relationship with tissue pathology. We challenge such a unidimensional, sensory-physiological view of pain. In this paper we extrapolate from research on the psychology of pain, and apply the available knowledge to cancer pain in an effort to broaden the perspective of practitioners who treat pain in oncology patients.

Conventional treatment of cancer pain

Somatic therapies dominate the cancer pain control armamentarium (e.g. Baines & Kirkham, 1989; Portenoy, 1988). Foley and Inturrisi (1987) observe that analgesic drugs constitute the mainstay of cancer pain management and echo the call of the World Health Organization (1986) to educate health professionals on non-narcotic, narcotic, and adjuvant options in the pharmacologic intervention for pain.

Some psychologists have also adopted the position that cancer pain is largely a physical problem with psychological factors being only of secondary importance. For example, Dalton and Feuerstein (1988) conclude that:

> "Cancer pain, like all pain, must be understood in relation to physiological mechanisms initiating tissue damage and the biobehavioural factors affecting the initial and long-term response to such damage" (p. 145).

And there is a hint of necessity and sufficiency of pharmacological therapy in Cleeland's declaration:

> "Nondrug therapies should never be considered acceptable alternatives to a carefully planned analgesic program tailored to the specific needs of the patient. Should analgesics produce satisfactory relief of pain with acceptable side effects, the primary objective has been met, and no further need for therapy exists" (1987, p. 23).

Lip service to psychology

As noted, psychological principles and treatment strategies for cancer pain receive cursory coverage in the literature. In a recent review of practical aspects of cancer pain control (Portenoy, 1988), 26 pages are devoted to pharmacological and other medical approaches followed by one paragraph mentioning psychological approaches. Many other papers (e.g. Baines & Kirkham, 1989; Brigden & Barnett, 1987; Moulin & Foley, 1984) purport to address control of cancer pain in general and provide passing reference to psychological contributions such as depression and anxiety. Even when affective distress is noted as potentially related to symptom reporting and pain, the focus is one use of psychotropic medication (Mount, 1989). Psychological factors in body preoccupation, symptom appraisal, and subsequent symptom reporting (e.g. Pennebaker, 1982), all of which have been shown to play a significant role in pain unrelated to cancer, have not even been considered. The assumption seems to be that if a cancer patient reports pain, this report is directly tied to the disease. Thus, the patient's report is accepted as an accurate reflection of nociception.

When mentioned, psychological modalities such as relaxation, biofeedback, and hypnosis tend to be only briefly outlined following extensive discussion of the nature, route, and combinations of pharmacological agents, aspects of regional anesthesia, and neurosurgical procedures. This is certainly not commensurate with the voluminous material available in the literature on the psychology of pain. Perhaps *benign neglect* best captures the way that psychological principles have been regarded in the cancer pain literature. We do not mean to suggest that somatic therapies are dispensable in efforts to control cancer pain. On the contrary, we believe that they are essential; however, a broader perspective is needed whereby psychological principles and treatment modalities receive balanced coverage and sufficient consideration in keeping with their contributions to pain as a whole.

Limitations of biomedical approaches

Biomedical treatments of cancer pain can be extremely effective; however, they are not without shortcomings. Some of these will be briefly highlighted here, but the interested reader is referred to recent volumes (e.g. Foley & Payne, 1989; Raj, 1986; Wall & Melzack, 1989) for more detailed discussion.

The first issue pertains to efficacy. Data reported by Cleeland (1987) indicate that of several hundred patients treated pharmacologically for pain, $\frac{1}{2}$ experienced <70% relief, almost $\frac{2}{3}$ found their analgesics to be <30% effective, and 15% reported little pain relief from analgesics. Although it is arguable that the limited efficacy of medication stems from limitations of dosage, route, schedule, and combinations of drugs; it appears that for a significant minority of patients, analgesic medications provide inadequate pain relief.

The relative efficacy of narcotic analgesics must be tempered by their potential for adverse effects of varying severity. The most common side effect is constipation requiring the routine use of laxatives in those receiving narcotics. Narcotic analgesics also produce nausea and vomiting especially in ambulatory patients thus necessitating the use of anti-emetics. The most serious problem (fortunately quite rare in occurrence) is respiratory depression produced by morphine and opioid agonists, which can be fatal.

There is also the pervasive and troubling concern with tolerance whereby, over time, increasing doses of narcotics are required to achieve the original analgesic effect. Since analgesia is a logarithmic function of narcotic dose, this may require increasing the dose multiplicatively. And, at high doses, narcotics become extremely toxic. There has been a good deal of often heated debate about the trade-off between drug tolerance or addiction vs pain relief. Some state that tolerance does not present a problem when sufficient narcotics are administered orally on a regular rather than PRN (take as needed) schedule (Mount, 1976; Saunders, 1976). According to Foley (1985) there is undue fear among physicians and patients about drug dependence and addiction. Others, however, maintain that with early tolerance to narcotic analgesics the patient may not be able to derive adequate relief from pain in the late stages of the disease (Murphy, 1973). Laboratory studies demonstrate that tolerance does occur rapidly with increasing dosages eventually clouding the cognitive processes and blunting affect (e.g. Houde, 1974; Siegel, 1975, 1977). In the terminal stages of cancer, alleviation of pain, by whatever methods, must be given primacy. However, potent narcotics are not only prescribed at the terminal state but throughout the disease progression. Thus, the point along the disease progression needs to be taken into consideration when prescribing narcotics.

When narcotics prove unsatisfactory for control of cancer pain, surgical procedures often become a treatment option. Neurosurgical procedures have been implemented at virtually every site from the periphery to the central nervous system. Their success in providing lasting pain relief remains an open question and, as with any major surgery, iatrogenic risks arise. Sundaresan and DiGiacinto (1988) point out that cordotomies (sectioning of the spinothalamic tract) produce pain relief in 70–90% of patients but this percentage declines to 50% at 6 months and by 1 yr only 30% of patients report continued pain relief; this is compounded by the risk of dysesthesias that may disable 5% of patients, bladder dysfunction in 30% of patients with bilateral cordotomy, and a 5% mortality rate. The authors also point to the possible loss of proprioception in rhizotomies involving sectioning of the posterior sensory rootlets, and risks of diabetes insipidus and cranial nerve palsies following chemical hypophysectomies. In short, despite remarkable strides, current biomedical technology does not provide a panacea for all cancer pain patients at all stages of the disease progression.

Uniqueness of cancer

Cancer is a particularly frightening and unique disease conjuring overwhelmingly negative beliefs (Peters-Golden, 1982; Turk & Rennert, 1981). The major sources of distress for cancer patients are their uncertain medical status, fear of physical and functional deterioration, the threat of aggressive anti-cancer treatments, and the fear of intensifying pain, and ultimately death (Fishman & Loscalzo, 1987). The evidence for some basic assumptions about cancer are particularly worthy of examination as they are likely to influence how cancer is perceived both by patients and health professionals.

Assumption 1: cancer is inevitably lethal. The special status accorded cancer pain has much to do with its association with death. Taylor and Crisler (1988) note that while only 38% survive beyond 5 yr from a diagnosis of cancer, this malady is dreaded more than other life-threatening conditions such as heart disease which (at twice the mortality rate of cancer) is the leading cause of death in the United States. Many people diagnosed with cancer have a relatively good prognosis and there is reason to believe that the survival rates will increase with earlier diagnosis and treatment advances.

In a provocative essay, Sontag (1978) illuminates the unique status assigned to cancer in Western society. She likens cancer to the way tuberculosis was viewed prior to the 20th century, shrouded in myth, emaciating, insidious and tantamount to death:

> "Cancer patients are lied to, not just because the disease is (or is thought to be) a death sentence, but because it is felt to be obscene—in the original meaning of that word: ill-omened, abominable, repugnant to the senses. Cardiac disease implies a weakness, trouble, failure that is mechanical; there is no disgrace, nothing of the taboo that once surrounded people afflicted with TB and still surrounds those who have cancer. The metaphors attached to TB and to cancer imply living processes of a particularly resonant and horrid kind" (p. 9).

Assumption 2: cancer is inevitably extremely painful. For many patients cancer is viewed as synonymous with pain. For example, in a survey of 500 individuals, Levin, Cleeland and Dar (1985) found that 48% thought cancer to be extremely painful and 54% regarded pain as a priority concern. However, there is growing evidence that as prevalent as pain is in cancer, a significant number of patients experience little pain even in advanced stages of cancer. Turnbull (1979) expressed perplexity that 29% of lung cancer patients experienced little or no pain throughout the course of their disease. Ahles, Ruckdeschel and Blanchard (1984) noted that 82% of a sample of lymphoma patients reported no pain. Furthermore, they note that out of 208 ambulatory patients with cancer, only 33.5% had pain attributable to neoplastic disease, 6.7% had pain from cancer-related surgery, 11% had pain from non-cancerous sources. And, 48% did not complain of pain at all.

Over the years, health care providers have also evolved to share the belief that cancer patients will have severe pain. They are not surprised when patients report pain. Since complaints of pain fit the health care provider's expectancies, they are quite willing to accept the patient's report as a reflection of nociception justifying an increase in the dosage of analgesic medication. The patient's beliefs about the severity of pain from cancer are confirmed by the prescription of larger doses of medication. This kind of circularity has reinforced an erroneous view about the prevalence of pain in cancer.

The tendency of physicians to accept cancer pain at its face value can be contrasted with the field of chronic nonmalignant pain where the patient's self-reports are often considered to be biased by many factors. But many of these same factors (e.g. desire for attention, fear, demoralization) are operative in cancer pain to at least the same, if not greater extent. These psychological factors can influence behavioral communications of distress and suffering as well as pain—'pain behaviors' (e.g. self-reports, requests for medication, grimacing, moaning). Overt communication of suffering can elicit responses from health care providers as well as family and friends. This is not to imply that health care providers should disregard patients' reports but rather to reiterate that factors other than nociception may contribute to and modulate patients' reports.

Assumption 3: reports of cancer pain are directly linked to tissue damage. The assumption of an isomorphic relationship between tissue pathology and pain has been seriously challenged in the general pain literature but this point does not seem to have permeated the cancer pain literature. Cancer pain is commonly distinguished from chronic nonmalignant pain on the basis of its purported organicity (Levy, 1987/1988). It is generally characterized as exclusively somatic-based where there is activation of peripheral nociceptors as when tumors infiltrate on bones, visceral pain in which there is infiltration, compression or distension of thoracic and abdominal organs, and deafferentation pain due to injury to afferent neural pathways (Payne, 1987). Thus, the traditional specificity model of pain is pervasive in conceptualizing and treating cancer patients' reports of pain.

The unidimensional specificity view holds that the undifferentiated free nerve endings are the receptors that transmit noxious stimuli. Stimulation of peripheral nerves (A-delta and c fibers) transmit noxious stimuli to putative receptor substances and neural transmitters identified in areas of the dorsal horn of the spinal cord where pain fibers terminate. The spinothalamic tracts (lateral and ventral) transmit pain impulses to the brain. Spinothalamic fibers connect with several levels of the reticular formation (which played a role in arousal and attention) as they ascend from the spinal cord. Projections from the spinothalamic tract enter the thalamus and cortex. The cerebral cortex, periadequeductal gray matter in the brain stem, and the serotonin-releasing neurons in the raphe nucleus are involved in the descending modulation of pain signals and have a significant effect on neural transmission in the substantia gelatinosa of the dorsal horn, and are believed to play a major role in pain perception.

It has become apparent, however, that pain is more than a simple transmission of sensory signals from a pain source ascending the spinal cord to the brain. Rather, it is the net result of a series of complex interactions of neurophysiological and neurochemical processes permitting such psychological processes as motivation, emotion, and cognition and learning to modulate the pain perception, experience and subsequently behavioral response. The definition of pain adopted by the International Association for the Study of Pain (IASP, Merskey, 1986) comes to terms with the complexity of the pain phenomenon: pain is *an unpleasant sensory and emotional experience associated with actual or potential tissue damage, or described in terms of such damage* (p. S217). In this definition it is clear that although pain is viewed in terms of tissue damage, it is not solely dependent upon actual tissue damage. *Activity induced in the nociceptor and nociceptive pathways by a noxious stimulus is not pain, which is always a psychological state, even though we may well appreciate that pain most often has a proximate physical cause* (1986, p. S217).

The lack of one-to-one correspondence between pain and tissue damage is supported by at least three lines of evidence. First, tissue damage can occur without pain as in degenerative changes in the spine associated with aging and congenital insensitivity to pain (Sternbach, 1963). Conversely, pain can arise spontaneously in the absence of identifiable tissue damage as in causalgia and phantom limb pain (Melzack & Wall, 1982). Finally, psychological processes often distort the mechanistic relationship between pain and injury through situational meaning (e.g. Beecher, 1946), fear of pain (Philips, 1987), reinforcement (e.g. Fordyce, 1976), observational learning (Craig, 1986), and a host of other psychological variables.

The direct link between reports of pain and actual physical pathology in cancer patients remains somewhat equivocal. As early as 1920, Simmons and Daland noted that many patients indicated that the reasons they had delayed in seeking treatment for what were determined to be cancerous lesions was that they did not experience any pain. Several authors (Black, 1975; Woodforde & Fielding, 1970) have noted that the majority of cancer patients do not report pain until *after* they are made aware of their disease. Cassell (1982) cited an example of a patient whose pain could easily be controlled with codeine when the patient attributed the pain to sciatica, but required significantly greater amounts of medication to achieve the same degree of relief when he was told that the pain was due to metastatic cancer. Only rarely is pain the primary symptom bringing cancer patients to physicians initially. However, the frequency of pain complaints appears to be significantly increased following reception of the diagnosis of cancer. And even after the diagnosis, contrary to what might be expected from the sensory view of pain, Greenwald, Bonica and Bergner (1987) found only a weak association between pain intensity and stage (progression) of disease.

The sensory–physiological view of cancer pain ignores the advice of Melzack and Casey (1968) who suggest that:

> "The surgical and pharmacological attacks on pain might well profit by redirecting thinking toward the neglected and almost forgotten contribution of motivational and cognitive processes. Pain can be treated not only by trying to cut down sensory input by anesthetic blocks, surgical intervention and the like, but also by influencing the motivational-affective and cognitive factors as well" (p. 435).

POTENTIAL PSYCHOLOGICAL CONTRIBUTIONS TO CANCER PAIN MANAGEMENT

Numerous psychological variables have been implicated in the perception and report of pain. Several of particular import for cancer pain will be briefly discussed.

Expectancy

Anticipation of pain can lead to catastrophizing responses that augment perceived pain (Spanos, Radtke-Bodorik, Ferguson & Jones, 1979). Hall and Stride (1954), for instance, showed that when they used the word 'pain' in their instructions to the Ss—in which a thermal stimulus was the source of nociception—the Ss' anticipations were translated into greater sensitivity and lower threshold for noxious sensations than those of similar Ss who had received the same thermal stimulus but with a neutral instructional set. As noted earlier, cancer patients expect pain. It should be no surprise then, that these expectancies will have an influence upon the frequency and magnitude of reported pain.

Psychological interventions often manipulate expectancy variables to reduce perceived pain. The efficacy of placebos may be one illustration of the significant role of expectancy. In a survey of 15 studies involving more than 1000 Ss, Beecher (1961) found that pharmacologically inert substances presented as though they were potent drugs, were responded to favorably by about 35% of Ss across a variety of conditions including pain, nausea, and mood change. Byron and Yonemoto (1975) found that 77% of patients with advanced cancer obtained complete relief for 4 hr or more from pharmacological preparations that include no active analgesic medication. Beecher (1961) even demonstrated a placebo component in surgery.

Affective distress

Anxiety has been demonstrated to be both a cause and correlate of pain perception. In some individuals, anxiety can initiate a sequence of physiological changes that may actually produce nociception (Bonica, 1979). Emotional stress may directly affect nociception through corticofugal systems and accentuated sympathetic nervous system activity to provoke muscular spasm, vasoconstriction, visceral disturbances, or lead to the release of pain-producing substances in the periphery.

Alternatively, patients may not be able to differentiate sympathetic arousal symptoms associated with emotional stress from those that result from nociceptive stimulation. Thus, anxiety may exacerbate pain by altering the discriminability of physical sensations. In this way, perceptual biases may play a role in pain perception by lowering patients' thresholds for labelling sensory events as pain. That is, physiological arousal may be labeled as pain rather than emotional distress (Pennebaker, 1982). Several studies provide support for this process. For example, Malow, West and Sutker (1986) found that high anxious Ss were less able to discriminate between different intensities of noxious stimuli than low anxious Ss. Yang, Wagner and Clark (1983) reported that chronic pain patients who were experiencing high levels of psychological distress were less able to discriminate harmful from innocuous situations.

A number of investigators (e.g. Bowers, 1968; Jones, Bentler & Petry, 1966) have demonstrated that when anxiety about pain is reduced, the subjective experience of pain is also reduced. Barber (1959) has concluded:

> "It appears that some procedures that are said to reduce pain actually reduce anxiety, fear, worry, and other emotions that are usually intermingled with pain. For instance,

the pain relief that follows the administration of morphine and other opiates may be closely related to the reduction of anxiety or fear. Although the patient who has received the opiate may still experience pain sensations, the reduction in anxiety, fear or other emotions apparently leads him to report that pain is reduced" (p. 453).

In short, anxiety may directly affect both physiological parameters and the interpretation of sensory information either of which can influence and exacerbate pain perception. Therefore, reduction of anxiety may be as important a consideration as the nature, quantity, and route of administration of analgesic medication.

Symptom interpretation

Any event, whether environmental or a physical sensation, can be described in two ways. First, in objective terms of the event, and second, in terms of the personal meaning of the event for the individual based on attitudes, beliefs, cognitive information processing style, and prior learning history (Turk & Salovey, 1985). Personal meaning is the product of an individual's appraisal of both the event and his or her own coping resources (Lazarus & Folkman, 1986). Much of the diversity in people's responses to threatening events or ambiguous sensations is related to variations in the appraisal process. An individual's appraisal influences emotional arousal and the behavioral response to a situation or sensation.

As noted by Lazarus (1966):

". . . the more ambiguous are the stimuli cues, the more important are general belief systems in determining the appraisal process" (p. 134).

Cancer is, by its very nature, an ambiguous disease. The disease is of unknown origin, its course is unpredictable and erratic, the likelihood of arresting the disease is uncertain, and the physical sensations created both by the disease and the treatments are often vague and diffuse.

Cancer patients often become withdrawn and introspective. When patients have cancer, they become sensitized to, continually monitor, and preoccupy themselves with bodily sensations. Bodily sensations serve as a constant reminder of the disease, with all that it connotes, and are capable of being interpreted or misinterpreted as 'pain' (Pennebaker, 1982) as well as leading to over-reaction and even outright panic (Clark, 1986; Rachman, Levitt & Lopatka, 1987). In one study, Ahles *et al.* (1983) noted that cancer patients experiencing pain interpreted the sensation as an indication of disease progression. Constant awareness of noxious stimulation and the belief that it signifies disease progression may render even low intensity pain less bearable by giving it a nagging, unpredictable, unavoidable and uncontrollable quality (Cassell, 1982).

LeShan (1964) characterized the 'universe of the patient in chronic pain' as being similar to a nightmare

". . . terrible things are being done to him and he does not know if worse will happen; he has no control and is helpless to take effective action; no time-limit is given . . .".

The psychological state of the individual is likely to have an impact on their perception of noxious sensations whether associated with cancer *per se*, emotional distress, or both.

Perceived controllability

Attribution of control, whether by oneself or another, is another factor that influences the perception of nociception or noxious stimuli.

"Personal control is a belief about how one can interact with the world; it may take the form of believing that one can affect actual outcomes, choose among them, coping with their consequences, and/or understand them . . . personal control is catalyzed by novel and challenging events; similarly lack of personal control becomes salient in the face of overwhelming aversive events" (Peterson & Stunkard, 1989, p. 820).

Imparting a sense of personal control to the patient, may lead to reduction in narcotic medication requirements. For example, Hill, Kornetsky, Flanary and Wikler (1952) reduced anxiety in their

Ss by allowing them to have control over termination of noxious stimuli. They demonstrated that morphine diminished pain reactions more when the anxiety level of the S was initially high and when Ss were allowed to control pain eliciting stimuli. When initial anxiety was lower, morphine had less demonstrable effect on the Ss' pain thresholds. In the context of cancer, the perception of uncontrollability may modulate analgesic efficacy.

In clinical studies, several investigators point out that perceived control, that is, the belief that one has control, whether veridical or not, is sufficient to induce pain relief (e.g. Hijzen, Slangen & Van Houweligew; 1986; Holroyd, Penzien, Hursey, Tobin, Rogers, Holm, Marcille, Hall & Chila, 1984). Hill, Saeger and Chapman (1986) used patient-controlled analgesia (that allows the patient control over the administration of analgesic medication by means of a drug-infusion pump that is connected to the patient by means of a catheter) for cancer patients undergoing bone marrow transplantation where there is severe pain for several weeks. They found that those connected to the pump used approximately one-third as much morphine to achieve equivalent level of pain control compared to those who received the narcotic by means of nurse-administered injection. Having control over an aversive event appeared to play an important role in the effect of morphine on pain reduction.

In summary, specific psychological variables can be manipulated to reduce over-reaction to sensory information as well as to render cancer pain more tolerable. There are two broad approaches to pain management that can be applied to cancer pain control. These fall mainly into behavioral and cognitive domains. A common and central ingredient to both, however, is the sense of control they instill in patients (Turk & Holzman, 1986). We will briefly review the behavioral and cognitive–behavioral approaches with cancer pain in mind; the interested reader is referred to Fordyce (1976) and Turk, Meichenbaum and Genest (1983) for more comprehensive discussion of behavioral and cognitive–behavioral perspectives and treatment approaches, respectively.

Behavioral principles

In the traditional disease model, pain is linked to underlying pathology or a nociceptive stimulus. As Fordyce (1974) has observed, when diagnostic efforts fail to reveal a sufficient organic factor or when organically-based intervention is ineffective, the pain comes to be viewed as psychogenic, hysterical, hypochondrical, malingering or as a pschophysiological reaction in which the underlying pathology is simply shifted from a body site to the cortex. The operant model, however, asserts that pain is inferred from overt behaviors such as moaning, grimacing, gait and posture abnormalities, and verbal complaints. These overt communications may be shaped by external consequences—operant conditioning. Specifically, the behaviors are frequently reinforced by rewarding consequences such as attention and support from others, relief from responsibilities, euphoria and other positive effects of medication, and financial compensation.

Philips (1987) has also suggested that avoidance learning may occur so that the person in pain may avoid certain activities (usually physical exercise) once associated with pain. Not surprisingly, Ahles, Blanchard and Ruckdeschel (1983) noted less walking and standing in cancer patients with pain than cancer patients without pain. It is difficult to determine, however, whether the reduction in activity is a result of tissue damage, nociception, pain, or fear of pain. Avoidance of activity can indirectly influence perceptions of pain by leading to isolation and self-preoccupation as well as directly affect nociception by fostering physical deconditioning.

Empirical evidence has already been obtained regarding the efficacy of treatment programs based on operant principles for chronic nonmalignant pain patients (as reviewed by Turner & Romano, 1984). Until recently; however, little attention was given to operant factors as they might relate to cancer pain (Keefe, Brantley, Manuel & Crisson, 1985). It is quite plausible, however, that positive reinforcement (e.g. attention, concern, support) might have the effect of maintaining and increasing the behavioral manifestation of distress. The operant approach is designed to modify illness behavior associated with pain rather than the subjective experience of pain, by breaking the contingency between pain behaviors and rewarding consequences, while simultaneously building a contingency between 'well behaviors' and positive reinforcement. This includes altering medication from a pain-contingent to a time-contingent basis.

There is no intrinsic reason, however, why the same behavioral principles applied to pain syndromes not associated with malignancies could not be viewed as pertinent to cancer pain. The maladaptive illness behavior of cancer pain patients is often reinforced by well-meaning significant others and may be extinguished using the same operant principles described above. Reports of pain should not be ignored as they may be related to nociception or disease progression (Turk & Flor, 1987); however, once these possibilities are ruled out, then the role of operant factors needs to be entertained.

Vicarious learning may also play an important role in cancer pain. Craig (1986, 1988) has demonstrated the role of modeling in the behavioral expression of experimental and acute pain. In one study, Fagerhaugh (1974) noted the potent effects of observational learning on pain behavior and distress in a burn unit. In this study, patients who had been one the unit longer 'modeled' appropriate behaviors for newly-admitted patients. Appropriate behaviors included suppression of overt distress except at times of designated treatments (i.e. debridement of the burn sites). Similar modeling principles might be considered and utilized for cancer patients on palliative care units and hospices; conversely, the negative effects of modeling pain behaviors by patients needs to be examined in any clinical situation that brings patients into interactions with one another (e.g. while waiting for chemotherapy or radiation therapy).

Cognitive–behavioral perspective

Specific cognitive variables such as expectancy and controllability have already been the subject of discussion. The cognitive–behavioral approach, however, is a broader approach that warrants mention here. It incorporates information-processing principles while recognizing the intimate connection between cognition, affect, physiology and behavior. Turk and his colleagues (Turk & Meichenbaum, 1989; Turk & Rudy, 1989) have suggested that the cognitive–behavioral perspective is based on five central assumptions:

(1) Individuals are active processors of information, not passive reactors;
(2) Thoughts (e.g. appraisals, expectancies) can elicit or modulate mood, affect, physiological processes, influence the environment, and serve as impetuses for behavior; conversely, mood, physiology, environmental factors and behavior can influence thought processes;
(3) Behavior is reciprocally determined by the individual and environmental factors;
(4) Individuals can learn more adaptive ways of thinking, feeling, and behaving; and
(5) Individuals are capable and should be involved as active agents in change of maladaptive thoughts, feelings, and behaviors.

Cognitive–behavioral interventions are active, time-limited, structured forms of treatment designed to help patients identify, reality test and correct maladaptive, distorted conceptualizations and dysfunctional beliefs. Patients are taught to recognize the connections linking cognitions, affect, physiology, and behavior, together with their joint occurrences. Cognitive–behavioral therapists are concerned not only with the role that patients' thoughts play in contributing to the symptom but, equally important, the therapist is concerned with the nature and adequacy of patients' cognitive and behavioral coping repertoires, since these affect intrapersonal and interpersonal situations and responses to the patient (Turk & Meichenbaum, 1989; Turk *et al.*, 1983).

The use of cognitive techniques that covertly influence pain through the medium of thoughts has had a long history (for a review see Turk *et al.*, 1983). These techniques span several varieties of imagery, cognitive restructuring, self-statements and attention-diversion (Fernandez & Turk, 1989; Wack & Turk, 1984) involving mechanisms of information reappraisal, distraction, or both. In short, cognitive techniques are methods designed to modify dysfunctional appraisals, interpretations, and expectancies or to train specific adaptive coping techniques.

The application of the cognitive–behavioral perspective to cancer patients and cancer pain has been described by several authors (e.g. Cleeland & Tearnan, 1986; Fishman & Loscalzo, 1987; Turk & Rennert, 1981). Turk and Rennert (1981) recognized the value of multi-component treatment regimens tailored to specific stages in the course of pain. They proposed a 'cognitive social-learning treatment' package for cancer pain, in which rational self-statements, attention–diversion, relaxation, problem-solving, operant conditioning, and self-regulation techniques are carefully integrated with somatic treatments to deal with pain and emotional distress. As Turk and Rudy (1989) suggest, the cognitive–behavioral perspective that focuses on the individuals appraisals, interpretations, and expectancies, as well as physiology and environmental influences may be more essential than any specific techniques. The various cognitive (coping skills training) and behavioral (e.g. relaxation, biofeedback) strategies may have their greatest impact by increasing the patients perceptions of control and thereby combating anxiety and demoralization.

SUMMARY AND CONCLUSION

In summary, psychological principles and variables have been found to be important in perception of pain and behavioral responses for diverse pain syndromes, both acute and chronic. Moreover, cognitive and behavioral modalities have been effectively used in the management of non-malignant pain of an acute or chronic nature. However, these approaches have seldom been incorporated into treatment of patients with cancer pain. It has been argued that this is primarily a result of some misconceptions that cancer pain is unique by virtue of its association with impending death and that cancer pain is largely related to organicity and therefore best treatable by biomedical methods. Pain, however, as discussed throughout this paper, is a perception subject to modulation by numerous psychological variables, prominent among which are controllability, expectancy, anxiety, appraisal processes, and contingencies of reinforcement. The manipulation of such variables can help patients to reinterpret noxious sensations as less intense, to relabel physical perturbations in terms other than pain, and to engage in well-behaviors. The successful use of such techniques also adds to a sense of control that can further alleviate suffering.

Not everyone, however, should be expected to respond uniformly. There may be predispositional factors for instance that determine the effectiveness of perceived control in alleviating pain (Weisenberg, Wolf, Mittwock, Mikulincer & Aviram, 1985) and there may be somatic factors that play a major role in pain severity. Therefore, such variables should be used judiciously and tailored to the needs of individuals just as narcotics should not be used as sufficient interventions for cancer pain.

It must also be added that psychological approaches for cancer pain management are likely to be time-consuming and involved for both patient and practitioner. Some patients may also be resistant to such intervention for fear that it connotes that their pain is 'all in their head'—a remonstrance frequently heard among chronic nonmalignant pain patients. On the contrary, it must be emphasized that pain is a multidimensional experience with sensory as well as cognitive and affective components affected by environmental contingencies, and each of these needs to be selectively addressed by a multifaceted approach giving broader consideration to both biomedical and psychosocial contributors and treatments. It is important to acknowledge the reminder of Davis, Vasterling, Bransfield and Burish (1987) that the association between pain and psychological distress in cancer patients may be one of reciprocal causality. The occurrence of psychological distress may influence the patient's perception of pain, whereas the occurrence of pain may contribute to the patient's psychological distress.

Pain associated with cancer shares much in common with pain in general. It is a multidimensional phenomenon that consists of cognitive, affective, behavioral, as well as physical contributors. Thus, we believe that the most appropriate treatment of cancer pain is by an interdisciplinary team that includes psychologists along with a range of other health care professionals (e.g. physicians, nurses, physical therapists, pharmacologists) (see also Cleeland, Rotondi, Brechner, Levin, MacDonald, Portenoy, Schutta & McEniry, 1986; Jay, Elliott & Varni, 1986).

Psychologists should be encouraged to tackle not only traditional issues of depression or be brought in to intervene as a last resort when all physical modalities have been exhausted. Instead, they can play an important role simultaneous with the use of biomedical modalities as well as to assist patients in understanding the role of their appraisal processes, body preoccupation, environmental contingencies, along with and how such factors can contribute to distress, pain perception, and suffering (Bonica, 1982; Davis et al., 1987). Psychologists can also teach patients a range of cognitive and behavioral techniques to increase the patient's sense of control over the disease and thereby reduce the demoralization frequently encountered in cancer patients. Psychologists may serve as consultants to the other members of the treatment team by alerting them to the role of cognitive and behavioral factors in the report, maintenance, and exacerbation of suffering.

We could not close this paper without the hackneyed plea for additional research. The majority of the empirical studies reported above that were used to buttress our thesis concerning the important but often neglected role of psychological factors in symptom perception, reporting, and behavioral responses were not conducted with cancer patients. Thus, our extrapolations, speculations, and suggestions as to the role of psychological factors and psychologists in cancer pain must be viewed with some caution. However, we see little to justify the current view of cancer pain as uniquely different from other types of clinical pain. The sensory–physiological view that has been seriously challenged in the general pain literature can be readily challenged in the context of cancer pain.

Our examination of the pain literature in general as well as the cancer pain literature leads us to a conclusion that is in marked contrast to that recently drawn by Dalton and Feuerstein (1988) who suggest that:

> "what is currently published suggests that biobehavioural factors play a modest role in cancer pain experience in adults" (p. 145).

We believe that there is sufficient knowledge, even at this time, to warrant greater attention to the psychological variables and principles that we have reviewed in both research and treatment of cancer pain patients. In our view, these variables appear to play a much more significant role in cancer pain then would be expected from reading the cancer pain literature.

REFERENCES

Ahles, T. A., Blanchard, E. B. & Ruckdeschel, J. C. (1983). The multidimensional nature of cancer-related pain. *Pain*, **17**, 277–288.

Ahles, T. A., Ruckdeschel, J. C. & Blanchard, E. B. (1984). Cancer-related pain—I. Prevalence in an outpatient setting as a function of stage of disease and type of cancer. *Journal of Psychosomatic Research*, **28**, 115–119.

Baines, M. & Kirkham, S. R. (1989). Cancer pain. In *Textbook of Pain* (Edited by Wall, P. D. and Melzack, R.), pp. 590–597. New York: Churchill Livingstone.

Barber, T. X. (1959). Toward a theory of pain: Relief of chronic pain by prefrontal leucotomy, opiates, placebos, and hypnosis. *Psychological Bulletin*, **56**, 430–460.

Beecher, H. K. (1946). Pain in men wounded in battle. *Annals of Surgery*, **123**, 96–105.

Beecher, H. K. (1961). Surgery as placebo: Quantitative study of bias. *Journal of the American Medical Association*, **176**, 1102–1107.

Black, R. G. (1975). The chronic pain syndrome. *Surgical Clinics of North America*, **55**, 999–1011.

Bond, M. R. (1985). Cancer pain: Psychological substrates and therapy. *Clinical Journal of Pain* **1**, 99–104.

Bonica, J. J. (1979). Cancer pain: Importance of the problem. In *Advances in Pain Research and Therapy* (Edited by Bonica, J. J. and Ventafridda, V.), Vol. 2, pp. 1–12. New York: Raven Press.

Bonica, J. J. (1982). Management of cancer pain. *Acta Anaesthia, Scandinavia*, **26**, 137–143.

Bonica, J. J. (1984). Management of cancer pain. In *Recent Results in Cancer Research* (Edited by Zimmerman, M., Drings, P. and Wagner, G.), Vol. 89, pp. 13–27. Berlin: Springer.

Bowers, K. S. (1968). Pain, anxiety and perceived control. *Journal of Consulting and Clinical Psychology*, **32**, 596–602.

Brigden, M. L. & Barnett, J. B. (1987). A practical approach to improving pain control in cancer patients. *Western Journal of Medicine*, **146**, 580–584.

Byron, R. & Yonemoto, R. (1975). Pain associated with malignancy. In *Pain Research and Treatment* (Edited by Crue, B. Jr), pp. 127–131. New York: Academic Press.

Cassell, E. J. (1982). The nature of suffering and the goals of medicine. *New England Journal of Medicine*, **306**, 639–645.

Clark, D. (1986). A cognitive approach to panic. *Behaviour Research and Therapy*, **24**, 461–470.

Cleeland, C. S. (1987). Non-pharmacological management of cancer pain. *Journal of Pain and Symptom Management*, **2**, S23–S28.

Cleeland, C. S. & Tearnan, B. H. (1986). Behavioral control of cancer pain. In *Pain Management: A Handbook of Psychological Treatment Approaches* (Edited by Holzman, A. D. and Turk, D. C.), pp. 193–212. New York: Pergamon Press.

Cleeland, C. S., Rotondi, A., Brechner, T., Levin, A., MacDonald, N., Portenoy, R., Schutta, H. & McEniry, M. (1986). A model for the treatment of cancer pain. *Journal of Pain and Symptom Management*, **1**, 209–215.

Craig, K. D. (1986). Social modeling influences: Pain in context. In *The Psychology of Pain* (Edited by Sternbach, R. A.), pp. 67–95. New York: Raven Press.

Craig, K. D. (1988). Consequences of caring: Pain in human context. *Canadian Psychology* **28**, 311–321.

Dalton, J. A. & Feuerstein, M. (1988). Biobehavioral factors in cancer pain. *Pain*, **33**, 137–147.

Davis, M., Vasterling, J., Bransfield, D. & Burish, T. G. (1987). Behavioural interventions in coping with cancer-related pain. *British Journal of Guidance and Counselling*, **15**, 17–28.

Fagerhaugh, S. (1974). Pain expression and control on a burn care unit. *Nursing Outlook*, **22**, 645–650.

Fernandez, E. & Turk, D. C. (1989). The utility of cognitive coping strategies for altering pain perception: A meta-analysis. *Pain*, **38**.

Fishman, B. & Loscalzo, M. (1987). Cognitive–behavioral interventions in managment of cancer pain: Principles and applications. *Medical Clinics of North America*, **71**, 271–287.

Foley, K. M. (1985). The treatment of cancer pain. *New England Journal of Medicine*, **313**, 84–95.

Foley, K. M. & Inturrisi, C. E. (1987). Analgesic drug therapy in cancer pain: Principles and practice. *Medical Clinics of North America*, **71**, 207–232.

Foley, K. M. & Payne, R. M. (Eds) (1989). *Current Therapy of Pain*. Philadelphia: Becker.

Fordyce, W. E. (1974). Pain viewed as learned behaviour. In *Advances in Neurology* (Edited by Bonica J. J.), Vol. 4, pp. 415–422. New York: Raven Press.

Fordyce, W. E. (1976). *Behavioural Methods for Chronic Pain and Illness*. St Louis, Mont.: Mosby.

Fox, B. H. (1978). Premorbid psychological factors related to cancer incidence. *Journal of Behavioural Medicine*, **1**, 45–133.

Greenwald, H. P., Bonica, J. J. & Bergner, M. (1987). The prevalence of pain in four cancers. *Cancer*, **60**, 2563–2569.

Hall, K. & Stride, E. (1954). The varying response to pain in psychiatric disorders: A study in abnormal psychology. *British Journal of Medical Psychology*, **27**, 48–60.

Hijzen, T. H., Slangen, J. L. & Van Houweligew, H. C. (1986). Subjective, clinical and EMG effects of biofeedback and splint treatment. *Journal of Oral Rehabilitation*, **13**, 529–539.

Hill, H. F., Saeger, L. C. & Chapman, C. R. (1986). Patient controlled analgesia after bone marrow transplantation for cancer. *Postgraduate Medicine* August, 33–40.

Hill, H. E., Kornetsky, C. H., Flanary, H. G. & Wikler, A. (1952) Effects of anxiety and morphine on discrimination of intensities of painful stimuli. *Journal of Clinical Investigation*, **31**, 473–480.

Holroyd, K. A., Penzien, D. B., Hursey, K. G., Tobin, D. L., Rogers, L., Holm, J. E., Marcille, P. J., Hall, J. R. & Chila, A. G. (1984). Change mechanisms in EMG biofeedback training: Cognitive changes underlying improvement in tension headache. *Journal of Consulting and Clinical Psychology*, **52**, 1039–1053.

Holzman, A. D. & Turk, D. C. (Eds) (1986). *Pain Management: A Handbook of Psychological Approaches*. New York: Pergamon Press.

Houde, R. (1974). The use and misuse of narcotics in the treatment of chronic pain. In *Advances in Neurology* (Edited by Bonica, J. J.), Vol. 4, pp. 527–536. Raven Press, New York.

Jay, S. M., Elliott, C. & Varni, J. W. (1986). Acute and chronic pain in adults and children with cancer. *Journal of Consulting and Clinical Psychology*, **54**, 601–607.

Jones, A., Bentler, P. & Petry, G. (1968) The reduction of uncertainty concerning future pain. *Journal of Abnormal Psychology*, **71**, 87–94.

Keefe, F. J., Brantley, A., Manuel, G. & Crisson, J. E. (1985). Behavioral assessment of head and neck cancer pain. *Pain*, **23**, 327–336.

Lazarus, R. S. (1966). *Psychological Stress and the Coping Process*. New York: McGraw–Hill.

Lazarus, R. S. & Folkman, S. (1984). *Stress, Appraisal, and Coping*. New York: Springer.

LeShan, L. (1964). The world of the patient in severe pain of long duration. *Journal of Chronic Diseases*, **17**, 119–126.

Levin, D. N., Cleeland, C. S. & Dar, R. (1985). Public attitudes toward cancer pain. *Cancer*, **56**, 2337–2339.

Levy, M. H. (1987/1988). Pain control research in the terminally ill. *Omega*, **18**, 265–279.

Malow, R. M., West, J. A. & Sutker, P. B. (1986). A signal detection analysis of anxiety and pain responses in chronic drug abusers. Paper presented at the annual meeting of the American Psychological Association, Washington, D.C.

Massie, M. J. & Holland, J. C. (1987). The cancer patient with pain: Psychiatric complications and their management. *Medical Clinics of North America*, **71**, 243–258.

Melzack, R. & Casey, K. L. (1968). Sensory, motivational and central control determinants of pain: A new conceptual model. In *The Skin Senses* (Edited by Kenshalo, D.), pp. 423–439. Springfield, Ill.: Thomas.

Melzack, R. & Wall, P. D. (1965). Pain mechanisms: A new theory: *Science* **50**, 971–979.

Melzack, R. & Wall, P. D. (1982). *The Challenge of Pain*. New York: Basic Books.

Merskey, H. (1986). Classification of chronic pain: Descriptions of chronic pain syndromes and definitions of pain terms. *Pain* (suppl. 3), S1–S226.

Moulin, D. W. & Foley, K. M. (1984). Management of pain in patients with cancer. *Psychiatric Annals*, **14**, 815–822.

Mount, B. M. (1976). The problem of caring for the dying in a general hospital: The palliative care unit as a possible solution. *Canadian Medical Association Journal*, **115**, 119.

Mount, B. M. (1989). Psychological and social aspects of cancer pain. In *Textbook of Pain* (Edited by Wall, P. D. and Melzack, R.), 2nd edn, pp. 610–623. New York: Churchill Livingstone.

Murphy, T. (1973). Cancer pain. *Postgraduate Medicine*, **53**, 187–194.

Payne, R. (1987). Anatomy, physiology and neuropharmacology of cancer pain. *Medical Clinics of North America*, **71**, 153–167.

Pennebaker, J. W. (1982). *The Psychology of Physical Symptoms*. New York: Springer.

Peters-Golden, H. (1982). Breast cancer: Varied perceptions of social support in the illness experience. *Social Science and Medicine*, **16**, 483–491.

Peterson, C. & Stunkard, A. J. (1989). Personal control and health promotion. *Social Science and Medicine*, **28**, 819–828.

Philips, H. C. (1987). Avoidance behavior and its role in sustaining chronic pain. *Behaviour Research and Therapy*, **25**, 273–279.

Portenoy, R. K. (1987). Optimal pain control in elderly cancer patients. *Geriatrics*, **42**, 33–40, 44.

Portenoy, R. K. (1988). Practical aspects of pain control in the patient with cancer. *CA-Cancer Journal for Clinicians*, **38**, 327–352.

Rachman, S., Levitt, K. & Lopatka, C. (1987). Panic: The links between cognitions and bodily symptoms—I. *Behaviour Research and Therapy*, **25**, 411–423.

Raj, P. P. (1986). *Practical Management of Pain*. Chicago: Yearbook.

Saunders, C. (1976). Control of pain in terminal cancer. *Nursing Times*, **72**, 1133–1135.

Siegel, S. (1975). Evidence from rats that morphine tolerance is a learned response. *Journal of Comparative and Physiological Psychology*, **89**, 498–506.

Siegel, S. (1977). Morphine tolerance acquisition as an associative process. *Experimental Psychology: Animal Behavior Processes*, **3**, 1–13.

Simmons, C. C. & Daland, E. M. (1920). Cancer: Factors entering into the delay in its surgical treatment. *Boston Medical and Surgical Journal*, **183**, 298–303.

Sontag, S. (1978). *Illness as a Metaphor*. New York: Farrar.

Spanos, N. P., Radtke-Bodorik, H. L., Ferguson, J. D. & Jones, B. (1979). The effects of hypnotic susceptibility, suggestions for analgesia, and the utilization of cognitive strategies on the reduction of pain. *Journal of Abnormal Psychology*, **88**, 282–292.

Sternbach, R. A. (1963). Congenital insensitivity to pain: A critique. *Psychological Bulletin*, **60**, 252–254.

Sundaresan, N. & DiGiacinto, G. V. (1988). Antitumor and antinociceptive approaches to control cancer pain. *Medical Clinics of North America*, **71**, 329–348.

Taylor, C. M. & Crisler, J. R. (1988). Concerns of persons with cancer as perceived by cancer patients, physicians, and rehabilitation counselors. *Journal of Rehabilitation*, January–March, 23–28.

Turk, D. C. & Flor, H. (1987). Pain > pain behaviors: Utility and limitations of the pain behavior construct. *Pain*, **31**, 277–295.

Turk, D. C. & Holzman, A. D. (1986). Commonalities among psychological approaches in the treatment of chronic pain. Specifying the meta-constructs. In *Pain Management: A Handbook of Psychological Treatment Approaches* (Edited by Holzman, A. D. and Turk, D. C.), pp. 257–268. New York: Pergamon Press.

Turk, D. C. & Meichenbaum, D. (1989). Cognitive–behavioral approach to the management of chronic pain. In *Textbook of Pain* (Edited by Melzack, R. and Wall, P. D.), 2nd edn, pp. 1001–1009. New York: Churchill Livingstone.

Turk, D. C. & Rennert, K. S. (1981). Pain and the terminally-ill cancer patient: A cognitive social learning perspective. In *Behavior Therapy in Terminal Care: A Humanistic Approach* (Edited by Sobel, H.), pp. 95–124. Cambridge, Mass.: Ballinger.

Turk, D. C. & Rudy, T. E. (1989). An integrated approach to pain treatment: Beyond the scalpel and syringe. In *Handbook of Chronic Pain Management* (Edited by Tollison, C. D.), pp. 222–237. Baltimore Md: Williams & Wilkins.

Turk, D. C. & Salovey, P. (1985). Toward an understanding of life with cancer: Personal meanings, psychosocial problems, and coping resources. *Hospice Journal*, **1**, 73–84.

Turk, D. C., Meichenbaum, D. & Genest, M. (1983). *Pain and Behavioral Medicine: A Cognitive–Behavioral Perspective*. New York: Guilford Press.

Turnbull, F. (1979). The nature of pain that may accompany cancer of the lung. *Pain*, **7**, 371–375.

Turner, J. A. & Romano, J. M. (1984). Evaluating psychologic interventions for chronic pain: Issues and recent developments. In *Advances in Pain Research and Therapy* (Edited by Benedetti, C., Chapman, C. R. and Moricca, G.), Vol. 7, pp. 257–296. New York: Raven Press.

Wack, J. T. & Turk, D. C. (1984). Latent structure in strategies for coping with pain. *Health Psychology*, **3**, 27–43.

Wall, P. D. & Melzack, R. (1989). *Textbook of Pain*, 2nd edn. London: Churchill Livingstone.

Weisenberg, M., Wolf, Y., Mittwock, T., Mikulincer, M. & Aviram, O. (1985). Subject versus experimenter control in the reaction to pain. *Pain*, **23**, 187–200.

Woodforde, J. M. & Fielding, J. R. (1970). Pain and cancer. *Journal of Psychosomatic Research*, **14**, 365–370.

World Health Oganization (1986). *Cancer Pain Relief*. Geneva: World Health Organization.

Yang, J. C., Wagner, J. M. & Clark, W. C. (1983). Psychological distress and mood in chronic pain and surgical patients: A sensory decision analysis. In *Advances in Pain Research and Therapy* (Edited by Bonica, J. J., Lindblom, U. and Iggo, A.), pp. 901–906. New York: Raven Press.

CASE HISTORIES AND SHORTER COMMUNICATIONS

An application of behavior modification technique to a problem of chronic pain

(*Received* 24 *June* 1967)

INTRODUCTION

THE CASE study reported here treats as operants aspects of what we term "pain behavior". It describes applications of operant methods (Ayllon and Michael, 1959; Haughton, 1962) to modifying environmental contingencies to pain behavior and illustrates preliminary results.

Responses by others to overt pain behavior accompanying the subjective experience of pain may serve to reinforce or to extinguish aspects of that behavior. When the pain behavior occurs with some consistency over a protracted period of time, as in chronic pain problems, the environment may come to be shaped in such a way as to reinforce the pain behavior and thereby sustain it. In a hospital, overt expressions or demonstrations of discomfort are frequently followed by attention from professional personnel, just as at home family members may respond with attention and ministering behavior. If one can modify such environmental responses, pain behavior itself may be modified.

The case study reported was carried out in a comprehensive medical rehabilitation department of a teaching hospital.

Mrs. Y is a 37-yr-old, married, white female, high school graduate with one child, a teenage son. Her husband is a bright, upward mobile, school administrator. Since 1948, approximately 1 yr after her marriage, she has had virtually constant low-back pain and has been decreasingly able to carry out her normal homemaking activities.

At the time of admission to the hospital, she complained of a continuous aching pain in the low back which increased with any activity. She reported her maximum continuous period of activity without an interval of reclining rest was approximately 20 min. When one of these episodes of pain occurred, typically she ceased all activity, reclined on her bed or couch, took pain medication, and cried until the pain subsided. These episodes elicited much solicitous and ministering behavior from husband and son.

Medically, during the 18-yr history of back pain, the patient had undergone four surgical procedures. The first of these (1951) was removal of a herniated disc, which removed the symptoms of root irritation, but did not completely remove the localized back pain. The final operation (1962), a lumbosacral spine fusion, left her with a stable spine. A careful evaluation revealed no neurologic deficit. No signs of nerve root irritation were elicited.

It was decided that Mrs. Y's pain behavior would be treated as an operant. A treatment schedule was designed to modify her pain behavior and increase her general level of activity. The major reinforcers under our control were medication, attention, and rest.

When admitted, the patient was taking 4 or 5 habit-forming analgesic tablets per day when she experienced pain. Such a regime has the effect of reinforcing pain behavior, with chemotherapeutic relief and attention from prestige figures. Her medicine regime was shifted from a pain to a time contingency program; i.e. medication was given at specified time intervals. Medication was never given when she complained of pain unless the complaint coincided with elapse of the time interval.

A color and taste masking vehicle was added to her medication. After the patient was solidly established in an activity regime, the narcotic content was decreased and by 40 days after admission was deleted altogether, without knowledge of the patient or nurses. Then the doses were decreased to every 4 hr, and 1 week later the dose in the middle of the night was omitted.

All treatment staff (physicians, nurses and other ward personnel, occupational therapist, physical therapist, and rehabilitation counselor) were instructed to be as neutral and socially unresponsive as possible to complaints by Mrs. Y. of pain and discomfort (Ayllon and Michael, 1959). When the patient was observed participating in any kind of activity, other than lying in bed, the staff was instructed to make a positive effort to be friendly and socially responsive. They were instructed to be lavish in their praise of daily increases in her activity level. Thus, pain behavior received a minimum of social reinforcement while activity was maximally reinforced.

An occupational therapy program was designed which emphasized rest as the reinforcer. Mrs. Y was given the task of constructing a close-weave luncheon cloth on a standard 36-in. floor loom. The task demanded considerable movement of her arms and legs and was accomplished sitting, a position she had described as one of her most painful. At the outset she was instructed "to work as long as you can." Several days of observation established her base line as approximately 25 threads within her 20 min activity tolerance. She was then instructed that each day she was to add ten more threads before she could leave occupational therapy to return to the ward to rest. At the end of 13 days she had completed a sizable tablecloth and was working continuously for more than 1 hr. She was then started on a new task which involved the construction of a small Turkish knot rug. At this point her rate of activity was so rapid and so efficient that she was able to complete this and several other occupational therapy projects before a stable base line of activity could be established. By the 30th day after admission she was working voluntarily for the full period of available occupational therapy time which was slightly under 2 hr.

A program was developed to increase her walking. A minimal physical therapy program of body baker and mild massage to the lower back area was begun. Concomitantly, on the ward she was assigned a daily walking schedule of 200-ft laps around the ward in the morning and again in the afternoon. Her initial trials demonstrated a base line of approximately 10 laps before she would complain of intolerable fatigue and/or pain. She was instructed to report to the nurses at the outset and completion of each series of laps. This provided a check on the reliability of her lap elapsed time recordings. It also alerted the ward staff to apply appropriate social reinforcement to this activity (Meichenbaum, 1966). The immediate reinforcers for the walking task were rest upon completion, social attention and praise from ward personnel both during and following her striding around the ward, and her own record, which she could observe herself and show to others. She was started at sets of 10 laps in the morning and 10 in the afternoon. Approximately every 10 days she was instructed to increase the number of laps in each set by five. At the end of seven weeks she was walking 25 laps or 5000 ft both morning and afternoon in very nearly the same time it had taken her to do 10 laps at the outset. She reached a walking speed approximately twice that of normal (Bard and Ralston, 1959).

Mrs. Y was given a small notebook to keep near her at all times in which she recorded unscheduled activities and their duration, in minutes. The staff referred to it often and made positive references to her daily increases in extra-schedule activities. The total number of minutes spent in activity each day, both scheduled and unscheduled were tabulated daily.

An approximate baseline of Mrs. Y's prehospitalization activities was provided by her husband who submitted a list which he felt was representative of her typical activities. It indicated a nonreclining activity schedule averaging approximately 2 hr per day. The balance of her day was spent reading, watching TV or sleeping.

Mrs. Y was seen daily for 10–15 min to construct graphs from her own records showing her daily progress. These sessions served to provide social reinforcement for her progress, as well as quality control checks on each component of the program.

At the outset of treatment, it was specified that her case would not be accepted unless her husband made himself available no less than 1 hr per week. He was seen by the same psychologist who was seeing the patient. The general outlines of the program were described to him. His cooperation was readily obtained. He was instructed on specific ways of being non-responsive to pain behavior and the importance of making reinforcing responses to her activity behavior.

He was asked to keep records of the amount of time she was engaged in active pursuits, rather than reclining and resting, when she was home on weekend passes. These records provided checks against Mrs. Y's records and served as reminders to him to be selectively responsive to activity and inactivity or pain behavior. They also served as a source of reinforcers to him in that he could observe tangible evidence of changes in her behavior as the treatment program went along. The length and frequency of passes granted to the patient to go home were increased on succeeding weeks. Concomitantly, sessions with the husband were used to explore specific activities which could be added during the times Mrs. Y was on pass. These included homemaking, cooking, washing, ironing, grooming, visiting with friends and relatives, and dining out.

Despite these various measures designed to provide generalization of her increasing levels of activity, when Mrs. Y moved to outpatient status there was, at first, a sharp drop in her activity and a sharp increase in her overt complaints of pain, as well as in the accompanying reclining behavior. She soon returned to her pattern of steady increase in activity. Figure 1 shows the record of her activity since admission.

At the time of this report the program had consisted of eight weeks of inpatient care and 23 weeks of decreasingly frequent outpatient visits. She was being seen once a month for a brief recheck. The family had acquired a second car and she was taking driving lessons so as to be independently mobile in the community.

DISCUSSION

Results with this case suggest that the modification of some environmental contingencies influenced pain behavior. The methods described consider questions relating to whether the pain is "real" as irrelevant. The question dealt with is whether modification of environmental responses to pain behavior can produce measureable changes in that behavior and in other behavior identified as limited by virtue of the presence of a chronic pain problem.

The results suggest judicious use of three potential reinforcers (medication, rest and social attention), commonly available in medical settings, can produce significant effects on behavior relating to chronic pain.

There has been a marked increase in her activity level and virtual disappearance of complaints of pain in a period eight weeks of comprehensive care following 18 yr of decreasing activity, during the past 5 yr of which she was in a state of virtually total immobilization. Fairly effective control has been gained over environmental responses to her behavior. How long these new patterns will continue remains to be seen.

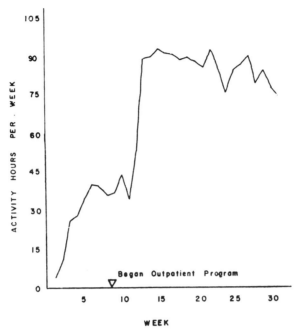

FIG. 1. Hours of non-reclining activity per week.

Acknowledgements—This study was supported in part by VRA Research and Training Grant RT-3.

Department of Physical Medicine and Rehabilitation,
University of Washington, School of Medicine,
Seattle, Washington

WILBERT E. FORDYCE
ROY S. FOWLER
BARBARA DeLATEUR

REFERENCES

AYLLON T. and MICHAEL J. (1959) The psychiatric nurse as a behavioral engineer. *J. exp. Analysis Behav.* **2**, 323–334.
BARD G. and RALSTON H. J. (1959) Measurement of energy expenditure during ambulation, with special reference to evaluation of assistive devices. *Arch. phys. Med. Rehabil.* **40**, 415–420.
HAUGHTON E. (1962) Shaping participation in occupational therapy. Paper given at the Third International Congress World Federation of Occupational Therapists. November, 1962, Boston, Massachusetts, mimeo.
MEICHENBAUM D. H. (1966) Sequential strategies in two cases of hysteria. *Behav. Res. & Therapy* **4**, 89–94.